A Portrait
Cast in Steel

Plate 1. Pouring molten steel from the ladle into the molds, around 1917. *Courtesy of the Ohio Historical Society, Inc. Columbus, Ohio.*

A Portrait Cast in Steel

Buckeye International and Columbus, Ohio, 1881-1980

Mansel G. Blackford

CONTRIBUTIONS IN ECONOMICS AND ECONOMIC HISTORY, NUMBER 49

GREENWOOD
PRESS

WESTPORT, CONNECTICUT
LONDON, ENGLAND

Library of Congress Cataloging in Publication Data

Blackford, Mansel G., 1944–
  A portrait cast in steel.

  (Contributions in economics and economic history,
ISSN 0084-9235 ; no. 49)
  Bibliography: p.
  Includes index.
  1. Buckeye International (Firm)—History.
  2. Columbus (Ohio)—Economic conditions. I. Title.
  II. Series.
  HD9519.B82B57   338.7'669142'0977157   82-6114
  ISBN 0-313-23393-4 (lib. bdg.)   AACR2

Library of Congress Catalog Card Number: 82-6114
ISBN: 0-313-23393-4
ISSN: 0084-9235

First published in 1982

Greenwood Press
A division of Congressional Information Service, Inc.
88 Post Road West
Westport, Connecticut 06881

Printed in the United States of America

10 9 8 7 6 5 4 3 2 1

Copyright Acknowledgments

Grateful acknowledgment is given for permission to use the following material previously published by the author:

Excerpts in chapters 1 and 3 from "Small Business in America: Two Case Studies," Paul Uselding, editor, *Business and Economic History: Papers Presented at the Twenty-Fifth Annual Meeting of the Business History Conference* (Urbana: University of Illinois Press, 1979), pp. 9-15. Used with the permission of the publisher.

Excerpts in chapter 3 from "Business Growth and Technological Change: Buckeye Steel Castings, 1881-1916," James H. Soltow, editor, *Essays in Economic and Business History* (East Lansing: Michigan State University Business Studies, 1981). Used with the permission of the publisher.

Excerpts in chapter 3 from "Scientific Management and Welfare Work in Early Twentieth Century American Business: The Buckeye Steel Castings Company," Robert L. Daugherty, editor, *Ohio History* 90 (Summer, 1981), 238-58. Used with the permission of the publisher, Ohio State University, Columbus, Ohio.

Excerpts in chapter 8 from "An Inside Look at the Merger Process through Oral History," in Jeremy Atack, editor, *Business and Economic History*, (Urbana: University of Illinois Press, 1981), pp. 57-69. Used with the permission of the publisher.

FOR KIM AND RANDY

CONTENTS

ILLUSTRATIONS

Illustrations depict work and life at Buckeye Steel between 1914 and 1917.

THE PRODUCTION PROCESS

LIFE AT BUCKEYE STEEL

TABLES

PREFACE

"That scholars know far too little about the history of small enterprise is a truism," observed the historian Ralph Hidy in 1970.[1] This situation continues today. Business and economic historians have prepared numerous studies of large corporations, but few of small or medium-sized ones. James Soltow's fine study of New England metal fabricators and machinery makers, which Hidy pointed to as an example of what could be accomplished in this field, remains one of the very few full-scale efforts to examine the history of small business in the United States.[2] Most recently, the seventeen essays comprising *Small Business in American Life*, edited by Stuart Bruchey, have increased our understanding of the development of small business.[3] Yet, much remains undone. Scholars still know relatively little about the history of small business or the role it has played in the social and economic growth of the United States.

This neglect of small business is lamentable. Small business is worthy of study for its own sake. As Hidy noted, "from colonial times to the present, the little businessman has carried out basic functions in American society."[4] In 1970 small businesses, as defined by the Small Business Administration, accounted for about 37 percent of America's Gross National Product and employed roughly 40 percent of its workforce.[5] Then, too, by comparing the special characteristics of the evolution of small business to those of big business, scholars can gain a more complete understanding of the overall development of the American business system.

My study examines the evolution of Buckeye International from its formation as a small business in Columbus, Ohio through its growth to become a medium-sized, diversified corporation with facilities across the United States. Beginning as a malleable iron producer during the 1880s, Buckeye hovered on the brink of failure for about a decade. However, the company's management soon saw the importance of what was then the growth industry of its day, American railroads. In the early 1890s Buckeye started producing cast iron couplers for railroad cars, and, as trains became longer and heavier, it changed to stronger cast steel couplers in the twentieth century. Steel couplers and other railroad car parts long remained Buckeye's major products. Only in the 1960s and 1970s did new challenges lead Buckeye's management to enter additional fields—plastics, communications, precision metal parts, and juvenile products. In this expansion Buckeye became a diversified corporation quite different from what it had been just a short time before. Finally, after a long existence as an independent business, Buckeye lost its corporate identity in a merger with Worthington Industries, another diversified firm, in 1980.

This work analyzes Buckeye's history as a business, but it examines as well the important roles Buckeye played in the growth of the American steel-castings industry and the development of Columbus, Ohio.[6] From the outset, Buckeye was a leader in the changes transforming the steel-castings industry in the late nineteenth and early twentieth centuries, and this study looks at the corporation's place in that industry. Buckeye's history was also affected by its relationship with the rest of its hometown, Columbus, Ohio, and this work probes the interrelationships in the development of the company and that community.

The first chapter of the study investigates Buckeye's founding and early struggle for survival in the years 1881 through 1894, a period in which the company came close to failing. Chapters 2 and 3 examine Buckeye's emergence as a major corporation in America's steel-castings industry during the years 1895 through 1921. They analyze the firm's pattern of growth and its reasons for success. In the many problems it faced, Buckeye was typical of newly formed small businesses, then and now. But, Buckeye was also atypical, for the company did prosper and grow; most new businesses fail. In fact, by the time of the First World War, Buckeye had become one of Columbus's largest industrial employers, with some 2,000 workers. No single factor explained this success. Tapping the national railroad market for its products was an essential first step, a move made possible by the personal connections of Buckeye's management with the Rockefeller family. Other factors proved important as well, not the least of which was the harmonious relationship between Buckeye's officers, the company's labor force, and the rest of the Columbus community. Buckeye's officers won recognition as social, political, and cultural leaders in Columbus in the early 1900s, and this recognition helped their company in concrete, tangible ways.

Chapters 4 and 5 deal with the years 1922 through 1959. In this period Buckeye first attained maturity as a leader in the steel-castings industry and then entered a time of decline. The company's commitment to the railroad market produced large profits through the 1940s, but the cyclical and shrinking nature of this market after the Second World War spelled trouble for steel-castings companies. Buckeye's officers lacked the foresight needed to change with the times, and their company came close to foundering in the late 1950s. This lack of vision was due in part to noneconomic factors. As political, social, and cultural leaders in Columbus, Buckeye's officers had become too complacent, too satisfied with the status quo. While admirable in the support of their community, they failed to perceive changes occurring beyond its boundaries. Even as their company declined in relative importance in Columbus's economy, Buckeye's management played ever-larger roles in the city's affairs.

Finally, the last four chapters analyze Buckeye's emergence as a diversified corporation in the 1960s and 1970s. In these two decades a new management at Buckeye led their company into many areas beyond the corporation's traditional railroad market. Some changes also took place in the relationship between Buckeye and Columbus; but here there was more continuity than change, as Buckeye's officers remained deeply involved in community affairs. Buckeye's management was generally successful in its diversification drive, perhaps in a way too successful. They soon discovered that their corporation was the target of takeover attempts. After fending off several unfriendly efforts, Buckeye's officers agreed to a proposal by Worthington Industries. Worthington acquired Buckeye in 1980, and Buckeye went out of existence as an independent entity.

My history of Buckeye should appeal to several audiences. It will be intrinsically interesting to anyone curious about the development of the steel industry . More importantly, Buckeye's history is

well worth examining precisely because it analyzes the evolution of
a small company and the roles which that company played in the
development of its community. My study investigates in rich detail
the relationship between the firm's strategy and the nature of its
management, the company's daily operations, the business's
marketing and technologic advances, the corporation's labor force,
and the roles Buckeye played in community affairs. Buckeye's history illustrates well the close connections between economic and social changes in the United States.

Notes

1. Ralph Hidy, "Business History: Present Status and Future Needs,"
Business History Review 44 (Winter 1970): 494.
2. James Soltow, "Origins of Small Business: Metal Fabricators and
Machinery Makers in New England, 1890-1957," *Transactions of the
American Philosophical Society* 55 (December 1965): 1-58.
3. Stuart Bruchey, editor, *Small Business in American Life* (New York:
Columbia University Press, 1980).
4. Hidy, "Business History," p. 494.
5. United States, Small Business Administration, *Annual Report, 1970*
(Washington D.C., 1971), p. 25.
6. On the relationship between business and urban development, see
Burton W. Folsom, Jr., *Urban Capitalists: Entrepreneurs and City Growth
in Pennsylvania's Lackawanna and Lehigh Regions, 1800-1920* (Baltimore:
Johns Hopkins Press, 1981).

ACKNOWLEDGMENTS

Many people helped make this study a reality, and I would like to thank them for their aid. Special thanks should go to the management of Buckeye International. They opened their corporate records to me and allowed me to write as I have seen fit without any restrictions. Their eagerness in explaining the workings of the steel-castings industry and their willingness to endure lengthy interviews also proved to be most helpful. Several people merit particular thanks. John G. McCoy, Buckeye's chairman of the board, and Rowland C.W. Brown, past president and chief executive officer at Buckeye, deserve my thanks for approving and actively supporting this project. Lewis I. Day, a retired senior vice-president and former acting chief executive officer at Buckeye, was of great assistance. His constant encouragement, his aid in locating company records, his personal knowledge of the company's past forty years of history, and his help in setting up interviews were indispensable.

Still others were of great aid. Andrea Lentz, who acted as a research assistant throughout the project, was particularly helpful in assembling information about Buckeye's officers and in unraveling the links between Buckeye and the rest of Columbus. Nobuo Kawabe, a research assistant during the spring of 1978, spent many tedious but worthwhile hours checking items in newspapers and trade journals. Albro Martin and Nelson Lichtenstein read and commented upon the history in manuscript form, and their suggestions improved it for publication. Finally, I wish to thank The Ohio State University for releasing me from teaching duties during the spring of 1978 to engage in research on this history.

I am, of course, solely responsible for any errors of fact or interpretation in this work.

A Portrait Cast in Steel

chapter 1

THE IRON YEARS, 1881–1894

Buckeye International—by 1979 a diversified corporation with annual sales of $162,000,000—had inauspicious beginnings.[1] Buckeye
International evolved out of the Buckeye Steel Castings Company
which, in turn, had developed from a number of malleable iron
companies. Until the 1890s these predecessors, like most new businesses then as now, were unprofitable and short-lived. Buckeye's
forerunners produced a wide range of malleable iron products and
sold most of them in central Ohio. In doing so, they faced fierce
competition and, lacking any specialty items, had a hard time carving out and holding onto a market niche for their goods. Chronically
short of capital, Buckeye's predecessors led tenuous and unstable
lives. Yet, they did survive and grow. Through the development of
new products and markets, they laid the foundation upon which
Buckeye's later success could be built.

The Origins

Buckeye's early growth occurred against a background of rapid-
fire developments in the iron and steel industries. Adopting the
British practice, American iron makers began to substitute coke for
charcoal in the smelting of pig iron during the 1840s. With this
development and with the growth of markets for iron, America's
iron production rose from 165,000 tons in 1830 to nearly 1,000,000
tons thirty years later. By 1890 about 70 percent of the United

Part of this chapter was presented as a paper at the 1979 Business History Con-
ference in New Orleans; the paper has been published as: "Small Business in
America: Two Case Studies," Paul Uselding, editor, *Business and Economic
History: Papers Presented At the Twenty-Fifth Annual Meeting of the Business
History Conference* (Urbana: University of Illinois Press, 1979), pp. 9–15. Used
with permission.

States' pig iron was being produced with coking coal, making possible the output of high-quality pig iron on a large scale, and in that year America's pig iron production surpassed that of England for the first time. In 1900 American blast furnaces turned out over 15,000,000 tons of pig iron. Steel production lagged behind that of iron, but the use of the Bessemer process after the Civil War greatly reduced the costs of making steel and led to a tremendous expansion in steel production. The output of steel in the United States soared from less than 70,000 tons in 1870 to over 4,000,000 tons just twenty years later. The open-hearth process, which gradually supplanted the Bessemer process in many steel mills during the late nineteenth and early twentieth centuries, further stimulated steel production by allowing the mills to use the phosphoric ores which the Bessemer process could not handle. By 1900 American steel production had leaped to nearly 12,000,000 tons. It was in these exciting times that Buckeye began its existence.[2]

Buckeye's lineage can be traced back to the company of Murray-Hayden which was formed in Columbus during 1881. This business was a partnership of John F. Murray, Neville G. Hayden, and William H. Hayden, Jr., with Zelotes Wood joining as a partner in 1882. As would be true of many of those involved with Buckeye at a later date, the partners in Murray-Hayden had close personal and business ties with the Columbus business community. These connections were particularly strong in the case of the Haydens, whose family was long established in Columbus. Peter Hayden had moved to Columbus in 1836, and by the mid-1840s his iron foundry was employing 100 men. Over the next forty years, he and his family went into a broad range of commercial and industrial enterprises, including railroads, hardware, saddlery, coal mining, and banking. At the time of his death in 1888, Hayden was one of Columbus's foremost businessmen.[3]

William H., Jr. and Neville Hayden began their careers in 1879–81 as foreman and clerk, respectively, in P. Hayden and Sons, which operated an iron foundry at the corner of Scioto and Broad Streets in downtown Columbus. John Murray had been a salesman for Patton Manufacturing in the late 1870s. This firm produced "enameled, tinned, turned, and plain" hollow ware, and it was through this business that Murray came to know the Haydens. Zelotes Wood probably also learned of the Haydens through his work, for before joining the partnership he had been a general fire insurance agent who specialized in insuring Columbus businesses.[4]

Murray-Hayden manufactured malleable iron products in a small foundry in downtown Columbus at the corner of Randolph and West Streets (near the intersection of today's Gay Street and Grant Avenue). One of some half-dozen similar companies in Columbus, Murray-Hayden experienced only limited success. In fact, the partnership dissolved soon after its formation, as several members left in search of more promising prospects. Wood formed his own malleable iron works and for a number of years operated a foundry just across the street from the Murray-Hayden location. Murray went into several businesses in the 1880s and 1890s. He became the proprietor of a cigar company, the owner of two saloons, and the head of the Columbus Fire and Accident Notification Company. With the defection of Murray and Wood, the firm of Murray-Hayden disappeared in mid-1883.[5]

Undaunted by their early lack of success, the Haydens reorganized their company as Munson-Hayden, another partnership, in July of 1883. In this venture the Haydens were joined by Charles E. Munson and George D. Linn. Munson had been born and reared in Zanesville, Ohio and came to Columbus in 1882. Linn had begun his career as a bookkeeper for Murray-Hayden at about the same time.[6] The company purchased a new downtown tract of five acres on Russell Street (just off North Fourth Street) from James Kilbourne and Felix Jacobs.[7] While not large when compared to Buckeye's later landholdings, this location allowed the fledgling company to spread out. Just to the north was Kilbourne and Jacobs, one of Columbus's leading manufacturers; to the south lay a lumber yard; to the west, a horseshoe factory; and to the east, railroad tracks.[8]

Here Munson-Hayden established a small foundry and opened for business. Over the next three years the company turned out a variety of malleable iron products, nearly all sold locally, and most for amounts of less than $100. In May 1884, for example, Munson-Hayden had thirty-two customers. Most of these were in central Ohio, with only two or three beyond the state's boundaries. The largest sale came to $3,157 for Champion Iron Fence; the smallest, ten cents for the Columbus Brass and Pipe Works. Since railroads were later to become Buckeye's major customers, it is worth noting

that Munson-Hayden made no sales to railroads during its three
years of existence. It remained, like Murray-Hayden before it, a
general malleable cast iron company.[9]

As one Buckeye executive later observed, "business was not very
successful" at Munson-Hayden.[10] The times did not favor new
companies. The United States was suffering from a business recession in the mid-1880s, and this recession adversely affected the nation's iron and steel industries. Pig iron production dipped from
5,147,000 tons in 1883 to 4,530,000 tons two years later.[11] Columbus was hit hard by the recession. The city's population growth
slowed, and bank clearings, a reliable economic indicator, after rising from $44,100,000 in 1880 to $69,700,000 in 1884, fell to
$69,500,000 a year later. Some businesses were forced to close their
doors, including the Columbus Rolling Mill Company which
employed 400 men at the time of its failure in 1884.[12] Munson-
Hayden led a shaky existence. Charles Munson lent the company
$1,700 in 1884 and $6,800 a year later. Yet, even with this fresh
capital, the business posted losses in 1885 and 1886.[13] Thoroughly
discouraged, Munson left the partnership, forcing its dissolution in
1886. While never again actively involved in its management, Munson remained a stockholder until his death in 1927.[14]

Wilbur Goodspeed and Buckeye Malleable Iron

Major Wilbur F. Goodspeed, who has traditionally been considered the "father" of Buckeye Steel Castings by those associated
with the company, spearheaded the reorganization of Munson-
Hayden. Born in Massillon, Ohio in 1836, he moved with his family
to Haydenville, Massachusetts seven years later, where he attended
school and became acquainted with members of the Hayden family. Goodspeed returned to Massillon in 1850 to continue his
schooling and to work in his brother-in-law's wholesale shoe house.
Striking out on his own, Goodspeed served for a year as a clerk in a
New York boot and shoe establishment in 1853, and then opened
his own shoe business in Cleveland. He stayed in this line of work
until 1861, when he enlisted as a private in the Army of the
Cumberland in the Civil War. Goodspeed served with distinction,
rising to the rank of major in 1864. Returning to the shoe trade
after the war, Goodspeed became a salesman and then a partner in
Burgert, Adams, and Company, a Cleveland wholesaler, but in

1876 he left this firm to join a rival company as a traveling agent. Four years later, the restless Goodspeed forsook shoes for the post of United States marshal for the northern district of Ohio. Shortly after taking this position, Goodspeed, a widower, married Harriett Howe, the daughter of William W. Howe, a well-known Toledo businessman.[15]

Of average height, Goodspeed was stocky and solidly built. While favoring a mustache, he eschewed the beard so fashionable in his time. Like most businessmen trying to project an impression of solidity, Goodspeed dressed conservatively, with a gold watch chain strung across his blue vest coat. A touch of flair crept into his headgear, however. Instead of the traditional top hat, he normally sported a more daring derby.[16]

Precisely how Goodspeed became interested in Munson-Hayden is unclear, but he probably learned of the company from the Haydens, who were close enough friends to attend his wedding in Toledo in 1883. Alternately, he may have heard of the business from acquaintances he had made while in business in Cleveland or while serving as United States marshal. At any rate, Goodspeed came to Columbus and reorganized Munson-Hayden as the Buckeye Malleable Iron Company, a venture incorporated under Ohio's general incorporation laws in September 1886. For $15,000 Goodspeed bought out Munson's share of Munson-Hayden and merged it into Buckeye. Goodspeed had at least two reasons for going into the iron business. His term as marshal was due to expire in two years, at which time he would once more be looking about for something to do. More importantly, Goodspeed had been loaning money to Munson-Hayden, and he probably became increasingly involved in the business in an attempt to protect his investment.[17]

Initially capitalized at $60,000, Buckeye Malleable Iron received backing not only from Goodspeed, but also from the same sources that had financed Munson-Hayden. Goodspeed acted as president and treasurer, Neville Hayden was general manager, while his brother William became vice-president. Talfourd P. Linn, an attorney for Outhwaite and Linn, acted as Buckeye's secretary.[18] Short of funds from the outset, Buckeye had only $14,000 in paid-in capital when it began business, and two years later the firm's stockholders were still some $10,000 short of paying in their full subscriptions.[19]

Shy of capital, Buckeye's founders faced the same problems as before. Like its predecessor, Munson-Hayden, Buckeye produced malleable iron goods for local markets, without a proprietary product to set it apart from its competitors. For example, in December 1887, Buckeye sold its goods to forty-five customers, ranging from tool companies to fence and to nail companies. Buckeye sold $2,677 worth of products to P. P. Mast Company, its largest customer that month, but most sales were small. More typical was the $2.96 sale of iron to E. R. Osgood and Company. The railroad market remained untapped. Buckeye lost $4,234 in 1887, and over the next three years its operations were generally unsatisfactory.[20]

It was the lack of a distinct market for its products that hurt Buckeye and its predecessors the most. As a newly begun small business, Buckeye needed to find a market niche to insulate its products from competition. In his study of metal-fabricating and machinery-making firms in New England between 1890 and 1957, the historian James Soltow found that the key to success for small businesses lay "in adapting to a niche in the market which afforded some degree of isolation from complete and direct competition with other firms both large and small."[21] This situation was also the case with Buckeye in the 1880s and 1890s.

Buckeye's officers were soon borrowing money from friends and family to stay afloat. In late 1890 they borrowed $5,000 from Joseph Outhwaite, George Linn's former law partner. This loan, combined with the $10,000 still owed Munson, proved to be a heavy burden. To lighten the load, the firm borrowed $15,000 from the estate of Goodspeed's brother-in-law, Charles T. Howe, of which Goodspeed was one of the trustees, and used the proceeds to pay off the earlier loans. This move reduced Buckeye's annual interest charges and spread out the payments on principal over another five years.[22] In the next few years, many of those associated with Buckeye, while continuing as stockholders and while remaining active in management, branched out into other more prosperous enterprises. William Hayden, Jr. became superintendent of the P. Hayden Saddlery Hardware Company in 1891 and also dabbled in real estate, while his brother Neville left the Columbus scene. T. P. Linn became a partner in the newly formed law firm of Outhwaite, Linn, McNaughten, and Gumble.[23]

If they thought the company's future unpromising, they miscalculated, for Buckeye's prospects were not as dismal as they seemed. The corporation's officers were taking steps to develop new products and to open up new markets.

Central in importance for Buckeye's future was the automatic coupler for railroad cars, a device already under development for some years in the United States. Well into the 1890s, most railroad cars employed "linch and pin" couplers, which were extremely dangerous to trainmen who had to step between railroad cars to couple them together manually. If the cars missed connections, the trainmen might be crushed, and either killed or maimed for life. The accident rate was high. As late as 1890 one of every 105 men directly engaged in handling trains was killed and one in twelve was injured—many of these mishaps due to coupler-caused accidents.[24] Automatic couplers, which could join cars without requiring trainmen to step between them, offered a solution to this problem. E. H. Janney is usually credited with designing and patenting the first automatic couplers in the late 1860s and early 1870s. Others entered this field, and numerous improvements were made over the next fifteen years. A great number of automatic couplers were designed, and ten or fifteen types were actually placed in service. The Master Car Builders Association, which was then a trade association representing most railroad car builders, adopted the general form of the automatic coupler as standard in 1887.[25]

Goodspeed was among those to see the potential of the automatic coupler. In 1889, together with James Timms, a pattern maker in the Hocking Valley Railroad's Columbus shops, he formed the Timms Automatic Car Coupler Company. Goodspeed had been assisting Timms in his attempts to design a usable automatic coupler, and their new company was set up "for the purpose of manufacturing car couplers and other car equipment."[26] Initially incorporated for only $5,000, the company had its authorized capitalization raised to $200,000 a few months later. Headed by Goodspeed as president, the company brought new investors into the picture, among them S. P. Peabody, superintendent of the C. & C. Midland Railroad and of Frost, Stearnes, and Company (a railroad contractor), Robert M. Rownd, the proprietor of Beall Manufacturing in Columbus and a member of the managing board of the Ohio Penitentiary, and W. A. Shore.[27] The corporation changed its name to the Buckeye Automatic Car Coupler Company in 1891.

The company began producing an automatic coupler known as
the "Trojan" in 1889 or 1890 and found a ready market for it.
Reaching beyond Columbus, the business sold its couplers to north-
eastern and Chicago-based railroads and to railroad car manufacturers. Personal connections were of utmost importance in securing
these sales. The Baltimore & Ohio Railroad, with Peabody now as
its general agent, accounted for one-third of Buckeye's orders in
1891. Peabody also traveled to Chicago in 1890 to try to persuade
the Western Railroad Association to buy exclusively from Buckeye.[28]
    The Buckeye Automatic Car Coupler Company was a techni-
cal success. In 1892 the *Railroad Gazette*, a nationally read trade
journal, singled out Buckeye as producing "the highest grade of
malleable iron" products known for their "tenacity." A year later,
the same journal again praised Buckeye, noting that "this company
has no trouble in making automatic couplers that will stand the
Master Car Builders tests."[29] The number of stockholders in Buckeye Automatic Car steadily increased to nineteen in late 1894.
Moreover, since the Buckeye Malleable Iron Company produced
the couplers which Buckeye Automatic Car sold, the former firm
also began to prosper. In 1890 Buckeye Iron's stockholders boosted
their company's capitalization from $60,000 to $100,000. Significantly, the new stock certificates pictured a puffing railroad locomotive hauling a coal train through the countryside. A further capital increase to $200,000 was voted two years later.[30]
    Yet, economic problems remained. Both firms were still short of
capital. Buckeye Automatic Car periodically had to borrow money
for working capital from Columbus banks. Moreover, it obtained
longer-term loans at various times from Peabody and Rownd. Like
Buckeye Malleable Iron, Buckeye Automatic Car also borrowed
funds, some $10,000 from the Howe estates. Markets were another
perennial problem. Though Buckeye Automatic Car began tapping
the national market, its sales were small. Even in 1891 the company's total sales came to only $23,000.[31]
    Partial solutions to these problems soon appeared. In late 1892
Goodspeed successfully concluded negotiations with Frank Rockefeller and Thomas Goodwillie for aid in selling Buckeye's couplers.
Frank was John D. Rockefeller's brother and an executive with the
Standard Oil Company. Described by the historian Allan Nevins as
"genial, adventurous, quick to love and hate," Frank Rockefeller

was always on the lookout for new opportunities. So was Good-willie. In the early 1880s he had been an independent oil refiner in Cleveland, and by 1892 Goodwillie had joined Standard as head of its refined oil department in Cleveland.[32] In November 1892 the stockholders of Buckeye Automatic Car agreed to give Rockefeller and Goodwillie each $15,000 worth of their corporation's stock. Moreover, Rockefeller and Goodwillie were to share in any future increase of the company's stock, in proportion to these holdings. In return for this gift of stock, Rockefeller and Goodwillie promised to use their influence to persuade railroads to buy Buckeye couplers. As the legal agreement stated, "Rockefeller and Goodwillie hereby agree to use their best endeavor to secure the introduction and use upon railroads of the said couplers of the said corporation and in all ways to advance the interests of said corporation."[33]

Exactly how Goodspeed came to know Rockefeller is uncertain, but it was probably through Goodspeed's friendship with Good-willie. Both Goodspeed and Goodwillie belonged to the Cleveland Gatling Gun Battery, a military and social organization formed in 1878 in the wake of the nationwide railroad strikes of the previous year. Goodspeed may also have known Rockefeller directly. Like Goodspeed, Frank Rockefeller had served for four years in an Ohio outfit during the Civil War, and he may have known Goodspeed either during the war or after it as a member of the Grand Army of the Republic. Then again, both men had been Cleveland business-men and may have gotten together in this manner. Finally, Good-speed could have come into contact with Rockefeller through his United States marshal's job, for the position had political and eco-nomic, as well as legal, significance in the 1880s.[34]

Congressional legislation also aided the two Buckeye companies. In 1891 and 1892 the Congress considered several bills designed to require the use of automatic couplers by railroads. However, the opposition of railroad executives, who testified that automatic couplers had not yet been perfected, and of yardmen, who told of difficulties encountered in using automatic couplers, killed the measures.[35] Nonetheless, continued discussion, which emphasized the benefits accruing to railroads through the increased inter-changeability of cars as well as the improvement in safety for train-men, changed the situation. In late 1892 the Committee of Safety Appliances of the American Railway Association, the national railroad trade association, came out, as its chairman put it, "distinctly and emphatically in favor of safety couplers."[36] Finally, in 1893 the Congress passed the Safety Appliance Act which required all railroad cars used in interstate commerce to adopt within five years "couplers coupling automatically . . . without the necessity of men going between the ends of the cars."[37]

Buckeye Malleable Iron and Buckeye Automatic Car benefited from these developments. Pushed by Goodspeed, Timms designed a new coupler designed to meet the specifications laid down by the Congress. In early 1893 Buckeye Automatic Car began producing the new "Buckeye" coupler, and by June of that year some 2,000 cars were equipped with it. Buckeye Malleable Iron took on a new life. In 1894 its letterhead could proudly show a plant of five buildings with six smokestacks belching black smoke into the sky. There is some truth to the cliché that nothing succeeds like success. With its newly found prosperity, Buckeye Malleable Iron attracted additional stockholders who brought in fresh capital, thus making further expansion possible. As the original officers and stockholders of the company brought in their friends and business acquaintances, the corporation's list of stockholders swelled to twenty-nine by late 1894.[38]

Many of the newcomers to Buckeye were up-and-coming Columbus businessmen: John G. Deshler, vice-president of the Deshler National Bank; David Greene, the secretary-treasurer of the Case Manufacturing Company (a maker of mill machinery); Felix Jacobs and James Kilbourne, vice-president and president, respectively, of the Kilbourne and Jacobs Manufacturing Company; and D. T. McNaughten, a partner in Linn's law firm. However, Buckeye also attracted important new investors from beyond Columbus: the Chester Pierce family of Rochester, Vermont; James Barnett, a Cleveland businessman; and George P. Welch, of Sterling, Welch, and Company in Cleveland.[39]

The Buckeye Malleable Iron and Coupler Company

Emboldened by their successes during the early 1890s, the stockholders of Buckeye Malleable Iron and Buckeye Automatic Car decided to join forces through the formation of a new company. They accomplished this with the incorporation of the Buckeye Malleable Iron and Coupler Company on November 19,

1894. Set up "for the purpose of manufacturing, purchasing, and selling malleable iron castings, steel castings, and other iron castings for general use," the company had seven incorporators: Goodspeed, Rownd, Timms, Deshler, T. P. Linn, Peabody, and Orland Smith, president of the Columbus Transfer Company. These men also acted as Buckeye's first officers, with Goodspeed serving as president and treasurer, Deshler as vice-president, and Linn as secretary.[40] Buckeye Malleable Iron and Coupler Company quickly merged its two predecessor companies into the new corporation.[41] Capitalized at $500,000, Buckeye Malleable Iron and Coupler began business with forty-seven stockholders inherited from Buckeye Malleable Iron and Buckeye Automatic Car.[42]

By 1894 those founding Buckeye had survived the most perilous years. They were well on the way to raising adequate financing for the company. Even more importantly, they had developed a new specialty product, the cast iron automatic coupler, and through their personal connections they were beginning to sell it in the national rather than local market. In its survival, Buckeye was already proving to be an unusual small business. The attrition rate for small businesses in America has always been high. In their study of Poughkeepsie, for instance, Clyde and Sally Griffin found that of the 1,530 firms evaluated for credit by R. G. Dunn and Company between 1845 and 1880, some 32 percent lasted for only three years or less, and only 14 percent survived for twenty years or more. "Most businesses faded rapidly," the Griffins have observed, "only a few were very promising ventures at the onset."[43]

The founding of Buckeye Malleable Iron and Coupler and the operations of its predecessor companies occurred as part of industrial advances in Columbus. Ohio's capital since 1816, Columbus owed its early growth to politics and commerce. After 1870, however, Columbus became an industrial center as well. In the last three decades of the nineteenth century, Columbus businessmen solved many of the problems hindering the growth of their industrial ventures. Columbus's population rose from 31,000 to 126,000, providing a larger market for locally manufactured goods. Then, too, the spread of regional railroad lines like the Hocking Valley Railroad linked Columbus with other areas throughout Ohio. This occurrence opened southeastern Ohio's iron and coal reserves to development, and mining in this area provided Columbus with its first major market for industrial products. Most importantly, interstate railroads, especially the Pennsylvania and the Baltimore & Ohio, provided connections with the rest of the nation, allowing companies like Buckeye to sell to the national market. By 1890 fifteen railroads entered Columbus, and the shrill whistle of their steam locomotives had come to sound like a sweet melody to the city's appreciative businessmen.[44]

While still primarily a commercial and political center, Columbus was broadening its economic base in the late nineteenth century. Buckeye was one of twenty-three malleable iron companies, foundries, and machine shops in Columbus in 1887. The value of the combined output of these plants was $937,000, and the companies employed 658 men. While a small business in national terms, Buckeye was already becoming a substantial local enterprise. No records exist giving the number of employees at Buckeye at this time. But, of the companies mentioned above, only two, Buckeye and one other firm, were malleable iron companies, and the combined employment of the two companies was 180 men. The value of their combined annual output was $173,500. Clearly, Buckeye was emerging as one of the larger local industrial ventures, a trend that would continue in the next few decades.[45]

Yet, industrial progress was uneven, for national recessions and depressions interrupted Columbus's industrial growth. As we have seen, the recession of the mid-1880s slowed business development in Columbus. Even more shattering was the depression which affected the entire United States between 1893 and 1896. This depression severely retarded industrial development. In the years 1893 through 1897, some 800 banks failed, industrial production fell by about 25 percent, and at least 20 percent of the industrial work force was unemployed.[46] The iron and steel industries suffered, with pig iron production dropping from over 10,000,000 tons in 1892 to 7,500,000 tons two years later.[47]

Like the rest of the nation, Columbus was hurt by the depression. As business slackened and unemployment rose, the city faced what one newspaper reporter labeled "the tramp problem." As he noted with dismay in November 1894 (when Buckeye was being formed), "every night a large number of unfortunates apply for lodging at the city prison."[48] By this time, some efforts were underway to alleviate the distress. The city was employing about 1,000 men on public works projects.[49] Yet, Columbus was not as hard hit as many industrial centers. "Columbus had weathered the gale," the *Ohio State Journal* could accurately observe, "a great deal better than many other cities of the same class throughout the country." Despite the depression, people in Columbus spent $2,000,000 on private building construction in 1894. Among the new structures was the Wyandot Building, the first Chicago-style skyscraper in Columbus.[50] Some even found time to laugh at the economic situation. On Halloween the YMCA sponsored a "hard-times party" featuring "refreshments in . . . harmony with the character of the party, consisting of crackers, pickles, onions, and water."[51] With a diversified economic base—government, trade, and industry—Columbus endured the depression years in relatively good shape.[52]

The depression slowed, but did not stop, Columbus's growth as a city, and Buckeye would develop as part of an urban environment. Columbus continued to evolve socially and economically during Buckeye's formative year, 1894. In January, W. G. Deshler donated $25,000 to the Columbus Female Benevolent Society for its home. Three months later the United Mine Workers opened its national convention in Columbus and promptly called for a general strike. In early May the Sells Brothers began their circus season in the city, and later in the month, Eugene Debs, soon to become a nationally known socialist leader, spoke to a large crowd at city hall. Cycling and harness races were favorite summer pastimes, while a campaign "to drive houses of ill-repute from Seventh Street" enlivened late August. Republicans swept the local and congressional elections in November. The *Ohio State Journal* was able to report the election returns from the outlying districts of Franklin County (of which Columbus was a part) a bit sooner than normal, for it arranged for members of the Columbus Wheel Club to bicycle into town with the results (through mud, as it had rained that day). The year closed with the directors of the YMCA deciding "not to introduce billiards at present," after considerable public and private discussion.[53]

It was, then, against a background of long-term growth and prosperity, tempered by temporary distress, that the Columbus businessmen met to found the Buckeye Malleable Iron and Coupler

Company, the immediate precursor of the Buckeye Steel Castings Company, in late 1894. Despite the depression, the future for their company and city seemed rosy. In a bit of boosterism, the *Journal* closed the year with the observation that "the outlook for the coming year is exceeding bright," and predicted that "Columbus will enjoy a year of unprecedented prosperity."[54]

Notes

1. Buckeye International, *Annual Report, 1979*, unpaged. All corporate records before 1958 have been donated to the Ohio Historical Society in Columbus, Ohio. Later records are available at corporate headquarters in Columbus, Ohio.

2. On the development of the iron and steel industries, see William T. Hogan, *Economic History of the Iron and Steel Industry in the United States*, vol. 1 (Lexington, Mass: D.C. Heath, 1971); Kenneth Warren, *The American Steel Industry, 1850-1970: A Geographic Approach* (London: Oxford University Press, 1973).

3. Peter Hayden moved to New York in the 1880s, but he remained deeply involved in Columbus businesses. For more on Peter Hayden, see *Columbus Dispatch*, April 7, 1888; Henry Hunker, *Industrial Evolution of Columbus Ohio* (Columbus: The Ohio State University Press, 1958), p. 37; *Ohio State Journal*, April 7, September 2, 1886; *New York Times*, April 9, 20, 1888.

4. G. J. Brand and Company, *Columbus City Directory* (Columbus), *1879*, pp. 146, 235, 345; *1880*, pp. 173, 280, 418; *1881*, pp. 182, 299, 443; Wiggins and McKillops, *Columbus City Directory* (Columbus), *1878*, p. 313.

5. Brand, *City Directory, 1882*, pp. 206, 342, 540; R. L. Polk, *Columbus City Directory* (Columbus), *1895-96*, p. 587; Williams and Company, *Columbus City Directory* (Columbus), *1883-84*, pp. 534, 832; *1884-85*, pp. 612, 615, 958.

6. *Ohio State Journal*, November 21, 1927; Williams, *City Directory, 1883-84*, p. 453.

7. "Bank Draft, July 3, 1883, Munson-Hayden to James Kilbourne and Felix Jacobs"; for the exact property boundaries, see "Mortgage Deed from Charles Munson *et al.* to Kilbourne Jacobs, July 5, 1883."

8. G. William Baist, *Baist's Property Atlas of the City of Columbus and Vicinity, Ohio* (Philadelphia: Baist Company, 1899), plan 11.

9. Munson-Hayden Company, *Trial Balance Ledger, 1883-86*.

10. A. H. Thomas, "Address to Sales Conference, January 5, 1939," mimeographed copy.

11. Hogan, *Economic History*, vol. 1, p. 184.

12. Columbus Board of Trade, *Annual Report, 1889* (Columbus), p. 74; Hunker, *Industrial Evolution*, pp. 39–51; Alfred E. Lee, *History of the City of Columbus*, vol. 1 (New York and Chicago: Munsell and Company, 1892), pp. 331–32.

13. "Memorandum," undated, in *Stock Ledger, 1886, Buckeye Malleable Iron Company*; Munson-Hayden Co., *Trial Balance Ledger*, 1883–86.

14. Columbus *Dispatch, Columbus 400: Men of the Ohio Capital* (Columbus: Columbus *Dispatch*, 1896), p. 35; *Ohio State Journal*, November 21, 1927.

15. Precise biographic information about Goodspeed is surprisingly difficult to find. But see: Columbus *Citizen*, February 4, 1905; Columbus *Dispatch*, February 4, 1905; *Ohio State Journal*, February 5, 1905. Goodspeed's career for 1865–1886 can be traced in Cleveland city directories. See: Cleveland Directory Company, *The Cleveland Directory for the Year 1881* (Cleveland), p. 208; Cleveland Leader Company, *Cleveland Leader City Directory* (Cleveland), *1866–67*, p. 119; *1868–69*, p. 171; W. S. Robinson Company, *Cleveland Directory* (Cleveland), *1871–72*, p. 189; *1872–73*, p. 196; M. B. Haven, *Cleveland Social Directory* (Cleveland), *1885*, p. 59.

16. Photographs of Goodspeed are available in the Buckeye Collection at the Ohio Historical Society.

17. "Agreement between Buckeye Malleable Iron Company and Charles E. Munson, September 2, 1886"; Cleveland *Leader*, December 27, 1883; Toledo *Blade*, December 27, 1883. Using records no longer in existence, Stephen C. Noland prepared a three-page historic sketch of Buckeye in 1934. In it he writes that Goodspeed "had from time to time loaned money" to Munson-Hayden. See Stephen C. Noland, "Sketch of the Buckeye Steel Castings Company," typewritten pamphlet, May 1, 1934, in Buckeye Collection, Ohio Historical Society. In his "Address to Sales Conference, January 5, 1939," A. H. Thomas, Buckeye's president, also claimed that Goodspeed had been "indirectly interested" in Munson-Hayden before he moved to Columbus.

18. Buckeye Malleable Iron Company, *Stock Ledger 1886*; Polk, *Columbus City Directory, 1889–90*, p. 122; Wiggins, *Columbus City Directory, 1887–88*, p. 154; *1888–89*, p. 116.

19. "Articles of Incorporation of the Buckeye Malleable Iron Company, September 1, 1886."

20. Buckeye Malleable Iron Company, *Trial Balance Ledger, 1886–87*; Columbus Board of Trade, *Annual Report, 1887* (Columbus), p. 75; Thomas, "Address, January 5, 1939."

21. James Soltow, "Origins of Small Business and the Relationships Between Large and Small Firms: Metal Fabricating and Machinery Making in New England, 1890–1927," in Stuart Bruchey, editor, *Small Business in American Life* (New York: Columbia University Press, 1980), p. 195.

22. "Agreement, Buckeye Malleable Iron Co. with W. F. Goodspeed and Charles L. Howe, trustees for the estate of Charles T. Howe, July 1, 1891"; "Minutes of Directors Meeting, Buckeye Malleable Iron Co.," April 10, 1891; and "Mortgage Deed, from the Buckeye Malleable Iron Co. to Joseph H. Outhwaite, October 29, 1890."

23. Polk, *Columbus City Directory, 1890–91*, p. 381; *1891–92*, pp. 348, 452; *1892–93*, pp. 320, 416.

24. Ari Hoogenboom and Olive Hoogenboom, *A History of the ICC* (New York: W. W. Norton, 1976), p. 34.

25. A. G. Williams, "The Development of the Automatic Coupler in America," *Baldwin Locomotive Magazine* (December 1928): 25–31; H. H. Wolfe, "History of the Automatic Coupler" (paper read at shop meeting, Buckeye Steel Castings, August 12, 1934).

26. "Articles of Incorporation, Timms Automatic Car Coupler Company, March 1, 1889."

27. Wiggins, *Columbus City Directory, 1887–88*, p. 701; *1888–89*, pp. 211, 409.

28. Timms Automatic Car Coupler, *Journal, 1889–92*.

29. *Railroad Gazette*, May 27, 1892, April 14, 1893.

30. Buckeye Malleable Iron Company, "Certificates of Stock Increase, August 5, 1890 and October 31, 1892"; Buckeye Malleable Iron Company, *Stockbook*; "Statement of Shares formerly owned in the Buckeye Malleable Iron Company," no date (probably late 1894).

31. Timms Automatic Car Coupler, *Journal, 1889–92*.

32. Allan Nevins, *John D. Rockefeller*, vol. 2 (New York: Scribners, 1940), pp. 187–88, 385–88, 681.

33. "Memorandum of Agreement Made this 25th day of November, 1892 by and between Orland Smith, S. P. Peabody, R. M. Rownd, James Timms and W. F. Goodspeed, parties of the first part and Frank Rockefeller and Thomas Goodwillie, parties of the second part." See also: Thomas Goodwillie to W. F. Goodspeed, October 5, 1892; V. P. Kline to W. F. Goodspeed, October 24, 1892; "Minutes of Conference of Original Stockholders of the Buckeye Automatic Car Coupler Company, November 25, 1892."

34. Unfortunately, neither the Rockefeller Archives in New York nor any of the Standard Oil archives shed any light on this question. For the connection between Goodspeed and Goodwillie see: James H. Kennedy, *A History of the City of Cleveland, 1796–1896* (Cleveland: S. J. Clark Publishing Company, 1896), pp. 433–34; *Constitution and By-Laws of Cleveland Gatling Gun Battery, June 26, 1878*, pamphlet in Case Western Reserve Library.

35. *Railroad Gazette*, November 13, 20, December 25, 1891, and January 15, March 25, April 1, 1892.

36. Ibid., December 16, 1892.

37. Ibid., February 17, 1893; Howard Gilbert, *The Development and Maintenance of A.A.R. Couplers*, pamphlet, 1948, n.p., in Buckeye Collection, Ohio Historical Society.

38. Buckeye Automatic Car Coupler Company to W. A. Mills, March 31, 1893; "List of Stockholders, Buckeye Malleable Iron Co.," undated, probably late 1894.

39. List of Stockholders," probably late 1894.

40. "Articles of Incorporation, Buckeye Malleable Iron and Coupler Company, November 19, 1894"; Polk, *Columbus City Directory, 1895–96*, p. 247.

41. "Minutes of the Board of Directors Meeting, Buckeye Malleable Iron and Coupler Company, November 19, 1894" (hereafter cited as "Directors Meeting" with date).

42. "Stockholders in the Buckeye Malleable Iron and Coupler Company, December 1, 1894."

43. Clyde and Sally Griffen, "Small Business and Occupational Mobility in Mid-Nineteenth Century Poughkeepsie," in Bruchey, *Small Business in American Life*, p. 126.

44. This analysis of Columbus's industrial growth is based on Hunker, *Industrial Evolution of Columbus*, chap. 3. But, see also Michael Speer, "Urbanization and Reform: Columbus, Ohio 1870–1900" (Ph.D. dissertation, The Ohio State University, 1972), chap. 1.

45. Columbus Board of Trade, *Annual Report, 1887* (Columbus, 1888), p. 75.

46. On the depression of the 1890s, see: Charles Hoffman, "The Depression of the Nineties," *Journal of Economic History* 16 (June 1956): 137–64; Samuel Rezneck, "Unemployment, Unrest, and Relief in the United States during the Depression of 1893–1897," *Journal of Political Economy* 61 (August 1953): 324–45.

47. Hogan, *Economic History*, vol. 1, p. 184.

48. *Ohio State Journal*, November 19, 1894.

49. Ibid., November 30, December 30, 1894.

50. Ibid., December 30, 1894.

51. Ibid., November 1, 1894.

52. Betty Garrett and Edward Lentz, *Columbus: America's Crossroads* (Tulsa, Oklahoma: Continental Heritage Press, 1980), p. 97.

53. *Ohio State Journal*, November 4, December 30, 1894.

54. Ibid., December 30, 1894.

chapter 2
FROM IRON TO STEEL,
1895-1921

> At 5 o'clock Tuesday afternoon the first heat was turned off
> from one of the furnaces in the new works of the Buck-
> eye Malleable Iron and Coupler Company in South Colum-
> bus. . . . Someone gave a signal and in a minute everyone in
> the building and out of it was on hand to watch the great crane
> as it lifted the smoking ladle and carried it to the furnace. Then
> at a touch the furnace itself slowly turned on its axis until the
> steel came pouring forth in a stream of liquid fire amid a cloud
> of fiery spray. It was a beautiful sight, indeed.[1]

With these vivid words, a reporter for the Columbus *Citizen* described Buckeye's entrance into the steel age in 1902. On October
14 of that year the corporation began changing from iron to steel
production, and by 1916 Buckeye's officers could observe that their
company was operating "the largest steel foundry in the world . . .
devoted entirely to the manufacture of steel castings for railroad
work."[2] From a small malleable iron company Buckeye emerged,
within the short span of twenty years, as a major corporation in
America's steel-castings industry.

Buckeye Enters the Steel-Castings Industry
Buckeye's evolution occurred as part of advances in the United
States' steel industry. As established markets—railroads, the construction industry, shipbuilding, and the oil industry—developed
further and as new steel-using industries, most importantly the
automobile and electrical machinery industries, grew up, the demand for steel soared. Between 1900 and 1920 American steel production rose from 11,400,000 tons to 47,200,000 tons annually, and
in the same years the United States' share of the world's production
of steel increased sharply from 37 to 59 percent.[3]

More specifically, Buckeye's growth took place as part of the rapid expansion of America's steel-castings industry. The industry began in Buffalo, Pittsburgh, and the Delaware Valley during the 1860s and 1870s. Progress was initially slow. The appearance of the castings, their imperfect surfaces, and the adherence of sand from the molds retarded their acceptance. Even more importantly, the cracking and porosity of the castings led to a high rejection rate. Moreover, the market for steel castings was small. The only major customers were railroads, and in this period even railroads used but a limited amount of steel castings. The industry came of age with the remarkable growth of railroads in the 1880s and 1890s. As new processes for the production of steel castings were developed, railroads came to use cast steel for couplers and other items. Steel castings also won increasing acceptance in shipbuilding and ordnance. From less than 2,000 tons in the early 1880s, the annual production of cast steel rose to 200,000 tons in the late 1890s. During the first two decades of the twentieth century, the steel castings business developed into one of America's major basic industries. Railroads remained the principal market, as car construction increasingly utilized steel in couplers, bolsters, wheels, and sideframes. Mechanical construction—especially cylinders for hydraulic presses, valves, and shafts—used more and more cast steel, as did ordnance and shipbuilding. The First World War further stimulated the industry. By 1919, some 825,000 tons of steel castings were being produced each year.[4]

After its founding in 1894, the Buckeye Malleable Iron and Coupler Company began operations in the plant on Russell Street in downtown Columbus which had been occupied by Munson-Hayden. This plant continued to turn out cast iron couplers during the 1890s.[5] Buckeye's business was a success from the beginning. Even in the depths of the depression of the mid-1890s, the company posted a "net gain" of $47,000 in 1895. As general economic conditions improved, so did Buckeye's earnings, which rose to $100,000 in 1896. To handle the company's increasing business, additions were made to the Russell Street foundry, and by 1897 Buckeye possessed assets of $515,000.[6]

Not even these additions gave Buckeye room enough to keep up with its expanding business. Moreover, as trains became longer and heavier, the malleable iron couplers could not handle the increased strains put on them. To solve this problem, Buckeye's management, like those of other coupler companies, decided to change to the production of the much stronger cast steel couplers.

In early 1898 Wilbur Goodspeed and T. P. Linn began looking for land upon which Buckeye could build a large, modern steel plant. A year later they acquired thirty-one acres just south of Columbus, and they purchased additional acreage in 1902. The land was west of Parsons Avenue, called in those days Smoky Row Road. Already an industrial area becoming known as Steelton, this region also contained the plants of the Federal Glass Company, Keever Starch, Columbus Woodenware, Carnegie Steel, and Columbus Iron and Steel.[7] Buckeye's relocation was part of a general migration of industry out of Columbus's downtown area. Land was simply becoming too expensive there for industry, and by the early 1900s factories had moved to emerging industrial districts around First Avenue and Fourth Street and South Parsons Avenue.[8]

Construction on the new plant proceeded smoothly, and the first heat of molten steel was poured in October 1902. By the end of 1903 the South Plant (as the Parsons Avenue plant was called) had become the center of Buckeye's operations and had a value of $670,000. In recognition of this shift, Buckeye's officers changed their company's name to the Buckeye Steel Castings Company, the name by which the corporation would be known for the next sixty-four years.[9]

The South Plant was initially housed in two main buildings. The foundry building, measuring 800 by 135 feet, enclosed two tilting open-hearth furnaces, one of ten- and one of twenty-tons capacity. The other major building, 500 by 135 feet, sheltered the finishing facilities. Auxiliary buildings housed the pattern-making area and the boiler plant. Buckeye purchased its raw materials—scrap steel, limestone, and pig iron (much of which came from Columbus Iron and Steel)—locally, melted them in its open-hearth furnaces, cast the resulting metal in molds, and finished the cast steel products in chipping and grinding rooms and in annealing furnaces which strengthened the steel through heat treatments.[10]

This construction was just the beginning of Buckeye's early-twentieth-century expansion. New facilities soon blossomed on land added to the original South Parsons' property. The company increased the number of open-hearth furnaces to four in 1905 and to five a year later.[11] Appropriations for capital improvements, needed because "the business of the plant has grown," came to around $100,000 annually between 1905 and 1912 (exclusive of sums for furnace construction) and paid for the building of or additions to the power plant, the pattern shop, the core room, a special coupler shop, and improved finishing facilities. As the South Plant expanded, the malleable iron works on Russell Street contracted its operations, and in 1910 the company sold it altogether.[12]

With Buckeye's growth came public recognition of the company's rising importance as part of Columbus's industrial base, a significance underlined by a decline in the number of malleable iron works, foundries, and machine shops in Columbus from twenty-three to twelve in the mid-1890s.[13] In 1907 the *Ohio Magazine* observed that Buckeye "is one of the largest makers in the country for railroad cars" and noted that "the plant of the company in South Columbus covers many acres of ground and has recently been almost doubled in size."[14]

The construction and start-up operations of the South Plant strained Buckeye's resources. As one officer remembered the situation, "the cost of the steel castings plant and the necessary additional working capital greatly exceeded the estimates," with the result that Buckeye's "liquid assets were depleted."[15] Even so, Buckeye continued to show net gains, $229,000 in 1905; and by 1906, a year singled out by Buckeye's president for "the satisfactory condition of the business," the corporation's output of steel castings reached 36,000 tons.[16]

Buckeye's progress did not come easily. Technical problems in the perfection of casting techniques cost Buckeye time and money. George T. Johnson, later Buckeye's president, recalled a typical early-day mishap in an address he gave in 1946. In 1907 Buckeye secured an order for 500 truck bolsters from a railroad car builder in St. Louis. Unfortunately, the center plates of the bolsters, as delivered by Buckeye, were out of round. As a result, Johnson and others from Buckeye were forced to spend several weeks in St. Louis chipping the plates by hand until they were the correct shape. "In order to keep us supplied with chisels," Johnson remembered, "a box of 75 was expressed every other day for over two weeks." It was on this job, he concluded, that he learned his "first lesson as to requirements of accuracy."[17]

Setbacks of this nature did not long slow Buckeye's growth, for, like others in the steel castings industry, Buckeye found the years 1906 through 1914 to be prosperous ones. Net earnings averaged $340,000 annually on average sales of $2,340,000 per year, a healthy 15 percent return.[18] The year 1912 marked the beginning of another major expansion drive at Buckeye, as some $450,000 were spent on improvements over the next two years.[19] With its modern steel plant in operation, Buckeye quickly became an important factor in the steel-castings industry. In 1909 about ninety companies produced 615,000 tons of steel castings in the United States, and of this total Buckeye's output was 46,000 tons. (For details on Buckeye's production figures, see Appendix 1 at the end of this study.) Throughout the next decade, Buckeye accounted for about 10 percent of the industry's annual production.[20] One of the five major coupler manufacturers in America, Buckeye was the third largest, as shown in Table 1.[21]

Table 1
Couplers Sold in the United States, 1908–1912

COMPANY	NUMBER OF COUPLERS SOLD	PERCENTAGE OF SALES
National Malleable	1,605,000	46
American Steel Foundries	786,000	23
Buckeye Steel	513,320	15
Gould Coupler	447,000	13
Monarch Steel Castings	93,000	3

SOURCE: Ernst and Ernst, "Report on Sales of Couplers," pamphlet in Buckeye Collection, Ohio Historical Society, p. 8.

However, Buckeye's advance was erratic. As the company came to produce increasingly for railroads, it found its fortunes tied ever closer to those of the railroads. When the railroads bought new cars, Buckeye prospered, and, since many railroads were modernizing their lines in the opening decades of the twentieth century, Buckeye generally did quite well. By the same token, however, when railroad purchases declined, Buckeye suffered. As railroads cut back their orders from 235,000 cars in 1912 to 146,000 cars a year later, Buckeye had to nearly curtail its cast steel production. The company operated its six furnaces at "full capacity" into June 1913. But then, as Buckeye's president noted, "business conditions changed rather suddenly," and the company had to begin shutting down its furnaces. In late June, four furnaces were still operating; by mid-September, two; and in December, only one. The dependence upon railroads as their main market would long trouble Buckeye's management. Only with a major diversification program in the 1960s and 1970s would they partially solve this problem.[22]

The First World War boosted the demand for steel castings in general and Buckeye's products in particular. To prepare for war work, Buckeye installed a six-ton Heroult electric furnace and constructed a forge plant.[23] These facilities were soon put to use. In mid-1917 Buckeye signed a contract to produce 2,000,000 pounds of gun forgings on the basis of "cost plus a reasonable profit," and additional contracts soon followed.[24] As the Columbus *Citizen* noted, Buckeye was one of fifteen "big new plants" producing gun forgings for the federal government, and the only one in Ohio. At the same time, Buckeye arranged with the Railroad Administration, a federal government agency running American railroads during the war, to produce couplers and other railroad parts for a 12 percent profit on actual investment.[25]

Buckeye's war work brightened its financial statements. With its production of steel castings soaring to 95,000 tons in 1917 and 73,000 tons in 1918, Buckeye had sales of close to $10,000,000 in each of those years, and by 1920 the firm's assets had risen to $9,100,000. However, because of the restrictive terms of the various government contracts, Buckeye did not reap excess profits from the war. Net earnings rose little faster than sales or assets during this period.[26] This situation stood in marked contrast to the much higher profits made by the larger steel companies, such as United States Steel and Bethlehem Steel, which secured more flexible, open-ended government contracts.[27]

Reconversion to peacetime production proved difficult for the steel industry. By 1920 the steel industry was operating at only 75 percent of its capacity, and a year later production had dropped precipitously to just 35 percent of capacity.[28] Buckeye suffered along with the other steel companies. Buckeye's forge plant was quickly dismantled, and the building was put to use as housing for the electric furnace. Buckeye's officers purchased some equipment which had been supplied by the federal government for the war effort for $50,000; but, for the most part, the company tried to shift rapidly to the production of railroad couplers and other railroad car castings. This task was hindered by a postwar recession. Railroad purchases of freight cars fell to 23,000 in 1921, a drastic decline from the 97,000 cars purchased the year before.[29] This turn of events hurt Buckeye. In mid-April 1921 the president reported to his directors that recent cutbacks in production had resulted in massive layoffs in the work force, leaving Buckeye with only "key people, who are in many cases not performing their regular duties, but anything to which they can turn their hand, which includes labor work." Even with this retrenchment, Buckeye had problems. As sales fell to $1,500,000, the company reported a loss of $370,000 for 1921.[30]

Buckeye had, then, built its basic steel plant by the end of the first two decades of the twentieth century. It was this facility, albeit with substantial renovations and additions, that would serve as the company's productive facility into the 1940s. Even as they developed their Columbus facilities, Buckeye's officers looked for opportunities elsewhere. Highly motivated, aggressive business-men, they sought additional expansion possibilities. Although few of their expansionary moves ultimately worked out, they indicate the buoyant optimism which characterized Buckeye's early years.

The first serious prospect for growth beyond Columbus came in 1908. During the fall of that year, Harry Scullin, the president of Scullin-Gallagher Iron of St. Louis, proposed to sell his company to Buckeye. After only a "casual observation which was made in walking through the plant in the course of an hour," Buckeye's officers offered him $2,250,000. They did not, however, consummate the purchase. Perhaps the price was too low for Scullin; or, more likely, those at Buckeye had second thoughts about the price. In making their offer, Buckeye's directors complained that they had had "no opportunity to make a thorough inspection of your property with a view of ascertaining definitely its capacity and efficiency." Buckeye's proposition contained numerous escape clauses, and the firm's management may well have used one to quash the purchase arrangement, after further examining the Scullin plant.[31]

This same scenario of seeming interest followed by inaction oc-curred a decade later. In 1920 S. P. Bush, who had become Buckeye's president twelve years earlier, visited Birmingham, Alabama to look over the Anniston Steel Company, a large cast

iron and steel manufacturer. Although Bush reported to his directors that Anniston was in an "unusually advantageous condition"
and that its purchase would help Buckeye improve its sales in the
South, the directors did not pursue the matter. The postwar recession was already affecting Buckeye, forcing a cutback in the company's growth plans.[32]

Somewhat more successful was Buckeye's search for land upon
which to build a steel plant in the Chicago area. Served by low-cost
water transportation and possessing a large labor force, this region
attracted a number of steel companies in the early 1900s.[33] In early
1909 Bush commented upon the possibility of constructing a "supplemental steel castings plant" near Chicago, and over the next two
years, company officers considered several sites. In late 1910 the
directors voted to buy eighty-four acres in East Chicago and instructed Buckeye's president to ask for bids to build a three- or
four-furnace plant at this location. However, nothing immediately
came of this venture, for Buckeye's officers decided to spend all of
their available money on the Columbus plant.[34] In fact, by 1917
Buckeye's management was trying to sell their East Chicago land.
Buckeye's officers waxed hot and cold over various proposals during the next three years, but found no one willing to pay the price
they wanted.[35] Then, in 1920 they once again considered building a
plant on the property and had an architect draft a plan for a comprehensive steel-castings plant designed to produce couplers and
other items for railroads. Again, as in the consideration given the
purchase of Anniston Steel, the business slump following the First
World War cut short the implementation of this plan.[36]

At the same time that they tried to purchase other steel castings
companies, Buckeye's management sought to control their sources
of raw materials. They did so for two basic reasons. First, they
wanted to lessen costs by eliminating the profits paid to independent suppliers of sand, limestone, and other materials. More importantly, they hoped to assure their company of steady supplies
during times of peak demand, something not always possible when
Buckeye had to compete in the open market for the materials.

In adopting a strategy of vertical integration, Buckeye's officers
were following in the footsteps of many late nineteenth-century
businessmen. Most notable in this respect was Andrew Carnegie,
the head of Carnegie Steel. Originally set up simply to produce steel

ingots, Carnegie Steel faced the same problems Buckeye would later encounter. Carnegie believed the prices he had to pay for his iron ore, coal, and other raw materials were too high, and he was incensed when he could not secure all of the raw materials he wanted when the market for steel was booming. Backward vertical integration was Carnegie's solution. In 1889 he gained control of the Frick Coke Company to assure his business of an adequate supply of coking coal at a low price, and seven years later he bought out the Rockefeller holdings in the Mesabi Range to gain a new supply of iron ore.[37]

Buckeye never went as far as Carnegie Steel, but Buckeye did take significant steps in the direction of vertical integration. The first moves were made in the years 1906 through 1907, when Buckeye, together with the Federal Glass Company, spent $100,000 to prospect for natural gas to fuel its operations.[38] Noting that it was "exceedingly difficult" to purchase enough limestone in times of peak demand, Buckeye's president also acquired a large quarry in Clark County, Ohio. By 1929, when Buckeye closed the quarry, 200,000 tons of limestone had been extracted.[39] Buckeye's management sought control over supplies of molding sand as well. In early 1910 the company's president decried "the great difficulties" in obtaining sufficient quantities of it, and three years later Buckeye bought a major interest in a company with extensive holdings of sand in Illinois.[40] Buckeye lacked the resources to control its supply of pig iron; the company purchased it in 5,000-ton lots from a variety of sources in Pittsburgh and central Ohio.[41]

While largely failing in horizontal integration, Buckeye was successful at vertical integration. In this respect, Buckeye's growth strategy differed from that of its major rivals in the early twentieth century—the National Malleable and Steel Castings Company and American Steel Foundries. While, like Buckeye, both of these corporations sought to control the sources of their raw materials, they also engaged in programs of horizontal integration.

American Steel Foundries was formed, as that corporation's historian has described it, as a collection of "eight different foundries scattered from the Mississippi to the Atlantic."[42] Incorporated in 1902, it was composed of four foundries in Pennsylvania, three in Illinois, and one in Ohio. In 1905 the company bought the Simplex Railway Appliance Company, and additional

purchases followed in later years. National Malleable began as the
Cleveland Malleable Iron Company in 1886. Expansion first occurred with the establishment of the Chicago Malleable Iron Company (later called Chicago Works No. 1) during 1873. Nine years
later, the Indianapolis Malleable Iron Company was formed, and
in 1890 the Toledo Malleable Iron Company came into existence.
While all of these companies were separate legal entities, their
ownership was substantially the same; and in 1891 they were
merged to become National Malleable. In 1902 the company constructed a second plant in Chicago, and eighteen years later it purchased the Missouri Malleable Iron Company.[43]

In their headlong expansion, these companies encountered financial problems that Buckeye did not face. Difficulties were most pronounced at American Steel Foundries. Thomas Drever, an early
comptroller for the company and later its chairman of the board,
recalled that during the years 1902 through 1905 "the company lost
money . . . and was on the verge of bankruptcy."[44] By focusing
nearly all of their energies and resources upon first building and
then continually modernizing their Columbus plant, Buckeye's officers were able to avoid being caught in this situation. They were,
in effect, following Andrew Carnegie's well-known advice: "Put
all your good eggs in one basket, and then watch that basket."
Although sometimes short of funds, Buckeye Steel watched its
basket well and never came near failing.

Financing Growth

The rapid twentieth-century expansion in Buckeye's operations
required heavy capital expenditures, for the steel industry has
always been capital-intensive. As has been typical of beginning
businesses in America, those founding Buckeye raised the needed
capital by persuading personal friends and business acquaintances
to invest in the company. They sold no stock through organized ex-
changes. Even if they had been able to make a public offering of
Buckeye's stock, it is unlikely that Buckeye's founders would have
done so. They looked upon Buckeye as *their* company, and, as is
again typical of newly formed businesses, were loathe to yield any
degree of control over it to outsiders.[45]

The late 1890s, when Buckeye expanded its iron works, were
prosperous years for the corporation. While Buckeye paid high

dividends, an average of 23 percent annually in the years 1898–1900, large sums were also reinvested as plant improvements. The building and expansion of the steel plant in the early 1900s also came largely out of retained earnings. Dividends, while averaging a healthy 10 percent between 1900 and 1915, fell from the earlier levels as more and more income went into plant construction. Only during the war years was this situation reversed, with dividends averaging 27 percent for the period 1916–20.[46]

Despite these impressive earnings, Buckeye, like many fledgling ventures, was cash poor. Company officers, anxious to expand their operations, sought more funds than retained earnings alone could provide. Buckeye occasionally borrowed from banks, especially as a way to secure working capital. Personal connections were of great importance in obtaining these funds. Between 1902 and 1905 Buckeye borrowed significant sums, ranging from $15,000 to $75,000, from two Columbus banks—the Deshler National, whose head, John Deshler was a Buckeye director, and the Commercial National, of which Goodspeed was president—in the form of four- and six-month renewable notes. In 1904 Buckeye also received a loan of $16,000 from the Colorado Iron and Steel Company, a Rockefeller concern.[47] A year later, Buckeye's directors authorized its president to borrow $250,000 for additional working capital, and in 1912 they approved his request to seek $150,000 to take care of maturing financial obligations.[48] It is unclear from the records still in existence whether or not these loans were actually obtained and used, but most likely they were. Borrowing continued, as Buckeye expanded its operations during the First World War. In 1917 and 1918 the company secured $100,000 and $85,000, respectively, in ninety-day renewable notes from the Hayden Clinton Bank, and sums of $65,000 and $100,000 were borrowed during the same years from the Liberty National Bank of New York, an institution in which one of Buckeye's officers had an interest.[49]

Buckeye's management obtained additional financing from stock sales, and the corporation's growth led to changes in its capital structure. In 1901 Buckeye's stockholders voted to increase their firm's capital stock from $500,000 to $1,000,000. Some $250,000 of the increase was paid out as a stock dividend, but the other $250,000 was reserved for new stock sales. And, during 1902 and 1903, Buckeye's directors authorized the sale of new shares of stock

to provide working capital for the steel plant.[50] Further reorganization occurred in 1906, when Buckeye's capitalization was increased to $2,500,000 through a 100 percent stock dividend in the
form of 6 percent preferred stock and the authorization of sale of
$500,000 worth of additional common stock.[51] Finally, in two
separate moves in 1920, Buckeye's authorized capitalization was
raised to $7,000,000. Most of this increase was paid out as
common-stock dividends, but some common stock was retained for
new sales.[52]

Buckeye's stockholders were pleased with their company's performance. Unlike most beginning enterprises, which struggle simply to survive, Buckeye combined healthy expansion with hefty
cash and stock dividends. While the number of stockholders increased steadily from 47 in 1895 to 149 twenty-five years later, there
was a basic continuity in the ownership of Buckeye's stock.[53]

Even in 1920 Buckeye's most prominent stockholders were
associated with the company as directors, officers, or employees.
The Goodspeed family continued to control a large block of stock,
as did S. P. Bush and his family. Several of Buckeye's assistant
plant superintendents and engineers owned smaller shares. Most of
Buckeye's original incorporators kept up their ties with the corporation, increasing their stockholdings and often acting as directors. Through ties of business and friendship, they brought in new
investors, many of whom were connected with railroads or iron and
steel concerns. For instance, R. S. Warner, the secretary-treasurer
of King, Gilbert, and Warner Company, a Columbus iron and steel
manufacturer, became a major shareholder and director in the late
1890s; and Nicholas Monsarrat, the president of the Hocking
Valley, the Louisville & Western, and the Toledo & Ohio Central
railroads, became a stockholder and director several years later.
John Deshler, who enlarged his stockholdings and was a director
for Buckeye's first twenty-six years, attracted other Columbus
bankers to the company. By 1921 the president of the Franklin
Loan and Savings Company, the cashier and vice-president of the
Hayden Clinton National Bank, and the president of the Ohio National Bank all owned substantial blocks of Buckeye stock.[54]

Still other investors came from beyond Columbus, particularly
Cleveland. The Thomas Goodwillie family steadily acquired more
shares in Buckeye. Most noticeable, however, was the rise in impor-

tance of Frank Rockefeller and his family. Rockefeller purchased stock throughout the 1890s and early 1900s, becoming one of Buckeye's largest stockholders. Goodwillie and Rockefeller, in turn, brought still other Cleveland residents into the Buckeye fold, most notably W. R. Woodford, the president of the Rail and River Coal Company.[55]

Marketing

The construction of the new steel plant and its successful financing might have come to nought had Buckeye's marketing efforts not also succeeded. Sales were, of course, essential for Buckeye's growth and development. As the company switched from iron to steel production, the nature of its sales operations changed, and these changes also led to alterations in Buckeye's relations with its competitors.

During the 1890s Buckeye relied upon both its own officers and commission merchants to sell its railroad couplers. Buckeye employed Frank Wirgman of Philadelphia and C.H.M. McKibbin of New York as its eastern sales agents during the mid-1890s.[56] This situation proved unstable, and in 1898 C. L. Perkins and Company of New York became Buckeye's eastern agent, a position it would hold into the twentieth century. At the same time, Buckeye signed Julian Yale and Company of Chicago as its western sales agent. Both usually received a 5 percent commission on their sales, based on the prices of couplers F.O.B. Columbus.[57] Buckeye's officers and stockholders were also responsible for many sales. In 1895, for instance, Thomas Goodwillie, carrying out the pledge he and Frank Rockefeller had made three years before, lined up the Great Northern Railroad for 5,000 car sets of couplers. S. P. Peabody, a Buckeye director and officer of the Baltimore & Ohio Railroad, not only kept his own line buying from Buckeye, but also convinced other firms, most notably the Pullman Palace Car, to do likewise.[58]

Though much of its output of malleable iron continued to be sold locally, an ever-increasing share went into railroad couplers for the national market. Comprehensive sales data for the 1890s have not survived, but fragmentary correspondence suggests the growing number of Buckeye customers throughout the United States: the Keokuk & Western; the Illinois Central; the Missouri, Kansas, & Texas; the Indiana, Illinois, & Iowa; the Fort Worth &

Denver City; the Elgin, Joliet, & Eastern; the Union Pacific; the
Cleveland, Loraine, & Wheeling; the Cleveland & Canton; and
the Northern Pacific; in addition to those lines already mentioned.[59]

Buckeye's sales efforts became more intricate in the twentieth
century. To handle the increasing complexity of their products,
Buckeye's officers assumed more of the responsibility for sales
themselves and depended less upon the work of independent commission agents. At the same time, Buckeye's officers sought to
reach agreements with other steel-castings firms on ways to
stabilize the market for their products. By 1915 Buckeye had two of
its own sales offices in operation, one in New York to serve
eastern railroads and another in Chicago for the western lines.

Jerry Bower opened the New York office in 1913. Bower, as
would be the norm for Buckeye's salesmen into the 1960s, worked
through personal connections. "He was always working with the
presidents and vice-presidents of railroads," remembered Marshall
Cooledge, another Buckeye sales representative. Bower belonged to
the "right" clubs and ate at fashionable restaurants. He was a
member of a special body called the Firemen, which was an informal social group made up mainly of Pennsylvania Railroad officers. Each year this group would get together and "have a blast
off."[60] Bower's character contributed to his success in sales. He
was an outgoing person. Before coming to Buckeye, he had been
with the New York Central Railroad, a consistently large Buckeye
customer for many decades.[61]

C. B. "Barney" Goodspeed started the Chicago office just
before the First World War. The son of Wilbur Goodspeed, he left
Buckeye for the army during the war years; after the war,
Goodspeed, while remaining a major Buckeye stockholder, left the
company to pursue a life in politics.[62] Fred Cooledge took his place
as head of the Chicago office. Born on a Michigan farm in 1878,
Cooledge grew up in rural areas. His greatest fun as a boy came, he
later recalled, from "fishing, swimming, playing baseball, coasting
downhill in the winter time." In general, though, the work was
hard, with "farm boys from about 14 to 16 years old receiving 50
cents" a day for their labor.[63] Cooledge put himself through the
Grand Rapids Business College, receiving his diploma in 1894. By
1898 Cooledge had become a clerk for the Flint & Pere Marquette

Railroad, headquartered in Milwaukee. Eight years later, he moved to Chicago as a clerk for Julian Yale and Company, Buckeye's western sales agent. Within a few years more, he joined Goodspeed in setting up Buckeye's independent sales office, at a salary of $100 per month, and in 1917 he took charge of the office himself.[64]

Cooledge drew heavily upon his railroad contacts in his sales work. As Cooledge later observed, experience with Julian Yale and the railroads "gave me *something* to start with."[65] He quickly built upon this foundation to become, as his son put it, a friend of "a lot of [railroad] presidents and vice-presidents." Entertaining was important in maintaining the personal contacts so essential in sales work, and "in those days money rolled around pretty free."[66] A very successful salesman, Cooledge headed the Chicago office into the 1940s.

Subordinate to the Chicago sales office was a branch in St. Paul, and its operations amply demonstrated the importance of knowing the right people. The office was a one-man show run by George MacPherson. Of Scotch ancestry, MacPherson moved from Canada to St. Paul in the woolen business. There he became a friend of the railroad magnate James Hill through his membership in the Minnesota Club, one of Hill's favorite retreats. Described by one of his business acquaintances as "tight, honest, old-fashioned," MacPherson got along well with Hill, and Hill persuaded MacPherson to enter the railroad supply business. In the years before the First World War, MacPherson acted as an agent for the Bethlehem Steel, Atlas Portland Cement, and Pressed Steel Car companies, as well as for Buckeye. When James Hill died in 1916, MacPherson continued to sell to the Great Northern Railroad through his friendship with Louis Hill, James's son, and in these later years MacPherson dealt exclusively in Buckeye products.[67]

Even as they set up a national sales network, the officers in Buckeye's home office in Columbus devoted much of their time to sales. Fred Cooledge remembered that Frank Rockefeller, Buckeye's president between 1906 and 1908, "visited with me in the office several times."[68] S. P. Bush, who had ties with several railroads, spent much of his time on the road arranging sales. In August 1908 his wife wrote him that she was pleased "that your trip to Baltimore was successful."[69] A few months later Bush was again traveling, this time to negotiate sales with the Pennsylvania and New

York Central railroads. "The NYC," he noted ruefully, "are not
quick in their methods and we all have to wait on them."[70] Nicholas Monsarrat, who headed the Hocking Valley and several other
Ohio railroads, while also serving as a Buckeye director, made
some of Buckeye's sales. Frank Rockefeller accounted for still
more. In fact, Buckeye's management found his service so valuable
that in 1908 they entered into a special sales agreement with him.
Under its terms, Rockefeller received a commission of $0.50 on
each pair of couplers sold to two western lines in which he had an
interest—the Chicago, Milwaukee, & St. Paul and the Missouri,
Kansas, & Texas railroads.[71]

Several reasons caused Buckeye's shift to direct sales. First,
Buckeye's officers were plagued with disputes between their sales
agents. In 1898, for instance, a major controversy broke out between the Julian Yale Company of Chicago and the C. L. Perkins
Company of New York over who deserved the commission for coupler sales to the Indiana, Illinois, & Iowa Railroad.[72] By establishing their own sales offices, Buckeye's officers hoped to end
disputes of this type. More important, however, was the growing
complexity of Buckeye's products after 1900, when Buckeye moved
into the production of new types of couplers and other car parts for
railroads. These were technologically sophisticated products, requiring men well versed in mechanical engineering to explain and
sell them to railroads. Few commission merchants had this training. Almost of necessity, Buckeye came to rely upon its own personnel for sales.[73]

Buckeye's new approach to sales paralleled similar developments
in many larger businesses across the United States. America's long-established system of wholesale and retail merchants broke down
in the late nineteenth and early twentieth centuries, for the merchants lacked the resources and expertise required by the high-volume flow of technologically complicated goods produced by an
industrial society. Reacting to the deficiencies in the United States'
distribution system, businessmen established their own sales
systems. When the traditional merchants failed to handle the increased production of his steel mills to his satisfaction in the 1890s,
Andrew Carnegie began relying upon his salesmen. By the same
token, when independent commission agents proved incapable of
adequately demonstrating and servicing their products, electric
companies set up their own sales outlets.[74]

Buckeye's product offerings grew increasingly complex as time went on. Most important was Buckeye's continued development of the automatic railroad coupler. In 1903 the company introduced its first "Major" coupler. Named after Major Goodspeed, it quickly replaced the older "Buckeye" models. With some modifications the Major coupler remained Buckeye's leading product until 1916. Breaking into the production of additional products for railroads, the company began experimenting with the casting of steel car wheels in 1905, only to abandon this line of work five years later. More successful was Buckeye's entrance into the manufacture of integral box side frames for railroad cars about 1907, and about six years later the company pioneered as the first maker of full channel section side frames, which soon replaced the older arch bar side frame in the industry. It was in this same period that Buckeye initiated production of railroad car truck bolsters, selling the first orders on the basis of a service guarantee for the life of the car.[75]

The increased complexity of Buckeye's products not only led to alterations in the company's internal sales organization, but also resulted in changes in its relationships with its competitors. As a manufacturer of malleable iron products in the 1890s, Buckeye had many competitors and faced an atomized market for its goods. As a producer of cast steel railroad parts in the early 1900s, Buckeye had fewer competitors and worked in a more concentrated market. Not surprisingly, Buckeye and its major competitors—National Malleable, American Steel Foundries, Gould Coupler, and Monarch Steel—worked closely among themselves and with their railroad customers to standardize their products and restrict competition within their industry.

The impetus for cooperation came from the railroads and car builders, whose greatest concern centered upon couplers. Railroads were anxious to further the interchangeability of cars and disliked the expense of keeping large stocks of different makes of replacement couplers on hand. As early as 1904, the president of the Master Car Builders Association, a trade association, complained that "one of the greatest expenses we have to-day is the maintaining of so large a number of different makes of couplers . . . to maintain cars running." A committee set up to study the problem reported a year later that this trouble could best be ended through the "universal use of but one design of coupler." The association kept up its agitation for the development of a standard coupler over the next five years. However, the production of a standard coupler by different coupler manufacturers required the pooling of patents, and this was a step the coupler companies (which, like Buckeye, were just really beginning large-scale casting of steel couplers) were reluctant to take.[76]

In 1911 the Master Car Builders renewed its quest for a standard coupler. Railroads, caught in a squeeze between rising costs and relatively stable railroad rates, now led the attack. Representatives of the New York Central, the Chicago, Minneapolis, & St. Paul, the Union Pacific, the Chesapeake & Ohio, the Pennsylvania, the New York, New Haven, & Hartford, and the Seaboard Air Line all came out for a standard coupler at the 1911 meeting of the Master Car Builders Association. The conference passed a resolution calling upon the Committee on Couplers and Draft Equipment "to invite representatives of coupler manufacturing companies to join with the Master Car Builders' Committee in designing and adopting one standard freight-car coupler."[77]

This time the coupler manufacturers responded favorably to these overtures. They were more firmly established in their industry and were eager to rationalize relations among themselves. Many had just engaged in lengthy and costly patent fights. Buckeye, for instance, was involved in patent disputes with nearly all of its competitors between 1902 and 1911. Most protracted was a suit begun in 1904 with National Malleable which was finally decided in Buckeye's favor five years later.[78] Coupler manufacturers hoped to avoid the expenses and annoyances of such controversies through the adoption of a single design.

At meetings between themselves and representatives of the Master Car Builders Association, the coupler manufacturers laid the groundwork for cooperation in 1911 and 1912. Most crucial was a conference on May 15, 1912. At this meeting the coupler manufacturers agreed to pool their patents, an essential first step in the designing of a standard coupler.[79] The following month the Coupler Committee of the Master Car Builders Association began work on a standard coupler. Design and testing, carried on jointly with the coupler manufacturers, lasted another four years. Finally, in 1916 the Master Car Builders Association adopted what was known as the "Standard D" coupler as the only one that its members would purchase for freight cars.[80]

In preparation for the production of a standard coupler, the coupler manufacturers entered into an agreement to protect their rights and limit competition. Drawn up in July 1915 and revised fifteen months later, this agreement covered production and sales practices. Under its terms, the coupler manufacturers pooled all of their coupler patents. Moreover, they agreed to accept market shares for the sale of Standard D couplers proportional to their shares of the United States coupler market between 1908 and 1912. Finally, they agreed to charge identical prices for the Standard D coupler (the price was based on the price per ton of basic pig iron F.O.B., the Mahoning and Shenango Valley furnaces).[81]

This trend toward cooperation and avoidance of price competition was typical of America's basic steel industry as well as of the steel castings business. In the early twentieth century, United States Steel, which had been formed in 1901 with Carnegie Steel as its nucleus, dominated the industry. Through the "Gary dinners" of 1907–11 and then by more informal mechanisms in later years, United States Steel provided price leadership for the industry. The Pittsburgh Plus pricing system, which came into use around 1907, also dampened competition. Yet, despite price leadership by United States Steel and despite the Pittsburgh Plus system, some price competition remained in basic steel.[82]

The production and sales agreement for the steel-castings industry (at least for the production of railroad car couplers) remained in force for a long period of time and was quite effective. With some alterations it continued into the 1940s. Two factors explain its longevity. First, the coupler manufacturers set up a board of trustees, composed of one officer from each company, to police the agreement. If a company exceeded its market share in one year (and each company's books were open to the board), its share would be cut back in the succeeding year. Second, the board could deny a company access to the group's pool of patents. Since railroads agreed to buy only the Standard D coupler, and since access to these patents was required to produce the coupler, this power effectively enforced the agreement. The board could both penalize firms that violated the agreement and forbid new companies entry to the coupler market.[83]

By 1916, the first year for which comprehensive sales figures broken down by customer are available for Buckeye, the company had become a major seller of couplers, for which it had forty-eight customers. Some six railroads accounted for 86 percent of Buckeye's sales: the Baltimore & Ohio; the Chicago, Milwaukee, St. Paul, & Pacific; The Chicago, Rock Island, & Pacific; the Great Northern; the Norfolk & Western; and the Pennsylvania.[84] Buckeye's dependence upon a few major customers and the company's involvement in the coupler agreement paid short-term dividends. As we have seen, Buckeye was very profitable in the 1910s, and this profitability would continue in the 1920s. However, in the long run, these twin developments would retard innovation and lead to problems at Buckeye.

By 1921 Buckeye had emerged as a leader in the steel-castings industry. The company had clearly established itself as a major producer of cast steel car parts for America's railroads. Possessing a modern steel plant financed mainly from retained earnings, Buckeye was firmly grounded in Columbus and had begun to develop operations elsewhere. In part, Buckeye's growth derived from its management's ability to use technological innovations to overcome production problems and eagerness to maintain good relations with their corporation's labor force and the rest of the Columbus community. It is to these topics that we must now turn.

Notes

1. Columbus *Citizen*, October 15, 1902.
2. *The Buckeye Steel Castings Company*, pamphlet, February, 1916, unpaged, in Buckeye Collection, Ohio Historical Society.
3. William T. Hogan, Jr., *Economic History of the Iron and Steel Industry in the United States*, vol. 2 (Lexington, Mass.: D. C. Heath, 1971), pp. 649–51.
4. William P. Conway, Jr., *Cast to Shape: A History of the Steel Castings Industry in the United States* (Rocky River, Ohio: Dillon, Liederbach, 1977), chaps. 5, 6.
5. "Minutes of the Board of Directors Meeting, Buckeye Malleable Iron and Coupler Company, March 6, July 7, 1896" (hereafter cited as "Directors Meeting" with date). "Presidents Report for the Year Ending December 31, 1896" (hereafter cited as "President's Report" with date).
6. "Directors Meeting," January 14, 1896, January 12, 1897. "Minutes of Annual Meeting of Stockholders, Buckeye Malleable Iron and Cou-

pler Company, January 10, 1899'' (hereafter cited as "Stockholders Meeting" with date). For more detail on Buckeye's finances, see Appendix 2 of this book.

7. "Directors Meeting," January 11, 1898, May 24, 1899, September 22, 1902; *Modie and Kilmer's Folio Atlas of Franklin County, Ohio, 1910: Folio 10, Marion Township.*

8. Betty Garrett and Edward Lentz, *Columbus: America's Crossroads* (Tulsa, Oklahoma: Centennial Heritage Press, 1980), p. 87.

9. The name was changed on October 3, 1903. See: "Directors Meeting," October 3, 1903; "President's Report," December 31, 1903.

10. *Foundry* 20 (April 1902): 73.

11. Ibid., 26 (March 1905): 50; "Directors Meeting," October 12, 1906.

12. "Directors Meeting," January 12, 1906, January 29, 1907, April 10, November 16, 1908, January 25, July 11, October 27, 1910, January 30, 1912.

13. R. L. Polk, *Columbus City Directory, 1895–1896* (Columbus), p. 921.

14. W. B. Jackson, "Industrial Columbus," *Ohio Magazine* 3 (1907): 463.

15. Quoted in "History of the Buckeye Steel Castings Company," undated, unpaged typescript manuscript.

16. "Auditor's Report on Buckeye Steel Castings, January 29, 1907"; "Note on Buckeye Steel Castings, 1907"; "Stockholders Meeting," January 19, 1904, January 17, 1905, January 30, 1906, January 29, 1907.

17. "Remarks by George T. Johnson at the Second Annual Meeting of the B.S.C. 25-Year Club, August 27, 1946," typewritten pamphlet, p. 4, in Buckeye Collection, The Ohio Historical Society.

18. "Stockholders Meeting," January 29, 1907, January 28, 1908, January 26, 1909, January 25, 1910, January 31, 1911, January 30, 1912, January 28, 1913, January 27, 1914, January 26, 1915.

19. "Directors Meeting," April 19, May 10, 1912. "Minutes of Executive Committee Meeting, Buckeye Steel Castings Company, October 1, 1912" (hereafter cited as "Executive Committee Meeting" with date).

20. Conway, *Cast to Shape*, pp. 46, 60; "Stockholders Meeting," January 25, 1909, January 27, 1920.

21. Ernst and Ernst, "Report on Sales of Couplers," pamphlet in Buckeye Collection, Ohio Historical Society, p. 8.

22. "Stockholders Meeting," January 27, 1914, January 26, 1915. For figures on railroad car purchases, see the annual statistical issue of the *Railroad Age*. On railroad modernization, see Albro Martin, *Enterprise Denied: The Origins of the Decline of American Railroads, 1897–1917* (New York: Columbia University Press, 1971), chap. 3.

23. "Directors Meeting," July 26, October 6, 1915; "Executive Committee Meeting," March 27, 1914, April 10, 1915; "Stockholders Meeting," January 26, 1915, January 25, 1916, January 30, 1917.

24. "Directors Meeting," November 30, 1917; "Executive Committee Meeting," July 11, 1917, April 6, 1918.

25. Columbus *Citizen*, July 30, 1918.

26. "Stockholders Meeting," January 29, 1918, January 28, 1919, January 27, 1920.

27. Robert Cuff, *The War Industries Board* (Baltimore: Johns Hopkins Press, 1973); and Melvin Urofsky, *Big Steel and the Wilson Administration* (Columbus: The Ohio State University Press, 1969).

28. Hogan, *Economic History*, vol. 3, p. 811.

29. "Executive Committee Meeting," November 30, 1918, October 6, 1919.

30. "Directors Meeting," April 15, July 8, 1921; "Executive Committee Meeting," April 14, 1921; Stockholders Meeting," January 31, 1922.

31. "Directors Meeting," October 29, 1908.

32. "Executive Committee Meeting," December 1, 1920.

33. Phyllis Bate, "The Development of the Iron and Steel Industry of the Chicago Area, 1900–1920" (Ph.D. dissertation, University of Chicago, 1948).

34. "Directors Meeting," January 26, 1909, January 25, December 31, 1910, January 31, 1911.

35. S. P. Bush to C. B. Goodspeed, February 7, 1917; Bush to Charles Sullivan, June 24, 1919; Goodspeed to Bush, July 10, 1917; Charles Sullivan to Bush, June 23, 1919. All these letters are in Buckeye Collection, Ohio Historical Society.

36. "B.S.C. Plant, East Chicago, 1920"; Bush to William Hastings, June 3, 1920.

37. Harold Livesay, *Andrew Carnegie* (Boston: Little, Brown, 1975); Joseph Frazier Wall, *Andrew Carnegie* (New York: Oxford University Press, 1970).

38. "Directors Meeting," July 5, 1907, January 28, 1908; "Memorandum on Agreement Between Buckeye Steel Castings Company and Federal Glass Company, May 30, 1906."

39. "Directors Meeting," January 27, 1913; "Executive Committee Meeting," February 12, 1914.

40. "Directors Meeting," January 25, 1910, February 21, 1913; "Executive Committee Meeting," October 1, December 14, 1912.

41. "Directors Meeting," May 24, 1909, April 7, 1910, April 15, 1915; "Executive Committee Meeting," October 27, 1908, September 14, 1909, March 25, 1912, January 4, 1913, January 17, 1914.

42. Franklin Reck, *Sand in their Shoes: The Story of American Steel Foundries* (Cleveland: no publisher given, 1952), p. 1.

43. Anonymous, *National Malleable and Steel Castings Company, 1868-1943* (Cleveland: no publisher given, 1943), pp. 1–16.

44. Reck, *Sand in their Shoes*, p. 18.

45. Roland Robinson, "The Financing of Small Business in the United States," in Stuart Bruchey, editor, *Small Business in American Life* (New York: Columbia University Press, 1980).

46. These figures are the dividend rates for the common stock alone. From 1907 through 1921, Buckeye also paid an annual 6 percent dividend on a preferred stock issue. These figures are derived from Buckeye's annual balance sheets which are reprinted in the minutes of the annual stockholders meeting.

47. Buckeye Steel Castings Co., *Notes and Bills Payable Notebook*, undated, unpaged.

48. "Directors Meeting," October 25, 1912; "Stockholders Meeting," January 17, 1905.

49. Buckeye, *Notes and Bills*.

50. "Directors Meeting," May 10, 1903, April 27, 1903; "Special Stockholders Meeting," April 24, 1901.

51. "Directors Meeting," March 2, 1906; "Stockholders Meeting," April 17, 1906.

52. "Directors Meeting," January 28, 1919; "Stockholders Meeting," January 28, 1919, March 23, November 17, 1920.

53. "Lists of Stockholders, Buckeye Steel Castings, 1895, 1920," in Buckeye Collection, Ohio Historical Society.

54. Ibid.; Polk, *Columbus City Directory, 1920*.

55. "List of Stockholders, 1920."

56. "Receipt from Office of the Secretary of the Commonwealth of the State of Pennsylvania, April 7, 1896"; R. M. Rownd to Orland Smith, August 7, 1894; Unknown to F. Rockefeller, January 2, 1897; all in Buckeye Collection.

57. C. L. Perkins to W. F. Goodspeed, January 9, 1899; Julian Yale to Goodspeed, September 22, November 4, 1898, November 15, 1899.

58. William Agell to Buckeye Malleable Iron and Coupler Company, February 25, 1897; W. F. Goodspeed to Angell, December 16, 1897; Unknown to W. F. Goodspeed, April 29, 1895.

59. Larger buyers, as was common at that time, received considerable rebates on their purchases. The Union Pacific, Northern Pacific, and Great Northern railroads were granted rebates of 5 to 12 percent in 1895.

60. Interview by the author with Marshall Cooledge, August 9, 1978.

61. Interview by the author with George Johnson, Jr., April 21, 1978.

62. Columbus *Citizen*, August 8, 1918.

63. Fred Cooledge, "Reminiscences," 1949; this manuscript is now in the Bentley Historical Library, Ann Arbor, Michigan.

64. A. S. Parrish to Nelson Barrell, January 20, 1894; L. C. Whitney to J. N. Barr, March 28, 1899; "Cooledge Chronology—Notes"; all in the Buckeye Collection, Ohio Historical Society.

65. Fred Cooledge, "Retirement Speech," at the Ohio Historical Society.

66. Cooledge interview, August 9, 1978.

67. Interview by the author with Charles Pigott, June 14, 1978.

68. Cooledge, "Retirement Speech."

69. Flora Bush to S. P. Bush, late August 1908, in the Buckeye Collection at the Ohio Historical Society.

70. S. P. Bush to Flora Bush, probably late October 1908, in the Buckeye Collection.

71. "Directors Meeting," April 30, 1909; "Executive Committee Meeting," March 24, 1908. This commission was later commuted to an annual salary of $7,500. While never very important when compared to domestic sales, Buckeye also made some foreign sales, mainly in South America. In 1915 Buckeye made Chipman Ltd. of New York its exclusive sales agent for South America. Having branches in Rio de Janeiro, Buenos Aires, and Santiago de Chile, Chipman received a 15 percent commission on all sales of Buckeye products. See S. P. Bush to Chipman Ltd., Exporters, July 23, 1915.

72. Julian L. Yale and Company to the Buckeye Malleable Iron and Coupler Company, September 22, 1898.

73. Bush, "Notebook"; "President's Report," December 31, 1903.

74. Glenn Porter and Harold Livesay, *Merchants and Manufacturers: Studies in the Changing Structure of Nineteenth-Century Marketing* (Baltimore: Johns Hopkins Press, 1971), chaps. 8–12.

75. "Directors Meeting," October 25, 1905, January 25, 1910.

76. Anonymous, *History of the Development of the Standard Coupler and the Standard Coupler Agreement* (undated pamphlet in Buckeye Collection), pp. 1–2. See also Howard Gilbert, *The Development, Operation, and Maintenance of A.A.R. Standard Couplers* (undated pamphlet in Buckeye Collection).

77. *Development of Standard Coupler*, p. 11.

78. "Directors Meeting," May 20, 24, 1909. For all the details of the case see: *National Malleable Castings Company* v. *The Buckeye Malleable Iron and Coupler Company and The Buckeye Steel Castings Company*, United States Circuit Court of Appeals, Sixth Circuit, November 30, 1908.

79. "Revised Minutes of Meeting of M.C.B. Committee on Coupler and

Draft Equipment and Coupler Manufacturers, Held at Altoona, May 15, 1912," typescript copy in Buckeye Collection.

80. *Development of Standard Coupler*, pp. 13-22.

81. Ibid., reprints the agreements, pp. 23-40. National Malleable, American Steel Foundries, Buckeye Steel, Gould Coupler, and Monarch Steel signed the agreement. See also "Executive Committee Meeting," June 4, 1915.

82. Walter Adams, "The Steel Industry," in Adams, editor, *The Structure of American Industry* (New York: Macmillan, 1954), p. 152; Gertrude Schroeder, *The Growth of Major Steel Companies, 1900-1950* (Baltimore: Johns Hopkins Press, 1953), p. 197; George Stocking, *Basing Point Pricing and Regional Development* (Durham: University of North Carolina Press, 1954), chap. 3; Kenneth Warren, *The American Steel Industry, 1850-1870* (London: Oxford University, 1973), pp. 196-97, 201.

83. *Development of Standard Coupler*, pp. 13-22. Less binding and more short-lived agreements were entered into by the manufacturers of bolsters in 1919 and car trucks in 1921. See "Directors Meeting," September 25, 1919 and "Executive Committee Meeting," July 28, 1921.

84. "Sales, Net Tons, Couplers and Swivel Yokes, 1916-1951," typescript.

chapter 3

THE QUEST FOR COMMUNITY

It was the management that held Buckeye Steel and its many activities together. Aggressive and innovative, Buckeye's officers were quick to adopt new production techniques and ways of dealing with their labor force. At the same time, they worked to establish harmonious relations with other segments of Columbus's population. Their success in these matters, combined with several other factors, assured Buckeye's development as a major company in the steel-castings industry.

Buckeye's Management

To direct their company's work, Buckeye's original incorporators elected a president, who also served as the firm's general manager; a vice-president; a secretary-treasurer; and seven directors (all of whom were company officers or major stockholders in the firm). As Buckeye grew, new officers were added. In 1902 the stockholders elected a second vice-president, and three years later they set up an executive committee to meet monthly "as an advisory committee to the president and executive officers." A third vice-president was added in 1911. Below this top management, the steel plant was run by an assistant general manager and a superintendent.[1] Most of Buckeye's top management worked their way up through the ranks, winning advancement within the company. All were major stockholders in Buckeye, and nearly all stayed with the company for long periods of time. In fact, most left the corporation only upon their death or retirement.

Monetary rewards helped keep officers with Buckeye. Salaries were high for the time. The president received $6,000 in 1895, $20,000 in 1899, and $25,000 annually between 1913 and 1921. The vice-presidents usually served without pay. The secretary-treasurer made $1,500 in 1897, $6,000 in 1913, and $10,000 seven years later. The assistant general manager received $7,500 in 1909, but $19,000 in 1920; and the plant superintendent's salary rose from $6,000 to $17,000 during the same years.[2] These salaries compared well to those paid by other corporations. A survey by Harvard University showed that the chief executive officers of companies capitalized at $1,500,000 or more received average salaries of $9,958 during the years 1904 through 1914.[3]

Company officers benefited in other ways. In 1909 Buckeye began setting aside 10 percent of its net earnings as a bonus for its officers each year, and in that year the bonuses came to $12,000 for the president, $7,500 for the assistant general manager, $5,000 for the superintendent and $3,500 for the secretary-treasurer. In 1912 and 1920 Buckeye's officers were permitted to buy their company's stock at below its market value on generous credit terms. Finally, specific officers received still other considerations. T. P. Linn, a director, acted as legal counsel for the company at $3,600 annually by 1916, and, as we have seen, Frank Rockefeller received payments from Buckeye for couplers sold to railroads in which he had an interest.[4] More than a desire for monetary gain, however, motivated those at Buckeye.

As was increasingly the case in American business, Buckeye's officers were well-educated professionals with a deep interest in their work. This trend toward professionalization was most apparent in the changing backgrounds of the presidents. Wilbur Goodspeed, president between 1886 and his death in early 1905, was an entrepreneur with relatively little formal education and no professional training. Frank Rockefeller, who succeeded Goodspeed and remained president through 1907, had a public school education through age sixteen before going off to the Civil War as a private. By way of contrast, S. P. Bush, Buckeye's president during the years 1908 through 1927, had an extensive professional education, combined with practical training on the job. Born at Brick Church, New Jersey in 1863, Bush first attended public school and then the Stevens Institute of Technology, graduating with a degree in mechanical engineering in 1884. Bush began work as an apprentice in the shops of the Pittsburgh, Cincinnati, Chicago, & St. Louis Railroad (the Pennsylvania's affiliate between Pittsburgh, Columbus, and St. Louis) at Logansport, Indiana. He labored in the Columbus shops of the same line between 1885 and 1888, rising to assistant engineer for motive power in 1889 and master mechanic of the Columbus shop two years later. He transferred to the Pennsylvania Railroad as general superintendent of motive power for the line's southwest system in 1894, then moved to the Chicago, Milwaukee, & St. Paul Railroad in 1899, and finally to Buckeye as a vice-president in 1901.[5]

This same combination of professional education and practical training characterized the other Buckeye officers. John C. Whitridge, who was the firm's assistant general manager during the 1910s and a vice-president in 1920 and 1921, was born in Richmond, Indiana in 1872. He attended that town's Earlham College before going to Purdue University, where he received a bachelor's degree in mechanical engineering in 1895 and a master's degree three years later. During his spare time at college, Whitridge worked with the maintenance engineers for the Pennsylvania Railroad in his home town. Leaving college, he became an assistant for D. S. Barnes, a consulting engineer in Chicago, before joining Buckeye in 1902.[6] Like Whitridge, A. H. Thomas, who served as Buckeye's plant superintendent during the 1910s, was born and grew up in Richmond, Indiana. Moreover, he also received an engineering education at Purdue. Thomas worked on the Pennsylvania, on the Baltimore & Ohio, and on the Chicago, Milwaukee, & St. Paul railroads before beginning at Buckeye.[7]

Finally, Buckeye's officers stayed with the company, because they enjoyed the kind of life they and their families could lead in Columbus. Although it was rapidly growing and suffered from social problems, the city possessed, even in the 1920s, what one writer has recently described as a certain "ambience . . . a nice balance between urbanity and the solid farm philosophy that was so pervasive in the agricultural countryside."[8] For those who were well-off, life was quite pleasant. Those in Buckeye's upper ranks belonged to the "correct" clubs and took an active part in their city's social life. In 1912 Thomas belonged to the Columbus Club and the Ohio Club, and Whitridge was a member of the Arlington Country Club and the Columbus Club. (His wife belonged to the Columbus Art Association, Children's Hospital, and the Columbus Equal Suffrage Association.) As might be expected, Bush's affiliations were broader and more prestigious. In 1912 he headed the

Arlington Country Club, and he was active in the Automobile Club, the Columbus Club, the Columbus Symphony Association, the YMCA Businessman's Gym, the Assembly, and the Review Club. Mrs. Bush, in addition to the Assembly, belonged to Children's Hospital and the Columbus Gallery of Fine Arts.[9] Here they enjoyed lunches, teas, dinners, and balls and, in general, mingled with the "select" of Columbus.

For those who could afford it, travel offered a touch of variety to the local scene. Mrs. Bush often journeyed to Osterville on the seashore of Massachusetts to escape the summer heat and humidity of Columbus. Relatives and friends, many of whom were connected with Buckeye—Mrs. Charles Howe, Helen Deshler, Mrs. Wilbur Goodspeed, Daisy Hayden and others—frequently joined her, and they passed their time in luncheons, bridge, and swimming. "The bathing," Mrs. Bush wrote her husband in 1908, "is very fine indeed—safe and just enough sport for all purposes." Parties punctuated the otherwise sedate evenings. One Mrs. Goodspeed held was described as "quite a function." The Bush's children had a delightful time swimming, crabbing, rowing, and playing tennis and baseball. "The children are fine," Bush was informed by his wife, "and the change will be of lasting benefit to them. They do look so much better and thoroughly vigorous."[10]

The picture that emerges of Buckeye's management is that of fairly mature men who felt they knew what they wanted out of their work and life and how to get it. As a group, they were well educated for their time. (In 1900–1920 only 40 percent of America's business leaders had attended college, and still fewer had graduated.[11]) Most had extensive training on the job, usually with railroads, before coming to Buckeye in their thirties. For them Buckeye offered both a high pay scale and an opportunity to put their professional talents to good use. Beyond these factors, work and life in Columbus were appealing.

More than any other single individual, S. P. Bush typified Buckeye's early-twentieth-century management. He was a well-rounded person. An astute businessman, he was also involved in community affairs and national business events. "S. P.," as he was known at Buckeye, stood over six feet tall and had a powerful voice. As Albert Stock remembered him, Bush was "a snorter. . . . Everyone knew when he was around; when he issued orders, boy it went!''[12] Bush clearly enjoyed his life. Several companies, including the Pennsylvania Railroad, tried to lure Bush away from Buckeye, to no avail. "I hope you are as contented as you seem to feel," Flora Bush once wrote her husband.[13] He was. Bush's relaxed state of mind was, perhaps, most apparent in his dry sense of humor. In early December 1918 he wrote his wife, who was visiting relatives and friends, about the Christmas present he had purchased for her. "What do you think it is?" he asked. "Well, you can guess. A collar with a heavy chain to keep you at home."[14]

Scientific Management at Buckeye

One reason for Buckeye's success was the willingness, indeed the eagerness, of the company's management to adopt scientific management techniques in running their plant and dealing with their labor force.* Buckeye shared in and, in some cases, led the technologic advances which transformed the steel-castings industry in the opening decades of the twentieth century. In the operation of their plant, in their accounting practices used to monitor the work of the plant, and in still other ways, Buckeye's officers were in the forefront of change. In the late nineteenth and early twentieth centuries, an increasing number of businesses, particularly those engaged in heavy manufacturing, adopted the principles of "scientific management" as a way of removing production bottlenecks in their factories. Buckeye Steel was one of the corporations to embrace scientific management ideas.

Frederick Taylor is usually acknowledged as the father of scientific management in America, and Buckeye's management was well versed in Taylor's ideas. In the 1870s and 1880s Taylor worked at the Enterprise Hydraulic Works, Midvale Steel, and elsewhere to

---

*Parts of this section have been drawn from papers given by the author at professional conferences and were substantially published: Permission has been obtained from the publishers for use of "Business Growth and Technological Change: Buckeye Steel Castings, 1881–1916," at the Economic and Business History Conference, Los Angeles, April 26–28, 1979, published in *Essays in Economic and Business History* East Lansing: Michigan State University Business Studies, 1981; and for use also of "Scientific Management and Welfare Work in Early Twentieth Century American Business: The Buckeye Steel Castings Company," at the Economic and Business History Conference, Portland, Oregon, April 23–25, 1981, published in *Ohio History* 90 (Summer 1981): 238–58, by the Ohio Historical Society, Inc., Columbus, Ohio.

reestablish managerial control over the growing complexity of factory operations. In doing so, Taylor stressed three factors: the efficient layout of a plant to move material from point to point in a logical fashion, accompanied by the minute subdivision of labor; strict record keeping to speed the flow of materials through the plant; and detailed internal cost accounting to keep track of exactly what went on in a plant. In the early 1900s Taylor's ideas were well known in American business circles, and especially in the steel industry.[15] In addition to being familiar with Taylor's writings in general, Buckeye's officers knew of them through numerous articles in the *Foundry*, the major trade journal of steel-castings industry. Moreover, S. P. Bush may have known Taylor personally. Bush received a degree in mechanical engineering from the Stevens Institute of Technology in 1884, one year after Taylor.

Buckeye's steel plant was modern in construction. The buildings, put up by the American Bridge Company, were made of brick and structural steel. Steam power drove much of Buckeye's machinery, but direct current electricity, generated in the company's own powerhouse, drove many of Buckeye's overhead cranes and some of the finishing tools. The internal layout of the steel plant also bore the imprint of scientific-management thought, as every effort was made to speed the flow of work in process through the various stages of production.[16]

The production process began with the arrival of pig iron, scrap steel, limestone, sand, and other raw materials at the Buckeye plant. Once unloaded from the railroad cars by large cranes (magnetic cranes handled the scrap steel), they were routed via Buckeye's own intra-plant railroad system to their various destinations. Most of the sand went to the foundry, where it was shoveled by hand into the molds. The metal patterns for the molds had previously been made in Buckeye's pattern shop, which employed belt-driven, steam-powered machinery. Each mold consisted of two parts, a top (the cope) and a bottom (the drag). Meanwhile, some of the sand traveled to the core room, where universal core machines formed it into cores for the molds. The cores were then transferred to the foundry and placed inside the molds. With this step accomplished, workmen joined the copes and drags together. With the molds ready to receive it, molten metal was now needed. While the molds were being prepared, the pig iron, steel scrap, and limestone were sent to the foundry's furnaces to be melted down.[17]

Most steel-castings companies operated as open-hearth works in the early twentieth century. In 1909 about 92 percent of the United States' production came from open-hearth furnaces, and in 1919 about 85 percent. Open-hearth castings production become more and more of a science and less of an art as time passed. The steel "doctor" of the nineteenth century, a person who carefully guarded his recipe for a successful melt, gave way to the scientist and metallurgical engineer of the twentieth century. Even so, making steel castings remained an art, as well as a science, during Buckeye's early years.[18]

Buckeye engaged in both "basic" and "acid" open-hearth operations. For basic steel, the firm used a charge of 25 percent basic pig iron, 63 percent scrap steel, and 12 percent limestone; for acid steel the charge was 20 percent acid pig iron and 80 percent scrap steel.[19] Preparing and working the charges was a blend of art and science. Buckeye's plant superintendent gave detailed written instructions to his foremen on how to carry out their tasks, and the company set up a well-appointed laboratory to perform quality-control work. Despite this progress, many of Buckeye's operations were done on an ad hoc basis. In working the charge or batch, fracture testing alone was used to determine when the heat should be tapped. Moreover, the plant foremen still had considerable leeway in their operating instructions. In preparing a basic charge, foremen were given the following directions:

> (a) 1 box clean heavy metal stock in each door (b) limestone following (c) shop scrap as much as you can get in the furnace or heavy stock as much as you can in the furnace limited by the height of the scrap in furnace, being unable to get in with boxes (d) as soon as possible get rest of scrap in (e) pig iron last put in as soon as rest of charge melts low enough to get in the furnace.[20]

The same type of instructions informed foremen on how to work the charge:

> When about melted iron ore is added. The amount varies with the carbon as shown by fracture specimens taken from the first part of the heat. The ore is added from time to time until a low carbon fracture is obtained . . . lime is added from time to time until the phosphorous is removed.[21]

Buckeye was primarily an open-hearth operation, using seven twenty-five-ton-capacity tilting open-hearth furnaces by 1916; but the company experimented with other melting techniques as well. Electric furnaces were first used commercially in the United States in 1911. Authorities of the day rated electric furnaces superior to open-hearth, chiefly because electric steel was reported to be more elastic and more uniform in quality than open-hearth steel. Buckeye set up a Heroult electric furnace in 1915, under a licensing agreement with the United States Steel Corporation which controlled the American patents for the Heroult furnace. For an initial payment of $10,000 plus later royalties based on the tonnage produced, United States Steel agreed to share with Buckeye "its engineering knowledge and skill acquired in its prior extensive experiences and use of electric furnaces." United States Steel sent an engineer to Buckeye to set up the furnace, and Buckeye initiated its electric steel operations in 1916.[22]

Once thoroughly melted, the molten metal was poured from the furnaces into ladles. Called "tapping the heat," this process was a dramatic event. Proper timing was of the utmost importance. "Before you tapped a heat out, it had to be right," recalled Albert Stock, who began work at Buckeye in 1906 and who was in the foundry before the First World War. Once the melter, a skilled workman, determined that the batch of molten steel was ready, he signaled for the ladle to be brought by an electrically driven crane to the furnace. The heat was then tapped and the fiery steel poured into the ladle. This was *the* most exciting moment in the production of cast steel, replete with clouds of smoke and red and yellow flames. Stock remembered the process well:

> Then, we had whistles to blow. Number two furnace is ready, blow the whistle! Number three is ready! Then, [you] swing the lid off the ladle, all heated and ready to go. . . . Then, they tap it, and the molten [steel] will run in.[23]

As Stock indicated, workmen had prepared the large ladle earlier. They had lined the ladle with bricks and then covered the bricks with cement. Buckeye workers introduced an innovation in the lining process; they used a concrete gun to blow the outer lining on, rather than applying it by hand. Workers preheated the ladle before it received the molten steel, to prevent cracking of the lining. Once full, the ladle was conveyed by an electric crane to a position over the molds, and the still-liquid steel was poured into the molds, one at a time. After hardening in these molds, the cast steel couplers and other railroad car parts went to other buildings for finishing.[24]

Buckeye's finishing methods once again demonstrated the company's concern for modernity. The castings were removed—or as workmen phrased it, "shaken out"—from the molds by jarring machines, rather than by hand. Once out of their molds, the castings went to annealing furnaces where they received heat treatments to harden and strengthen them. Next, the castings had any sand adhering to their surfaces removed. Sandblasting equipment to clean castings became available around 1900, and Buckeye set up the industry's first fully equipped sandblast rooms soon after that. The now clean castings went to various buildings for finishing work, primarily grinding and chipping, to smooth edges and remove any abnormalities. The machinery in the chipping room was driven by compressed air, while the grinding machinery was electrically powered.[25]

Systematic testing of the finished products completed the production cycle. Buckeye maintained metallurgical and chemical laboratories to analyze its products and ensure a uniform quality for them. The metallurgical laboratory operated drop test and static test machines with 1,000,000-pound capacities. The chemical laboratory was equipped with experimental heat-treating facilities and with microscopic analysis equipment. In addition to quality-control work, these laboratories engaged in product-development work.[26]

Like officials of other manufacturing concerns, Buckeye's management tried to establish control over their increasingly complex operations through fairly sophisticated accounting systems.[27] Buckeye's officers engaged in detailed cost accounting, as they sought to pinpoint and lessen their company's production expenses. From 1902 on, the steel plant's superintendent figured out the cost per ton of steel melted, and apportioned this cost among the different production processes. A page from his plant notebook for April 1905, reprinted here as Table 2, shows how he broke down the costs.[28]

As can be seen, Buckeye's superintendent figured both fixed and

Table 2
Costs of Production for April 1905

Metal in mould	$ 49,266
Moulding	17,730
Core-making	4,873
Annealing and cleaning	3,419
Fitting and finishing	15,725
Patterns and drafting	414
Repairs to plant and equipment	5,266
Locomotive service, heat, light, and power	2,779
Selling expense	2,755
Shipping expense	989
Office expense	698
Superintendence	527
Miscellaneous expenses	2,691
Salary of officers	838
Advertising	250
Insurance and taxes	350
Freight	2,347
Testing	259
Total	$111,179
Add for defective castings	2,241

SOURCE: S. P. Bush, "Notebook, Years 1903–1905 Inc.," unpaged.

variable expenses in his accounting of costs. Buckeye was among the companies pioneering in the inclusion of indirect and overhead costs—selling, office, superintendence, and advertising expenses— as part of its costs of production. Many companies simply ignored these expenses. In handling depreciation, Buckeye's plant superintendent also took an approach quite advanced for his day. While not engaging in true capital accounting (few businesses had reached this level of sophistication), Buckeye's superintendent was figuring monthly charges for furnace repairs, building repairs, machinery repairs, and building depreciation as production costs as early as 1903. He explained his accounting methods in that year:

> For instance, we produced 18,500 tons of castings from the beginning of operations to Dec. 31, 1903. Total cost furnace repairs $12,129 = 70¢ per ton.

Repairs of buildings about $3,000 = 20¢ per ton.
Repairs of machinery about $6,000 = 35¢ per ton.
Depreciation of buildings figures at 3% per year.
Buildings are worth $200,000. Depreciation is $5,000 or 35¢ per ton.
Depreciation of machinery is figured at 10% per year.
Machinery is worth $250,000. So depreciation comes to $25,000 or $1.40 per ton.[29]

In their approach to business, Buckeye's management adopted the most modern methods. They experimented with novel melting techniques, laid out their new steel plant in a systematically efficient manner, and used the most up-to-date accounting methods as a check on their plant's operations. Buckeye's operations resembled those of late nineteenth-century Carnegie Steel. As at that much larger corporation, a concern for efficiency and reducing costs permeated the work of Buckeye's plant superintendents. Although personalities, personal whims, and luck continued to influence business decisions, especially in the realm of small and medium-sized businesses, as the American business system matured, rational considerations based upon concerns for efficiency and costs came to play larger roles.

Welfare Capitalism

"Labor will never be reasonably contented without a living wage that is economic; that is a wage that will permit of existence and some reasonable advance in civilization," S. P. Bush, Buckeye's president, wrote his company's directors in 1918. "Everyone in a community," he continued, "must have decent living conditions as well as facilities for education and recreation, and these the average industrial community has not supplied."[30] To improve this situation, Bush concluded, a business needed to do two things:

First, it should lead and assist in the particular community in which it is situated, in bringing about a wholesome community condition. Second, within the confines of its own operation and property it must provide all those conditions which make for fair dealing, health, efficiency, and a general outlook on the part of all, of confidence and helpfulness.[31]

In actions that would today be considered highly paternalistic, Buckeye's officers engaged in a broad range of what was then known as "welfare work," as they sought to improve labor relations and take part in community-development projects during the first two decades of the twentieth century.[32] The National Civic Federation, an association of businessmen, labor leaders, and government officials, offered a commonly accepted definition of welfare work in 1904.[33] Welfare work "involves special consideration for physical comfort wherever labor is performed; opportunities for recreation; educational advantages; and the providing of suitable sanitary homes." Moreover, it includes "plans for saving and lending money, and provisions for insurance and pensions."[34] Buckeye became active in all phases of the welfare work movement. Moreover, Buckeye's officers widened the definition to include, not only their own workers, but society in general.

Certainly, there was room for change, particularly in wages, hours, and working conditions for laborers in the steel industry.[35] The hours of work were long. As late as 1920 some 27 percent of the industry's labor force worked six days per week; 37 percent worked six days one week and seven days the next; with the remaining 36 percent engaged seven days each week. For their twelve-hour shifts workers received wages which were about average for laborers in manufacturing establishments. In 1910 they received $1.92 per day, a figure which had risen to $2.22 four years later.[36] The annual average wage for all types of steelworkers came to $697 in 1910, some $46 more than the average for all manufacturing industries in that year. Despite such innovations as the use of electrically driven machinery, work in the steel mills and foundries remained hard, dirty, and dangerous.[37]

Buckeye's wages were somewhat better than the average for the steel industry. In 1898–99 its work force earned an average annual wage of $528.[38] Five years later, the company's wage earners averaged $653, and the corporation's forty-two salaried employees (exclusive of officers) took home an average of $1,154.[39] The pay varied with the job. Foremen (there were eight in 1902) received an average of $4.50 per day in that year.[40] Below them were the other positions, as shown in Table 3.[41]

Wages rose in later years, particularly during the First World War, as Buckeye's management sought to keep its workers with the

Table 3
Buckeye's Payroll for December 17, 1902

DEPARTMENT	NUMBER OF MEN	DAILY WAGE
Pattern-Making	22	$2.85
Furnace platform	11	2.75
Mechanical	21	2.48
Office	9	2.15
Core-making	43	1.85
Chipping	128	1.77
Foundry	181	1.64

SOURCE: S. P. Bush, "Notebook, Years 1903–1905 Inc.," unpaged.

company. In late 1916 Buckeye's officers, noting that "it was becoming more difficult to obtain the necessary force of men," increased wages 10 percent.[42] Pressures for additional wage raises continued over the next few years, and in 1919 Buckeye's officers granted a general 10 to 13 percent increase "on account of the unprecedented high cost of living."[43] Buckeye's wartime experience paralleled that of other steel companies. The average wages of open-hearth workers across the United States more than doubled between 1914 and 1919, reaching $4.40 per day.[44]

Working conditions were about the same at Buckeye as elsewhere in the steel industry. The company operated two twelve-hour shifts, and changed to the eight-hour day only around 1922.[45] By today's standards, physical plant conditions were primitive. Adequate ventilation was a chronic problem. In 1917 Buckeye spent $12,000 for foundry ventilation "to give relief to the men working on the furnace platform."[46] While Buckeye had one of the most modern plants in the business, it lacked many of the amenities now taken for granted. Asked about work in the Buckeye foundry before the First World War, Albert Stock characterized it as hot, dirty, noisy, and physically demanding. It was, in short, "awful."[47]

Buckeye pioneered in the use of safety devices. Photographs of the plant taken between 1912 and 1919 show drive belts well shielded, workers wearing safety glasses, and multilingual safety bulletins prominently displayed.[48] Yet, accidents did occur. In 1915 and 1916 two men were crushed to death on the furnace platform "partly because of lack of sufficient room between the charging machine

and the north side of the structure.''[49] Stock later recalled that accidents were fairly common. One worker he knew died when caught
in the ropes of a tumbler; another was decapitated when an emory
wheel flew off. In fact, "I expect I could name you twenty killed
off" in industrial accidents, Stock concluded.[50] From about 1910
on, Buckeye had a safety officer who followed up on accidents to
prevent their recurrence. For instance, in 1917 the company spent
$14,500 to extend the furnace platforms five feet to eliminate the
cause of accidents in that area.[51]

Buckeye's involvement in welfare work took many forms, and
this involvement began early. The new steel plant operated a
medical office as early as 1903, and in twelve years this facility had
grown to include an emergency hospital staffed by a company doctor and nurses. By this time Buckeye had also built modern
washrooms and locker rooms and was running a company kitchen.
The corporation constructed a baseball field on vacant land adjoin-
ing the plant, and sponsored picnics at which, Stock later recalled,
"a little beer drinking" took place. Not everyone, however, participated in the picnics and athletics. After working all week, "the
boys," Stock remembered, "were pretty well played out and stayed
home." Buckeye's officers occasionally aided laid-off workers at
a time when there was, of course, no government unemployment
insurance.[52]

Like many corporations, Buckeye broadened the scope of its
welfare work during the First World War. In April 1917 the company began providing life insurance for all employees who had
been with the company two months or more. Three months later,
Buckeye's directors voted to purchase 108 acres of land opposite
the steel plant for $143,000 to provide adequate housing for its
employees.[53] During the First World War, Buckeye's management
also began working closely with the YMCA in sponsoring educational, social, and recreation activities for company employees.
Within the plant, ministers addressed monthly meetings in talks
"intended to be inspirational and educational." In addition, weekly
meetings were held in the various departments. Buckeye employees
were also encouraged to sign up for special courses offered by the
YMCA in such fields as mechanical drawing, electricity, and ac-
countancy in order "to render greater service to themselves and to
humanity."[54] Two weekly *Bible* classes enrolled about thirty em-

ployees each, and a music program led to the formation of bands, orchestras, choruses, and a horn quartette. A thrift program was set up to spur "the intelligent conservation of our financial, physical, and mental resources for the development of fuller, broader, happier, and more efficient lives." In particular, Buckeye encouraged its employees to buy homes "in good old Columbus town."[55]

The social and athletic program interested the greatest number of employees. Buckeye fielded teams in baseball, basketball, volleyball, bowling, trap shooting, horseshoe pitching, tennis, and track for competition in the YMCA league. The social program was also extensive. Four major social gatherings took place in 1919–20. Typical was an intershop picnic attended by 700 employees at Indianola Park on August 16, 1919. Athletic contests, including the 100-yard dash and "a watermelon race," took place; bands played, and the employees feasted on box lunches. A few months later, some 275 employees braved "fog and rain" to take part in "an enjoyable evening of music, readings, moving pictures, and refreshments" at Washington Park.[56]

Buckeye's officers took up welfare work for a variety of reasons. Many had a genuine desire to improve the working and living conditions of their employees for humanitarian reasons. Most notable in this respect was S. P. Bush, the son of an Episcopal minister. However, Buckeye's management also viewed welfare work as good business. In particular, they hoped that improved working and living conditions would lessen the turnover rate at their steel plant and, thus, decrease its costs of production. Buckeye's directors set up the life insurance program for their employees "to encourage the men to work more steadily" and to "promote loyal cooperation."[57] Similarly, Buckeye's officers bought the land for new housing because, as Bush put it, "Housing facilities must be provided near the plant if the Company is to have a satisfactory force of employees."[58] Finally, Bush and other Buckeye officials believed they had a duty to ensure that their employees would be loyal, patriotic Americans imbued with middle-class citizenship values.

This last concern was related to the changing nature of Buckeye's labor force. Fragmentary evidence suggests that the company's work force was composed almost wholly of native white Americans in the 1890s, which is not surprising, since the overall population of

Columbus was 90 percent native-born white in 1900. (Blacks made up only 7 percent of the total population, and few were then employed in manufacturing.)[59] This situation changed dramatically over the next two decades. Increasing numbers of immigrants and blacks moved to Columbus, and many of these newcomers were employed in manufacturing concerns. Blacks, in particular, came to Columbus in the war years. During the First World War, "a movement"—noted the secretary of the Ohio Manufacturers' Association, a Columbus-based trade association formed in 1910—was "started in the state providing for the distribution, housing, and employment of Negro laborers coming from other sections of the country."[60] Buckeye took part in this campaign. As Stock observed, "some of the guys went down South trying to get Negroes."[61] This effort succeeded. By 1919 Buckeye had at least 150 black employees, 7.5 percent of its total work force. The proportion of immigrants at Buckeye also rose, as Hungarians, Poles, Greeks and others joined the company's employ. In 1918 some 10 to 20 percent of Buckeye's workers were of foreign birth.[62]

Like some other manufacturing concerns around the United States, Buckeye undertook what was known as "Americanization work" among the foreign-born employees.[63] "A systematic effort was made," noted Buckeye's officers "to encourage them [immigrants] to attend night school, to take out naturalization papers, and to adopt American ideals and customs." Each Fourth of July the company held elaborate public celebrations to honor those employees who had become citizens during the past year.[64] Buckeye also maintained a special program of activities for its black employees. A savings club, musical organization, and *Bible* study groups grew up. Shop and intershop socials were well attended. One held in Glenmary Park in 1919 attracted 150 black workers from Buckeye "in spite of the inclement weather." Blacks joined other Buckeye employees on some of the athletic teams representing their company in the YMCA league (something quite unusual at a time when segregation was common in the United States), but they also formed their own all-black teams in baseball, basketball, volleyball, and track for intershop contests.[65]

Buckeye's officers carried their paternal concern for their workers over into a somewhat similar interest in the social and economic development of Columbus as a whole. Buckeye's officers played active roles in the development of Columbus's philanthropic organizations, in terms of both leadership and financial support. They also took part in the formation of local business groups designed to spur their city's growth.

Columbus expanded rapidly in the early twentieth century, as its population soared from 126,000 to 237,000 in the twenty years after 1900. Industrial growth lay behind much of this population increase. By 1914 the city had some 800 manufacturing plants employing 35,000 workers, and it had risen to fortieth place among the industrial centers in the United States. With 400 employees in 1904 and 2,000 twelve years later, Buckeye was one of the top ten employers in Columbus and one of the very largest industrial concerns.[66]

With growth came signs of modernity in Columbus. As one writer has recently described the transformation of Columbus in the early 1900s, "the village cocoon had burst wide open, revealing a small metropolis."[67] The downtown area changed, as steel-skeletoned skyscrapers began replacing the older cast-iron and brick buildings. In 1915 the old Deshler Block at the intersection of Broad and High Streets was torn down to make room for the new Deshler Hotel. Because of electrically illuminated arches which crossed above downtown streets, Columbus became known locally as the "Arch City." Though streets remained uncrowded by today's standards (traffic policemen regulated the flow of vehicles and pedestrians on downtown streets by turning large umbrellas lettered with "Stop" and "Go" on their sides), enough traffic developed to support a gasoline filling station at the corner of Oak and Young Street by 1913. With the development of electric street cars, the rest of the city began to uncramp and spread, leading to the growth of suburbs like Grandview, Bexley, and Upper Arlington.[68]

Entrepreneurs built major amusement parks for the city dwellers. The Olentangy Park, opened in 1896, boasted a theater capable of seating 2,248 for its shows, which included "all the leading vaudeville artists, as well as comic operas and minstrel stars." The park also had a boat house, dancing pavilion, and "a score of modern park amusements." It was a twenty-five-minute streetcar ride from downtown Columbus, located where Olentangy Apartments (just off High Street) are today. Minerva Park was about ten miles to the northeast. Its enticements were many: bowling alleys, a merry-go-round, a scenic railroad, a shoot-the-chutes, baseball fields, tennis courts, a pony track, and a large theater. As its advertisements boldly asserted, "modern park amusements are all supplied to accommodate the sporting man, the athlete, the old, the middle aged, and the young." It was a forty-minute trip by electric railway from downtown.[69]

There was, however, a darker side to this picture, for social problems accompanied the development of Columbus. Social services— garbage collection, street repairs, the provision of water and sewer mains—failed to keep pace with the city's growth. Still more galling, and perhaps more frightening, to Columbus business leaders was the discovery that poverty existed in their city.

In the nineteenth century most Americans viewed poverty as the result of the individual moral failings of those afflicted, not as the result of structural problems or inequities in society. The solution to the problem of poverty lay, most believed, in individual giving and charity to the "deserving poor," those whose poverty came about through some accident beyond their control and those who, with a little help, might be expected to become self-supporting again. Philanthropy became more highly organized in the opening years of the twentieth century, reflecting the growing complexity and organization of the businesses upon which it was coming to depend for financial support. And, as the problems of industrialization and urbanization became better understood, a growing number of people traced the origins of poverty to social rather than moral problems. Giving by organizations, particularly businesses, came to replace the earlier contributions from individuals as time progressed.[70] Columbus business and professional men sought to place charitable giving on what they viewed as a sound, efficient, business basis with the formation of the Associated Charities of Columbus in 1900. They set up this organization:

> To unite and harmonize all the charitable organizations of Columbus; to reduce vagrancy and pauperism and ascertain their causes; to prevent indiscriminate and duplicate giving; to secure the community against imposture; to see that all deserving cases of destitution are properly relieved; to assist all applicants in obtaining employment, and to make employment, as far as possible, the basis of relief.[71]

Many of those associated with Buckeye took part in the early activities of the Associated Charities, and the corporation began contributing directly to the organization in 1911. The Associated
Charities, in turn, distributed its funds to hospitals, children's
homes, dispensaries, and other charitable organizations, including
the Municipal Potato Patch Committee, throughout Columbus.[72]
Buckeye began making other corporate philanthropic contributions in the early 1900s. In 1907 the company's directors approved
"appropriations for charitable purposes" suggested by Bush. Five
years later, the company initiated a long-standing relationship with
the South Side Settlement House by donating $500 for its construc-
tion on Reeb Avenue. Buckeye's giving picked up during the war
years. The Children's Hospital received $1,000 in 1916, the Knights
of Columbus $3,000 and the Salvation Army $2,000 in 1919, and
the Boy Scouts $500 in 1920. By 1921 Buckeye's officers had placed
their corporation's contributions on a more systematic basis, giving
$12,840 for "various educational, semi-educational, charitable, re-
ligious, and semi-religious funds, objects, and institutions" through
donations to the Associated Charities.[73] The YMCA was a particular beneficiary of Buckeye gifts. Embodying ideals of Christianity,
education, and self-help, the organization was, as we have seen, directly involved in a broad range of activities for Buckeye employees. Between 1916 and 1921, Buckeye contributed $20,000 to the
YMCA and the YWCA. The company also supplied the site and
building for the South Side Industrial YMCA.[74]
Buckeye's officers were also active in city boosterism and the
work of business organizations. Bush, in particular, was especially
energetic. He helped reorganize the Columbus Chamber of Commerce in 1908 and was a charter member of the United States
Chamber of Commerce. A member of the executive committee of
the National Association of Manufacturers, Bush was, however,
best known for his work as head of the Ohio Manufacturers'
Association.[75] Formed in 1910, the Ohio Manufacturers' Association was set up "to promote the general welfare of the productive
industries in the State of Ohio" and "to oppose propositions that
would tend to restrain such development."[76] Bush served as the
body's second president during the years 1913 and 1914 and remained active in later times.
Bush was particularly important in the fight for Ohio's workmen's compensation laws, a major concern of the Ohio Manufac-

turers' Association. In 1911 the association concluded that Ohio's voluntary measure, just passed, was "probably the best law on the subject in the United States today" and urged employers to give it "hearty support." Relatively few did, however, and because of their recalcitrance, the voluntary approach, as association members agreed a year later, was "well nigh a failure." Only with the passage of compulsory legislation were many association members satisfied. Bush found praise for the Industrial Commission set up to oversee the operation of the new law for "endeavoring to administer the law efficiently and with fairness to all."[77]

Underlying all the welfare work of Buckeye's management was a vision of a harmonious society. As was true of many political, business, and labor leaders during the Progressive Era, Buckeye's management yearned for a society functioning smoothly without any friction or discord. They wanted the efficiency of their foundry to be replicated in the society around it. This desire was most apparent in S. P. Bush's thoughts and actions. He wanted labor and management to work together in mutual harmony for the benefit of both. "In a general way, labor discontent has grown," he once wrote, "out of the competitive system, which, when carried to extremes as it has been in this country, as well as in other countries, results in disaster to every interest whether employer or employee."[78]

More than the officers of most companies, Buckeye's management tried to change this situation. Precisely because their company was a medium-sized venture with strong ties to one locality, rather than a national giant with offices and plants scattered across the United States, Buckeye's management became intimately involved in welfare work. A favorable social environment would, they thought, aid them in the quest of their business goals, and they had no doubts about these goals. "It is fundamental," Bush wrote his fellow officers at Buckeye, "that those of superior intelligence, generally designated as leaders, will have to lead in any movement looking to an improvement."[79] With a certainty now lost, Buckeye's management equated the progress of their business with that of society as a whole.

The Successful Company

Progress was, in fact, made at Buckeye and in Columbus. By 1921 the formative years in Buckeye's history were ending; the company had survived the perils upon which most beginning firms in the United States founder.* Its management had established a market niche for the company's products and had set up a national, rather than simply local or regional, sales system. They had secured adequate financing for the corporation, and with this financing they had constructed an ultramodern production facility. Finally, they had initiated successful relations with their labor force and the rest of the Columbus community.

In its success Buckeye was an atypical beginning business. As we have seen, most new businesses failed within just a few years of their founding in the late nineteenth century. Even with the formation of the Small Business Administration, a federal government agency, in the 1950s to help new businesses get ahead, 60 percent of the business casualties of that decade were of firms less than five years old.[80] Throughout American history, beginning businesses have led marginal lives. No single factor ensured Buckeye's success; rather a combination of interrelated elements contributed to Buckeye's growth and development. Some of the factors were internal to the operations of the company, but others were external.

The most important internal factor was the nature of Buckeye's management. Buckeye's officers were vigorous men quick to adopt technological innovations. They were among the first to begin producing automatic couplers; and, when they built the steel foundry, they designed it along the most advanced lines that scientific management could provide. Perhaps even more significant were the personalities of Buckeye's officers. They possessed a toughness, an ability (to borrow a phrase from the historian James Soltow's study of small business) to "persist" in hard times.[81] They felt a sense of commitment to Buckeye. William Goodspeed came to Columbus to take over the company's faltering operations in 1886, because he had invested money in the firm which he could not afford to lose. S. P. Bush possessed a similar feeling of identification with Buckeye in the early twentieth century. "We have had hard times to bear," he wrote his wife about the business in 1908. "But, surely we should not care to have our lives easy," he concluded, for "there would be no accomplishment, no development."[82]

---

*Part of the analysis of Buckeye's success first appeared in Mansel Blackford, "Small Business in America: Two Case Studies," in Paul Uselding, editor, *Business and Economic History* (Urbana: University of Illinois, 1979), pp. 9–15. Used with the permission of the editor.

However, many other companies with officers just as determined as Buckeye's management have failed, and there was more to Buckeye's success than the character of its management. Bonds of personal friendship and business ties provided the corporation's officers with resources they repeatedly tapped to smooth over the rough spots in their company's early years. Many of Buckeye's officers, directors, and stockholders were leading Columbus businessmen, and they used their ties to the city's business community to secure financial support in both additional stock investments and bank loans. Personal friendships and business connections were still more important in carving out a market for Buckeye's products, especially the railroad car coupler. Nearly all of Buckeye's officers had worked for railroads before joining the firm, and most extended their railroad connections while with Buckeye. Bush, for instance, served as a director of the Pennsylvania, the Hocking Valley, and the Norfolk & Western lines—all of which were major Buckeye customers. Many of Buckeye's directors and stockholders, most notably Frank Rockefeller, were also connected with railroads and secured sales from them.

The availability of such ties may well be one of the keys to success in small business, even more than in big business. There is less margin for failure in small than in big business, and when a small business has problems, it needs help fast—help that can often only be secured from close personal and business friends.

External factors also led to Buckeye's success. Columbus was a fortunate location for Buckeye's operations. In Columbus, Buckeye possessed relatively easy and inexpensive access to the necessary raw materials and to markets for its finished products. Transportation by the Pennsylvania, the Baltimore & Ohio and other railroads was readily available at a reasonable charge. Moreover, the labor supply in Columbus was adequate, when supplemented by recruitment from the South during the First World War.[83]

External factors also helped create a market for Buckeye's products. The actions of the federal government, the passage of the coupler legislation of 1893, broadened the market for automatic couplers. Then, too, Buckeye's management had the good fortune of building and opening their steel plant during a prosperous time, for, with the exception of brief financial panics in 1907 and 1914, the first two decades of the twentieth century were expansionary years for the American economy. This situation held true especially for the railroad industry, as many lines sought to modernize. Buckeye was lucky to be in the right place at the right time.

Notes

1. "Minutes of the Board of Directors Meeting" (hereafter cited as "Directors Meeting"), January 17, 1907, January 31, 1911; "Minutes of the Meeting of Stockholders" (hereafter cited as "Stockholders Meeting"), January 14, 1902. Both are in the Buckeye Collection, Ohio Historical Collection.

2. "Directors Meeting," January 8, 1895, January 13, 1897, January 10, 1889, January 26, 1909, January 28, 1913, January 27, 1920.

3. F. W. Taussig and W. S. Barker, "American Corporations and the Executives: A Statistical Inquiry," *Quarterly Journal of Economics* 40 (November 1925): 19.

4. "Directors Meeting," January 26, 1909, January 24, 1910, January 30, 1911, January 29, 1912, January 27, 1913, June 23, October 11, 1920.

5. Columbus *Citizen,* February 9, 1948; Columbus *Dispatch,* February 9, 1948; *National Cyclopedia of American Biography,* vol. 40 (New York: J. T. White Co.), pp. 3334–35.

6. *National Cyclopedia,* vol. 26, pp. 490–91; Columbus *Citizen,* July 30, 1936.

7. Undated (1936?), unlabeled newspaper clipping in *Buckeye Scrapbook 1.*

8. George Condon, *Yesterday's Columbus* (Miami, Florida: E. A. Seeman Publishing, 1977), p. 101.

9. *Dau's Blue Book Columbus* (New York: The Dau Company, 1912).

10. Flora Bush to S. P. Bush, August 12, 19, 24, 1908, in Buckeye Collection.

11. William Miller, *Men in Business* (New York: Harper-Row, 1952), chap. 11

12. Interview by the author with Albert Stock, October 4, 1978.

13. Flora Bush to S. P. Bush, August 12, 1908, in Buckeye Collection.

14. S. P. Bush to Flora Bush, early December, 1918, in Buckeye Collection.

15. Numerous studies exist on the origins of scientific management. See: Alfred D. Chandler, Jr., *The Visible Hand* (Cambridge, Mass.: Harvard University Press, 1977), pp. 269–83; Samuel Haber, *Efficiency and Uplift: Scientific Management in the Progressive Era* (Chicago: University of Chicago Press, 1964); Leland Jenks, "Early Phases of the Management Movement," *Administrative Science Quarterly* 5 (December 1960): 421–47; Joseph Litterer, "Systematic Management: Design for Recoupling in

Manufacturing Firms," *Business History Review* 38 (Winter 1963): 369–81; Daniel Nelson, *Managers and Workers* (Madison: University of Wisconsin Press, 1975), chap. 4.

16. Some 300 glass plate negatives show every aspect of Buckeye's steel foundry operations for 1914–20; they are in the Buckeye Collection, the Ohio Historical Society.

17. Ibid.; *Buckeye Steel Castings Company,* pamphlet, unpaged, February, 1916, in the Buckeye Collection.

18. William P. Conway, Jr., *Cast to Shape: A History of the Steel Castings Industry in the United States* (Rocky River, Ohio: Dillon, Liederbach, 1977), p. 60.

19. S. P. Bush, "Notebook, Years 1903–1905 Inc." unpaged, in Buckeye Collection. The acid open-hearth process could use only pig iron which was very low in phosphorus; the basic process could use pig iron higher in phosphorus. See Steel Founder's Society of America, *Steel Castings Handbook* (Cleveland: Steel Founders Society of America, 1941), chap. 3.

20. Bush, "Notebook, 1903–1905."

21. Ibid.

22. "Buckeye Steel Castings Co.—United States Steel Co., Legal Agreement on Heroult Furnace, 1915."

23. Stock interview, October 4, 1978.

24. *Buckeye Steel Castings,* pamphlet; "Data on Ladle Lining, September 1917," typewritten pamphlet. Both in Buckeye Collection.

25. Glass plate negatives of the plant interior.

26. Ibid.; Bush, "Notebook"; Steel Founders Society of America, *Steel Castings Handbook,* p. 9.

27. On the history of accounting, see Chandler, *Visible Hand,* pp. 278–79; Samuel P. Garner, *The Evolution of Cost Accounting to 1925* (Tuscaloosa, Ala.: University of Alabama Press, 1954); H. Thomas Johnson, "Early Cost Accounting for Internal Management Control," *Business History Review* 46 (Winter 1972): 466–75; A. C. Littleton, ed., *Studies in the History of Accounting* (Homewood, Illinois: Irwin, 1956).

28. Bush, "Notebook, 1903–1905."

29. Ibid.

30. S. P. Bush to R. S. Warner, John Deshler, and T. P. Linn, March 6, 1918, in the Buckeye Collection.

31. Ibid.

32. On corporate community involvement, see Morrell Heald, *The Social Responsibilities of Business: Company and Community, 1900–1960* (Cleveland: Case Western Reserve University Press, 1970).

33. On welfare work in American business, see Heald, *Social Responsibility,* chaps. 1 and 2; Nelson, *Managers and Workers,* chap. 6.

34. Nelson, *Managers and Workers,* p. 101.

35. Katherine Stone, "The Origin of Job Structures in the Steel Industry," *Radical America* 7 (November–December 1973): 19–65.

36. United States Department of Labor, Bureau of Labor Statistics, "Wages and Hours of Labor in the Iron and Steel Industry, 1907 to 1920," *Bulletin 305* (Washington, D.C., 1922), pp. 5, 11. The figures for days worked per week are for all occupations at open-hearth furnaces. The figures for wages are for common (unskilled) workers at open-hearth furnaces.

37. David Brody, *Steelworkers in America* (New York: Harper & Row, 1960), pp. 48, 94.

38. Buckeye Malleable Iron and Coupler Company, *Payroll Cashbook, 1898–1899.*

39. "Note on Payroll, 1904."

40. Bush, "Notebook, 1903–1905."

41. Ibid. Unfortunately, no such detailed labor or personnel records have survived for later years, at least not until the 1960s. These wages were probably about the same or slightly higher than the average for the steel castings industry as a whole. In 1910 a melter averaged $5.00 per day, an assistant melter $4.00, a helper $3.00, and a laborer $2.00.

42. "Directors Meeting," December 16, 1916; "Executive Committee Meeting," February 26, May 2, 1916.

43. *Buckeye Steel Castings,* 1916 pamphlet; "Executive Committee Meeting," November 14, 1919; Henry Hunker, *Industrial Evolution of Columbus* (Columbus: The Ohio State University Press, 1958), p. 55.

44. U.S. Department of Labor, *Bulletin 305,* p. 11. This figure is for unskilled workers.

45. Bush, "Notebook."

46. "Executive Committee Meeting," March 7, 1917.

47. Stock interview, October 4, 1978.

48. Glass plate negative of the plant interior.

49. "Executive Committee Meeting," December 28, 1916.

50. Stock interview, October 4, 1978.

51. "Executive Committee Meeting," December 28, 1916.

52. *Buckeye Steel Castings Company,* 1916 pamphlet; Bush, "Notebook"; Columbus *Dispatch,* February 9, 1948; "Directors meeting," January 30, 1911, January 26, 1915; "Executive Committee Meeting," December 14, 1912; Stock interview, October 4, 1978.

53. "Directors Meeting," July 21, 1917; "Executive Committee Meeting," April 2, 1917.

54. Buckeye Steel Castings Company, *Industrial YMCA Activities, 1918–1920,* pamphlet, pp. 3, 16–17, in Buckeye Collection. Other courses were: blueprint reading, shop mathematics, steam engineering, auto-

mobile, welding, chemistry, business English, salesmanship, and English for Coming Americans.

55. Ibid., pp. 14–15, 18–19, 21–22.

56. Ibid., pp. 4–12.

57. "Executive Committee Meeting," April 2, 1917.

58. "Directors Meeting," July 21, 1917.

59. Buckeye, *Payroll Cashbook, 1898–1899;* Hunker, *Industrial Evolution of Columbus*, p. 41.

60. Ohio Manufacturers' Association (hereafter abbreviated as OMA), "Minutes of Executive Committee Meeting," July 11, 1917, in OMA archives, Columbus, Ohio. See also William Kaufman, *The Neighbors of the South Side Settlement* (Columbus: The Ohio State University Press, 1943), p. 40.

61. Stock interview, October 4, 1978.

62. Buckeye, *Industrial YMCA Activities,* pp. 13, 20.

63. On Americanization work in the United States, see Edward Hartmann, *The Movement to Americanize the Immigrant* (New York: Columbia University Press, 1948); Gerd Korman, *Industrialization: Immigrants and Americanizers* (Madison: University of Wisconsin Press, 1967).

64. Buckeye, *Industrial YMCA Activities,* p. 13.

65. Ibid., pp. 20–21.

66. "Directors Meeting," December 16, 1916; Hunker, *Industrial Evolution of Columbus,* pp. 51–56; "Note on Payroll, 1904."

67. Condon, *Yesterday's Columbus,* 52.

68. Ibid., pp. 75, 83, 85; Betty Garrett and Edward Lentz, *Columbus: America's Crossroads* (Tulsa, Oklahoma: Centennial Heritage Press, 1980), p. 107.

69. *Columbus, Ohio, 1900: Illustrated Guide to the City and Pleasure Resorts with Map and Street Railway Directions, Compliments of Columbus Railway Company,* undated, unpaged pamphlet at Ohio Historical Society.

70. Heald, *Social Responsibilities,* chaps. 1–2.

71. *First Annual Report of the Associated Charities of Columbus, 1900.* Available at the Ohio Historical Society.

72. Associated Charities of Columbus, *Annual Reports, 1900, 1903, 1911–12,* at Ohio Historical Society.

73. "Directors Meeting," October 25, 1907, April 24, 1919; "Executive Committee Meeting," December 14, 1912, March 25, 1916, May 17, 1919, April 20, 1920; "Stockholders Meeting," January 27, 1920, January 31, 1922.

74. "Executive Committee Meeting," November 21, 1916, March 25, 1919, April 20, July 6, 1920, April 30, 1921.

75. Columbus *Citizen,* February 9, 1948; Columbus *Dispatch,* February 9, 1948.

76. "Constitution, OMA, adopted November 10, 1910," OMA archives.

77. OMA, "Minutes of Annual Meetings," November 10, 1911, November 19, 1912, December 3, 1914, OMA archives.

78. Bush to Deshler, Linn, and Warner, March 6, 1918.

79. Ibid.

80. James Soltow, "Origins of Small Business: Metal Fabricators and Machinery Makers in New England, 1890–1957," *Transactions of the American Philosophical Society* 55 (December 1965): 1–58.

81. Ibid.

82. Samuel P. Bush to Flora Bush, 1908, in Buckeye Collection.

83. Alvin Ketcham, "The Foundry and Machine Shop Industry in Columbus," in *Columbus Manufacturers.* Typewritten copy in The Ohio State University Library.

WORK AND LIFE AT BUCKEYE STEEL

THE PRODUCTION PROCESS

Plate 2. Preparing the molds to receive molten steel, one of the first processes in making cast-steel products at **Buckeye's South Plant on Parsons Avenue, around 1917.** *Courtesy of the Ohio Historical Society, Inc., Columbus, Ohio.*

Plate 3. Ramming sand into the patterns to form the molds, around 1917. Molten steel would later be poured into the molds, and the molds defined the shape of cast-steel products. *Courtesy of the Ohio Historical Society, Inc., Columbus, Ohio.*

Plate 4. Lining the ladle by hand. The ladle was used to carry molten steel from the melting furnaces to the molds, around 1917. *Courtesy of the Ohio Historical Society, Inc., Columbus, Ohio.*

Plate 5. Lining the ladle by concrete-gun, a Buckeye innovation in the interest of increased efficiency, around 1917. *Courtesy of the Ohio Historical Society, Inc., Columbus, Ohio.*

Plate 6. Grinding a cast-steel part to remove abnormalities, a stage in the finishing process in making steel castings, around 1917. *Courtesy of the Ohio Historical Society, Inc., Columbus, Ohio.*

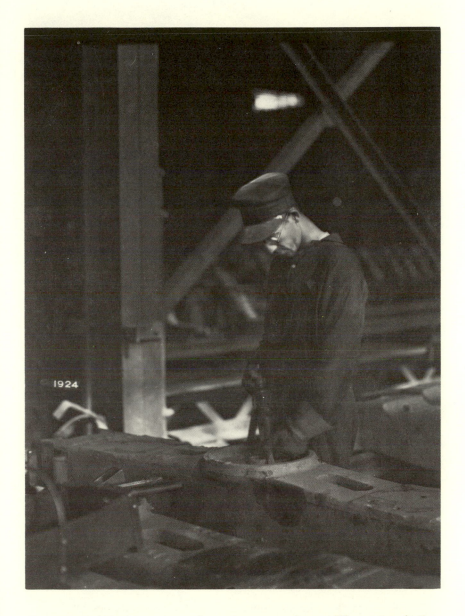

Plate 7. Chipping a cast-steel part to remove abnormalities, a stage in the finishing process in making steel castings, around 1917. *Courtesy of the Ohio Historical Society, Inc., Columbus, Ohio.*

Plate 8. One of Buckeye's automatic couplers in use, around 1915. The trainman did not have to step between the railroad cars to couple or uncouple them. *Courtesy of the Ohio Historical Society, Inc., Columbus, Ohio.*

LIFE AT BUCKEYE STEEL

Plate 9. The washroom at Buckeye's South Plant on Parsons Avenue around 1915. *Courtesy of the Ohio Historical Society, Inc., Columbus, Ohio.*

Plate 10. The locker-room at Buckeye's South Plant around 1915. *Courtesy of the Ohio Historical Society, Inc., Columbus, Ohio.*

85

Plate 11. Buckeye's track team for the YMCA league around 1915. Note the racial integration. *Courtesy of the Ohio Historical Society, Inc., Columbus, Ohio.*

Plate 12. One of Buckeye's plant baseball teams around 1915. *Courtesy of the Ohio Historical Society, Inc., Columbus, Ohio.*

87

Plate 13. A baseball game at Buckeye's South Plant around 1915. *Courtesy of the Ohio Historical Society, Inc., Columbus, Ohio.*

Plate 14. A multilingual safety poster inside Buckeye's South Plant around 1915. *Courtesy of the Ohio Historical Society, Inc., Columbus, Ohio.*

Plate 15. A Bible class meeting inside Buckeye's South Plant around 1915.
Courtesy of the Ohio Historical Society, Inc., Columbus, Ohio.

Plate 16. A reading class of Buckeye employees at the Southside YMCA around 1915. Note "Pluck and Luck" on the blackboard. *Courtesy of the Ohio Historical Society, Inc., Columbus, Ohio.*

Plate 17. An Americanization Day celebration at Buckeye's South Plant around 1917. *Courtesy of the Ohio Historical Society, Inc., Columbus, Ohio.*

chapter 4

MATURITY AND DECLINE IN THE STEEL CASTINGS INDUSTRY, 1922–1959

During the years 1922 through 1946, Buckeye Steel came of age. The company made few changes in its operations; rather, its development evolved along lines laid down in earlier times. As Buckeye matured, it continued its quest for excellence in steel castings. However, while perfecting technical processes, Buckeye's management failed to perceive changes occurring beyond the confines of their industry, and in the years after the Second World War this lack of vision threw Buckeye into a nearly fatal period of decline.

The Twenties

After the brief postwar recession ended, the American steel industry entered a period of substantial growth. The output of steel ingots in the United States rose from 47,000,000 tons in 1920 to 63,000,000 tons nine years later. Much of the increased demand for steel resulted from the production of flat rolled steel for new markets such as automobiles and household appliances. This production was made possible by two technological innovations: the electrification of steel plants and the development of continuous strip mills.[1]

During the 1920s the steel industry became increasingly concentrated and oligopolistic. In this decade the steel ingot production capacity of the "Big Three" companies—United States Steel, Bethlehem Steel, and National Steel—rose from 48 percent to 59 percent of the industry's total. By the same token, the ingot capacity of the twelve largest companies climbed from 63 percent to 84 percent of the total.[2] Regional shifts also occurred, as Chicago and the South emerged as major steel-producing regions, due in part to basic steel's switch from Pittsburgh Plus to multiple-basing point pricing in 1924.[3]

The steel-castings industry also grew in the 1920s. Cast steel production averaged 934,000 tons annually during the decade, a figure considerably higher than the output of earlier years. Railroads, shipbuilding, mining, and dredging machinery continued to take most of this output, but as in basic steel, consumer durable goods such as appliances and automobiles accounted for an increasing share. Not all companies benefited equally from this expansion, for the number of foundries grew even faster than the demand for their products. By 1922 some 237 foundries were making steel castings, and four years later 267 companies were in the business. As a result, overproduction plagued much of the steel-castings industry even before the 1930s. In particular, smaller companies turning out undifferentiated goods were having trouble by the late 1920s.[4]

As one of the United States' major manufacturers of cast steel railroad couplers and car parts, Buckeye did well in the 1920s. Although its share of the overall steel-castings business fell, Buckeye maintained its share of the coupler market, and both sales and earnings rose to heights well above those of the 1910s.[5] During these years Buckeye's operations continued to focus upon its steel foundry in Columbus. Buckeye's officers took no steps in radically new directions, but they did try to upgrade and modernize their plant, as in previous times, in the interest of increased efficiency. Plant improvements were most pronounced during the early 1920s. In 1923 Buckeye's directors approved an $830,000 improvement program needed "on account of the obsolescence of certain equipment, deterioration of buildings . . . and the general unbalanced and unsatisfactory condition of the plant." Specifically designed to "increase our open hearth capacity," the program would, the company's officers hoped, "put us abreast of the times and on an equal footing with our competition."[6] Further changes soon followed. In 1925 some $200,000 was spent to boost the plant's core-making capacity, and two years later $125,000 went for improvements to the pattern shop and sand equipment.[7] In the late 1920s Buckeye's officers expended an additional $170,000 to install waste heat boilers in their foundry; using heat from the melting furnaces, these boilers cost almost nothing to operate.[8] Land purchases enlarged Buckeye's Columbus property. In 1927 the company bought the property of the Carnegie Steel Company adjacent to the South Plant jointly with the American Rolling Mill Company.[9]

While Buckeye's officers centered their attention on Columbus, other operations occupied their time as well. In the mid-1920s they flirted with the possibility of acquiring the McConway-Torley Company, one of their competitors in the railroad coupler business. This purchase would have allowed Buckeye to increase significantly its share of the coupler market. Since the coupler agreement setting market shares for individual companies remained in effect, acquiring a competitor was about the only way a firm could boost its percentage of the business. However, the acquisition arrangements collapsed in late 1926.[10] In the following year, Buckeye's management considered buying the equipment and patents which the Ohio Steel Foundry Company of Lima, Ohio used in the manufacture of railroad car parts, but this possibility also fell apart in the final stages of negotiation. Just two years later, the National Malleable Iron and Steel Castings Company, probably eager to increase its share of the railroad business, tried to buy Buckeye, whose officers, however, rebuffed the offer.[11]

The 1920s, especially the mid-1920s, were prosperous years for Buckeye. As we have seen, the corporation's officers used some of the profits to modernize their steel plant. In general, however, they ran their business very conservatively. No major technologic advances were made during the decade; nor were any new products developed. Instead, the company paid out three-quarters of its net earnings as dividends. Much of the remainder, nearly $4,000,000 by 1931, was invested in federal government securities.[12] The entrepreneurial drive, so characteristic of Buckeye's management in earlier years, began dissipating in this decade.

The business situation for the steel-castings industry worsened in the late 1920s. In 1927 S. P. Bush, who continued as Buckeye's president, noted that "during the past two or thee years the advent of the motor truck . . . together with a very much more efficient railroad operation has made it unnecessary for the railroads to purchase so much equipment as they have in former years" and warned that this situation might cut into Buckeye's sales and profits. Still more vexing was price cutting. While the coupler agreement drawn up in 1915 and 1916 remained intact for most of the 1920s, it broke down in 1927 and 1928.[13]

John C. Whitridge assumed the presidency at Buckeye upon Bush's retirement in early 1928. Educated in mechanical engineering, Whitridge had worked his way up through the ranks at Buckeye, having started with the company twenty-six years earlier. He, too, recognized that his company and industry faced growing problems. In early 1928 Whitridge complained that "very severe competition and price cutting" had bitten deeply into his company's 1927 earnings, and in the following year he again decried "a marked reduction in the 1928 selling price due to severe competition and price cutting."[14] While realizing that Buckeye was in trouble, Whitridge, who remained president until his death in 1937, lacked the vision needed to solve these problems. Like the rest of Buckeye's management in the 1930s, 1940s, and 1950s, Whitridge was too narrow in his outlook and too comfortable with his life in Columbus to make necessary changes at Buckeye.

Buckeye's competitors reacted in a similar way to America's changing economic situation; for them, too, the 1920s were years of consolidation rather than innovation. National Malleable, like Buckeye, increased the capacity and efficiency of its existing plants, so much so, in fact, that it was able to transfer the production of the Chicago No. 1, the Toledo, and the East St. Louis plants to its other plants in Indianapolis, Cleveland, and Chicago.[15] American Steel Foundries did acquire new companies—the Galesburg Malleable Castings Company in 1921, the Damascus Brake Beam Company two years later, the Verona Steel Castings Company in 1926, the Eastern Steel Castings Company a decade later, and the McKees Rocks plants of the Pressed Steel Car Company in 1937—but these purchases were much less significant than those of earlier times.[16]

The Great Depression

The onset of the Great Depression of the 1930s exacerbated the problems Buckeye had encountered late in the previous decade. Between 1929 and 1932 the overall industrial production in the United States fell by one-half, and by 1933 at least one-quarter of the nation's industrial work force was unemployed.[17] The steel industry was hurt gravely, as the new markets developed in the 1920s—automobiles and appliances—cut back their orders for steel. America's output of steel fell precipitously from 63,000,000 tons in 1929 to just 26,000,000 tons in 1933, and during the same years the number of men employed in the steel industry decreased from

440,000 to 213,000. By 1932 the steel industry was operating at only 19.5 percent of its capacity.[18] As one Buckeye employee later remembered the situation, "things were pretty rough at the time; it was pretty bad."[19]

The early 1930s were disastrous for the steel-castings industry. As customers curtailed their orders, foundry after foundry banked its fires. The production of steel castings in the United States fell from 1,531,000 tons in 1929 to 312,000 tons four years later.[20] Companies like Buckeye which depended upon railroads for most of their business were particularly hard hit.[21] As railroad orders almost disappeared, Buckeye cut back its production severely; and, like American industry as a whole, Buckeye operated at a loss, as shown in Table 4.

Table 4

Buckeye Steel Castings, 1929–1932

	1929	1932
Castings output in tons	72,000	4,000
Sales	$7,000,000	$ 424,000
Net earnings	$1,257,000	($ 575,000)
Assets	$9,114,000	$6,445,000

SOURCE: The Buckeye Steel Castings Company, "Minutes of the Stockholders Meetings," January 16, 1930, January 23, 1933.

Faced with this situation, Buckeye's officers joined with their counterparts in other steel-castings companies in backing President Franklin Roosevelt's New Deal legislation. In particular, they supported the National Industrial Recovery Act (the NIRA), passed during the summer of 1933, which sought to bring about economic recovery by stimulating private business. Under its terms, the nation's antitrust laws were suspended, and businessmen, working with federal government officials, cooperated in drawing up "codes of fair competition" for their industries. These codes generally involved price fixing and the establishment of production quotas. Roosevelt and his advisors hoped the NIRA would boost business profits and, thus, spur economic growth in general. Adherence to the NIRA was voluntary, but most businessmen embraced the act as their savior.[22] After studying the legislation himself and taking part in conferences on it with the executives of other steel-castings companies, Whitridge recommended that Buckeye's officers accept the NIRA. They did. In July 1933 Buckeye's directors instructed the company's management to "cooperate in every possible way in the application of the act in its own operation looking to the successful administration of the new law," and five months later Buckeye's officers signed the code of fair competition drafted for the steel-castings industry.[23]

The federal government passed additional legislation of help to the steel-castings industry. The Reconstruction Finance Corporation, the Public Works Administration, and other government agencies set up by legislation passed in the early 1930s made funds available to railroads for the purchase of new cars and the repair of old ones. The Emergency Railroad Transportation Act of 1933, by allowing lines to avoid the duplication of facilities through the joint use of tracks and terminals, also promoted railroad recovery. Since railroads remained large purchasers of steel castings, these actions indirectly aided the steel castings industry.[24]

The mid-1930s saw some recovery of the American economy in general and the steel-castings industry in particular. Industrial production almost doubled between 1933 and 1936, and the nation's business corporations, which as a group had reeled under a $2,000,000,000 deficit in 1933, reported a $5,000,000,000 profit three years later.[25] American steel-ingot production recovered to an output of 57,000,000 tons in 1937.[26] The steel-castings industry shared in this turn of events, and in the same year produced 1,316,000 tons of steel, a figure considerably higher than the annual average for the 1920s.[27] Buckeye also did better. In early 1934 Whitridge noted that "for the first time in more than three years, the railroads are showing an interest both in repairs to present equipment and in the purchase of new equipment" and predicted that "as the equipment programs get under way, industries like ours should be benefited."[28] By 1937 Buckeye's steel-castings production had rebounded to 53,000 tons, and net earnings had risen to $1,046,000.[29]

Recovery was erratic, however. The United States plunged into a recession again in late 1937 and in 1938, and this recession crippled the steel industry. In 1938, the basic steel industry operated at only 30 percent capacity.[30] The steel-castings business was also badly injured. The railroad industry "fell out of bed," one Buckeye officer later remembered, and railroad orders nearly dried up.[31] As a result, Buckeye's output of castings fell to 9,000 tons that year, and the company once again operated at a loss.[32] Only in 1939 and 1940 did the steel-castings industry in general and Buckeye in particular begin their sustained recovery from the Great Depression.

Buckeye survived the 1930s in much better financial shape than most other companies. In the early part of the decade, the corporation's officers gradually sold the government securities purchased earlier and used the proceeds from these sales to cover their company's operating losses. They also used the sales of the government securities to allow continued dividend payments, despite the incurrence of operating losses. Buckeye missed no dividend payments on its preferred stock and passed payments on its common stock only in 1933–35 and part of 1938—a most unusual record for an American business during the 1930s.[33] Some changes occurred in Buckeye's capital structure. In 1925 a 4:1 common stock split had taken place, but in 1931 a more thoroughgoing recapitalization won approval. Buckeye's outstanding stock came to consist of three classes of issues: 10,000 shares of 6 percent prior preferred stock, 48,000 shares of preferred stock, and 240,000 shares of common stock.[34] The number of stockholders rose from 650 in 1936 to 1,212 three years later. While many of the stockholders continued to be directly connected to Buckeye or were Columbus and Cleveland businessmen, a growing number were investors with no ties to railroads or the steel industry. Buckeye was becoming less of a private club than in the past.[35]

The retrenchment of the 1930s affected Buckeye's landholdings in East Chicago. After briefly considering building a steel plant on the land, Buckeye's officers worked with several real estate firms to sell the land in the 1920s. Their efforts failed to bear fruit, mainly because, as one realtor complained, "your [asking] price appears to strike most prospects as rather high."[36] The coming of the Great Depression ended attempts to sell the land in the 1930s, but in late 1940 Buckeye's management sold all 108 acres to Linde Air Products.[37]

Despite the Great Depression, technological changes occurred in the basic steel industry at what one historian has called "a continually accelerated pace."[38] Particularly impressive was the construction of new hot strip mills and cold reduction plants to produce flat rolled steel. Some twenty hot strip and fifty-one cold reduction plants were built in the 1930s, and by 1939 flat rolled steel accounted for 38 percent of the total amount of steel produced in the United States, up from 25 percent nine years before.[39] This embrace of innovation did not extend equally to the steel-castings industry or to Buckeye Steel. Only a few new processes and products were developed in the Depression decade.

Buckeye remained a manufacturer of cast steel railroad car parts, and most new products the company brought out were simply modifications of older ones. Together with other manufacturers, Buckeye continued to produce the Standard D railroad freight car coupler during the 1920s. As train tonnage and locomotive power increased, railroads asked for still stronger couplers; so in 1931 Buckeye and other coupler makers began producing the Standard E coupler which featured stronger and more easily operated parts.[40] Most of Buckeye's attempts to move into new products proved abortive. In 1936 Buckeye considered entering into a licensing agreement with the Evans Product Company of Detroit for the production of railroad grade crossing barriers, but nothing came of this plan.[41] Four years later, Buckeye almost tooled up for the production of a new type of automatic transmission usable on trucks, buses, cars, and tanks. Buckeye's president favored this "because it gave some promise of a development in our product by diversification," but patent problems and the coming of war ended this experiment.[42]

Buckeye did move in a new direction in beginning the production of high-tensile alloy steels. These types of steel won favor because of their strength, ductility, and resistance to impact, abrasion, distortion, heat, and corrosion. Alloy steels were relatively new to the steel-castings industry. Only eight tons of alloy castings had been produced in 1910, but the 1920s witnessed a surge in their output. By the mid-1920s, about 70,000 tons were being turned out each year.[43] Buckeye shared in this advance. In the 1930s the company worked with other steel-castings companies and the Battelle Memorial Institute of Columbus, Ohio, a nationally known research institute, to develop new forms of high-tensile alloy steels, and in 1936–37 Buckeye sold 4,150 tons of such castings to railroads.[44]

For the most part, however, Buckeye's officers continued to manage their company conservatively in the 1930s. This conservatism allowed them to weather the Great Depression, but this approach hurt Buckeye in the long run. Buckeye's officers were more interested in using their corporation's earnings to pay dividends and make safe investments than to develop new products. In 1940 Buckeye remained what it had been twenty years before—a steel-castings company with its operations concentrated, even more than in the past, in one location. The corporation's steel plant had been improved, but no really new programs had been initiated.

The Second World War

The Second World War brought major changes to Buckeye's physical plant, daily operations, and relations with the federal government. A new sense of urgency and purpose ran through the firm. "The whole situation," remembered John Elder, then working his way up in Buckeye's mechanical department, "was considerably different" than it had been before.[45] Yet not even the war could change the nature of Buckeye's management or the types of products the company produced.

Federal government officials, working with business leaders, began preparing for war well before the bombing of Pearl Harbor. A host of government agencies was set up in 1940 and 1941 to coordinate wartime planning. During 1941 the government also began helping industry finance plant conversions for defense purposes. In 1942 the War Production Board (WPB), a federal government agency, centralized much of the government's economic war effort, and at the same time, the federal government offered additional incentives for industrial plant expansions, with the result that businessmen constructed as much new plant in 1942–45 as they had in the previous fifteen years. The government's war effort proved spectacularly successful in terms of economic production. Spurred by federal government expenditures, business poured out a plethora of war goods. By 1944 the United States was producing twice as much war material as the combined output of its enemies. Unemployment dried up in 1942 and 1943, and business profits, after taxes, rose from $6,400,000,000 in 1940 to $10,800,000,000 four years later.[46]

The steel industry shared in the wartime prosperity. Steel ingot production rose from 67,000,000 tons in 1940 to 89,600,000 tons four years later, as the industry operated at full capacity. Old plants were renovated and increased in size, and new mills were put up, especially in the Far West. In all, capital investment in the steel industry came to $2,680,000,000 during the war years, evenly divided between investments by the steel companies and the federal government through the Defense Plant Corporation.[47]

The steel-castings industry in particular benefited from the wartime recovery, as its foundries put out a wide variety of castings for the war effort. As the war increased the use of railroads (between 1940 and 1943 the amount of freight carried by railroads doubled and the number of passengers tripled), lines repaired old cars and bought new ones. In addition to railroad car parts, cast steel went into ordnance, tanks, ships, and, to a lesser degree, aircraft. The production of steel castings soared to nearly 2,000,000 tons in 1944, and the profits of steel-castings firms also rose. However, the work of the Office of Price Administration (OPA), which sought to set prices equitable to both the steel-castings industry and its customers, together with the annual renegotiation of profits made by the steel-castings companies on government contracts, prevented the making of excess profits.[48]

In their wartime experience, those at Buckeye were led by a new president. A. H. Thomas took over the position upon Whitridge's death in 1937. Like Whitridge, Thomas was trained in engineering and had been at Buckeye for many years before assuming the presidency. Described by a former Buckeye foreman as a "very quiet" person, Thomas was "a very fair, pretty easy-going" executive.[49] He was, one worker later recalled, "a square man, always honest, a good man."[50] His horizons were limited. He knew little of the world beyond Columbus. As Buckeye's Chicago sales manager remembered, "Thomas was good, but he never got out with you. I can't remember him ever leaving Columbus to come over here [Chicago]."[51]

Wartime plant expansion began at Buckeye in 1942. In early January, Thomas and representatives of other steel-castings companies, met with members of the Office of the Chief of Ordnance in Washington, D.C. to consider how best to increase the nation's steel-castings output. The Ordnance Department was particularly anxious to raise the production of cast steel tank turrets. Buckeye's officers suggested two ways by which they could increase their production. First, with the expenditure of $1,000,000 for improvements and extensions to their existing plant, Buckeye could, they

said, produce 500 tons of cast armor per month. Such improvements would have to be financed by the federal government, they
stated, "as we do not have sufficient resources for the purpose."
Under this plan, they predicted that armor deliveries could begin in
July. Alternately, the federal government, they pointed out, might
finance the construction of an entirely new plant on land Buckeye
owned next to its South Plant. It would cost more—$10,000,000
plus $4,000,000 for working capital—and it would take longer to
put into production, but it would be able to turn out 2,200 tons
each month.[52] Buckeye's officers much preferred the plan calling
for the erection of a new plant, recalled Lewis Day (then in general
accounting at Buckeye and later the company's acting chief executive officer), but the Ordnance Department "was interested in getting armor production started right now" and balked at the idea.[53]

After several more months of negotiations, Buckeye and the government agreed to a compromise plan. At the cost of $1,774,000,
Buckeye's existing facilities were to be extensively modified. The
company was to spend $760,000 for a 400-foot extension to the
main foundry building and a 300-foot addition to the finishing
building, together with changes in the railroad tracks serving these
buildings.[54] Like others expanding their facilities for war work,
Buckeye was to be permitted to amortize the costs of these additions over only five years. The federal government was to finance
directly all other improvements, including the new equipment in the
building extensions. Buckeye's expanded plant was designed to
produce 1,000 tons of cast steel armor per month (75 percent of this
tonnage was expected to be three-ton tank turrets) as well as parts
for railroad cars.[55]

Once approved by the federal government, construction began
quickly. Buckeye's yard gangs dug the building foundations by
hand, and company bricklayers (who usually spent their time re-
pairing furnaces) put the brick facings on the building extensions.[56]
In July 1942 Thomas reported that Buckeye's officers were doing
"everything in our power" to complete the extensions, but complained that "the time consumed by government procedure has
caused delays that were both disconcerting and discouraging."[57]
The construction of new facilities continued through 1943, but it
was not until early 1944 that Thomas could report that the plant expansion was "practically completed."[58] The facilities were finally

finished later that year—at a cost of $884,000 to Buckeye and $950,000 to the federal government.[59] Such construction delays and difficulties were all too common during the war years, with building materials and skilled labor in short supply. For instance, at the Homestead works in Pittsburgh, plant extensions began in the fall of 1941 but were not finished until three years later.[60]

However, even before they were completed, the new additions increased Buckeye's output of steel. During the second half of 1942 the company began making steel castings for tank armor and miscellaneous castings for the army, navy, and lend-lease programs. Tank armor castings continued to be Buckeye's major product in the first quarter of 1943, but for the rest of the year the company switched to the production of castings for railroad cars and ships, hawse pipes and cleats. In 1944 Buckeye's output consisted solely of railroad castings and special war castings. The company turned out no tank armor that year. By 1945 "war work" accounted for only 10 percent of the company's business. "Our regular products for the railroads of the country were our real source of business," reported Buckeye's president.[61]

The impact of the war upon Buckeye was mixed. The war revived Buckeye's financial fortunes. As the company's output of castings rose to about 66,000 tons per year, its sales and earnings perked up. However, increased income and excess profits taxes and the annual renegotiation of profits made on government contracts prevented any rapid increase in Buckeye's net earnings. In 1943, for instance, the company made net earnings of $621,000 on sales of $12,514,000.[62] The war caused no changes in Buckeye's basic patterns of production. Despite its large investment in new facilities, Buckeye remained more committed to the production of railroad castings than did other steel-castings companies. In 1940 railroad castings made up one-half of the tonnage of all steel castings produced in the United States, but during 1943 and 1944 they composed only one-sixth of the total.[63] Buckeye, except for late 1942 and early 1943, continued to produce primarily goods for railroads.

Reconversion and Decline

Buckeye experienced fewer immediate problems than many companies in reconverting to peacetime production.[64] In early 1943 President Thomas was already predicting that "upon the termination of war there will be a demand for our normal products for repairs and replacements of worn out car and locomotive equipment.''[65] Unlike many other businessmen who believed that a recession or depression would follow the cessation of war, Buckeye's officers were optimistic about the future. In 1945 Thomas reiterated his feeling that there would be "a good demand for our normal product" with the coming of peace, and Buckeye had once again turned almost solely to the production of railroad products by this time.[66]

Buckeye emerged from the war with a considerably enlarged plant acquired at relatively little expense. By October 1945 the company had amortized $392,000 of the $884,000 it had spent on the foundry and finishing building extensions. Moreover, under the terms of a presidential proclamation of September 29, 1945, Buckeye was allowed to respread the balance of its wartime capital expenditures over the period against which the original amortization was charged. The final result was that Buckeye made the building extentions for a net outlay of only $168,000 after taxes on income.[67] Buckeye's management was also able to purchase at low cost the equipment and improvements put in by the federal government. After extensive negotiation, Buckeye's officers secured $932,000 worth of government improvements for $67,000—which President Thomas noted with masterly understatement was "a price satisfactory to your management."[68] In fact, as Lewis Day, who was in charge of the negotiations for Buckeye, recalled, Thomas was so happy about the low purchase price that, when told what it was, "he just leaned back and roared."[69] Indeed, it may have been, as Day asserted, that Buckeye's management viewed the wartime extensions as "really an expansion of foundry capacity which could be used to great advantage once the war was over."[70]

In the late 1940s and the 1950s Buckeye developed along lines established in earlier years. Production for railroads continued to dominate Buckeye's activities, for Buckeye's officers failed to diversify their corporation's output of goods. Buckeye's reliance upon railroads was unfortunate, for by the 1950s railroads were a declining industry and, thus, a shrinking market for the products of steel-castings companies.

Buckeye's problems with the railroads did not immediately become apparent; the company enjoyed prosperity through most of the decade following the Second World War. Like many other American businesses, the company suffered from material shortages and the high price of raw materials in 1947. Nonetheless, the demand for new freight car equipment assured Buckeye of a fair year, an output of 51,000 tons of castings and net earnings of $875,000 on sales of $11,000,000.[71] Buckeye's problems eased in the following year. Production rose by about one-quarter, and net profits more than doubled in 1948.[72] By way of contrast, business fell sharply during 1949. In mid-October the plant was operating on the basis of only "a few heats per week," and the work force had been "greatly reduced."[73] Buckeye's output of castings dropped to 32,000 tons, and earnings fell precipitously.[74] The Korean War revived Buckeye's fortunes. Despite problems in obtaining enough raw materials and manpower, the steel plant was running at full capacity by late 1950 and continued to do so for the next two years. In addition to railroad equipment, Buckeye produced tank armor castings for the Ford Motor Company. When shortages developed in rolled steel, Buckeye also moved into the production of steel ingots suitable for rerolling. Spurred by the war, Buckeye's output soared to 65,000 tons of castings and 27,000 tons of ingots in 1951, a level of production nearly maintained in the following year.[75]

During these years, Buckeye introduced several new railroad products. In 1950 the company, in concert with other cast steel manufacturers, began producing the Type F railroad car coupler, a coupler stronger and more reliable than the older Type E. At about the same time, Buckeye developed an "easy-riding" four-wheel freight car truck known as the "Buckeye Cushion Ride." Designed to protect freight cars and their contents from the vibrations incurred at the higher speed trains were traveling in the postwar years, the "Cushion Ride" underwent testing in 1947 and 1948. By mid-1951 twelve lines were using it with "exceedingly good" results. The "Cushion Ride" won ever-wider acceptance as the decade progressed. By 1956 freight cars using the "Cushion Ride" had accumulated 100,000,000 miles service, and the "Cushion Ride" continued as a major Buckeye product in the 1960s.[76]

In actually designing new products, Buckeye's engineers generally started more "from the need of a railroad" than with their own ideas of what a product should be. As Leslie "Pete" Roberts, who served in product engineering at Buckeye between 1946 and 1977, explained, "sales and engineering . . . work[ed] hand-in-hand." Buckeye's salesmen kept the product engineers closely in touch with what the railroads wanted. In the late 1940s, for instance, Roberts accompanied Buckeye's eastern sales representatives on a trip to Philadelphia to confer with the engineers of the Pennsylvania Railroad. As a result of this meeting, Buckeye designed and produced two new castings for that line.[77]

Buckeye was able to develop and produce these new railroad items because of improvements in its physical plant. Buckeye came out of the Second World War with an enlarged plant, but a plant sorely in need of modernization. In 1946 George Johnson, who had become president that year, informed Buckeye's directors that the steel plant was fast "approaching that period in its history when major replacements were due both by reason of its physical deterioration and obsolescence," and he stated that the company's reserve of $4,156,000 would have to be spent "in the immediate future years to properly maintain the buildings and equipment for sound economic operation." He called for the immediate expenditure of $1,445,000 "to acquire added facilities and to enter more vigorously into the field of research for the improvement and development of the Company's products."[78]

Buckeye's management acted upon Johnson's advice over the next seven years, spending a total of $1,700,000 by the end of 1953. Buckeye's officers continued to upgrade the heat-treating facilities needed in the production of the high-tensile steel required in the new freight car couplers. They installed a wheelabrator to speed the finishing process and purchased an X-ray machine to modernize quality control. A new boiler for the power plant, diesel-electric locomotive cranes, new air compressors, and machine tools were other additions.[79] Few changes took place in the mid- and late 1950s. After the Korean War, Buckeye acquired $172,000 worth of armor-casting equipment for $57,000, and in 1956–57 the company installed new ladle cranes and air compressors. Finally, in 1958 Buckeye's president called for "a program of plant rehabilitation to insure that our buildings and equipment be kept in good shape." Responding to his requests, Buckeye's directors appropriated $300,000 to be spent over the next few years for a variety of purposes.[80]

Fewer improvements took place, in part because Buckeye's economic situation deteriorated in the mid- and late 1950s. As the

Korean War began drawing to a close, production, earnings, and net profits fell throughout 1952 and 1953. The year 1954 was little short of a disaster. Buckeye produced only 12,000 tons of steel, and reported its first loss since the days of the Great Depression.[81] Orders picked up again in the years 1955 through 1957, as railroads resumed buying. These were prosperous years for Buckeye. The company's annual production averaged 52,000 tons, and its average earnings came to $1,146,000.[82] This happy state of affairs came to an abrupt halt in 1958. A drop in railroad orders led to a drastic fall in Buckeye's output. In that year the company produced only 18,000 tons, and the firm once again plunged into the red.[83]

Buckeye's plight mirrored that of the steel-castings industry as a whole. Much of the industry remained tied to railroads, which took 38 percent of the industry's output in 1950–54 and 41 percent in 1963. Not surprisingly, the industry's production of steel castings, like Buckeye's, fluctuated considerably from year to year. While improvements were made in core making, molding, and finishing, they were more evolutionary than revolutionary in nature. Finally, it is worth noting that fifty-two steel foundries (there were 352 foundries producing steel castings in the United States in 1950) closed their doors between 1955 and 1965. Fully one-seventh of the firms in the industry went out of business in a single decade![84] Buckeye was in worse shape than most of the surviving companies. By 1962 Buckeye had fallen into the bottom one-third of the companies in the steel-castings industry when ranked by returns on sales or returns on investment.[85] Lewis Day, who had become Buckeye's comptroller in 1955, probably best described Buckeye's difficulties:

> In the late fifties something happened. Things seemed all at once to stand still. There was business, but the company was not growing. It was not modernizing. It was not replacing its equipment. . . . We were just cannibalizing the place.[86]

Buckeye's dependency upon the railroads, while serving the company well through the 1920s, hindered its long-run progress. It bred conservatism among many of Buckeye's officers, making them too willing to accept the status quo. Innovation, which had characterized Buckeye's early years, slowed in later times. Tied to a highly cyclical and declining industry, railroads, Buckeye encountered increasingly severe problems, until by the late 1950s the very survival of the company was endangered.

Sales

With few alterations taking place in Buckeye's product lines, the company's officers saw no need to change their sales methods. Buckeye's sales organization remained the same as in the late 1910s. The company's New York sales office handled orders for the eastern lines, while the Chicago office sold to railroads at points west. Marshall Cooledge, who took charge of the New York office in 1937, and Charles Pigott, who assumed control over the Chicago office in 1946, were Buckeye's most important sales representatives. George Johnson, Jr., operating out of the home office in Columbus, added significantly to the sales picture. In making sales, personal connections and service continued to be of most importance. Price competition, even for those items not covered by the coupler agreement, was uncommon.

Marshall Cooledge, the son of Fred Cooledge who was in charge of Buckeye's Chicago sales office for many years, was educated in engineering at the University of Illinois. After graduation, Cooledge worked for the Timken Roller Bearing Company until laid off during the Great Depression. Moving to Chicago, he joined the Illinois Emergency Relief Commission, and while on this job became close friends with Edward Ryerson. Ryerson, in turn, gave Cooledge a major position with his company, Ryerson Steel. Cooledge was at Ryerson Steel when offered command of Buckeye's New York sales office in 1937. Cooledge accepted the offer, and after "a little, short training period" in Columbus "to look over the plant" and "get acquainted with the engineering department," he moved to New York to take over Buckeye's operations from Jerry Bower. He remained at this post until his retirement in the 1960s.[87]

In making sales, Cooledge "worked from the bottom up." Using his knowledge of engineering, he visited the members of the mechanical departments of the railroads and, after talking to them, sought interviews with the railroad purchasing agents and vice-presidents. As he became established in the business, Cooledge found personal contacts to be of great use. "As you worked along," he explained, "you got to know all these fellows up to the top." Fairly soon, he noted, "presidents and vice-presidents were very close friends of mine." These contacts were of importance in winning orders, Cooledge later remembered: "Then you would have just sales contacts; well, he's a good buddy of mine, I'll give him an order."[88]

Charles Pigott had a strong railroad background before joining Buckeye. He grew up in Jackson, Tennessee, a division point for several railroads. While living in Jackson, Pigott got to know a number of railroad men. After several years of college in Mobile, Alabama, however, he moved to Chicago where he began work in a brass foundry. He gained additional technical knowledge by attending night classes at the Armour Institute and soon became the superintendent of the foundry, whose main products were valves and bearings for railroad locomotives. Pigott left the foundry in 1932 to begin work at United States Gypsum, which was interested in increasing its sales to railroads, and he was in charge of the company's railroad work until he was hired by Buckeye in 1946. Fred Cooledge was then responsible for Buckeye's Chicago sales office and, hoping to retire, was looking for someone to replace him. Pigott was recommended by a railroad official whom Cooledge knew, and Cooledge was immediately impressed by his railroad background. "With Gypsum," Pigott later remembered, "I called on every class one railroad in the United States."[89]

In securing orders, Pigott, like Marshall Cooledge in New York, placed great reliance upon personal relations with railroad men. Pigott later remembered his relations with the Illinois Central Railroad's purchasing vice-president as typical of his experiences. "I made a point of getting under his skin." The two men lunched together at the Union League Club, an exclusive men's club in Chicago, and played golf together at the South Shore Country Club. Not surprisingly, the Illinois Central began giving Buckeye orders in the mid-1950s. After his retirement in the 1970s, Pigott summarized what he believed had made him a successful sales representative:

> You have to have good delivery, good material. . . . Quality was absolutely necessary, but that was taken for granted. . . . You lived with your customer . . . being real close to them personally. If you could be real close friends with a purchas-

ing agent, he would want to have you in there. . . . You can't get away from the old personal contact.[90]

George Johnson, Jr., received his education as a history and literature major at Harvard University. After working for American Rolling Mill, IBM, and Anchor Hocking, he began at Buckeye in early 1946. The son of the company's president, Johnson operated from Buckeye's Columbus office in charge of sales for Ohio and southern railroads. Johnson later recalled that when a railroad announced that it was going to buy new cars, salesmen for the railroad supply companies eagerly competed for the orders. "It was just like Grand Central Station in the rush hour," he remembered, "everybody from all over the country would gather in the place." However, as Pigott and Cooledge also found, Johnson discovered that service, personal friendships, and past performance proved more important than price competition in making sales. Contacts had to be made before the railroad formally announced that they were in the market for new equipment. "By that time it was too late," Johnson observed, "if you hadn't done your homework by then, you weren't going to get anywhere."[91] As he further explained:

> Sales were made by living with the customer over a long period of time. . . . Sleeping with the customer . . . you live with him practically. . . . Service had a lot to do with it, because if you couldn't supply the coupler when a guy wanted it, he would go to someone else who had it, and then you would have a hard time getting back in. . . . Knowing people, that was probably most important.[92]

The regional sales offices had a fair degree of autonomy in their operations, but corporate headquarters in Columbus provided guidance and acted as a coordinating force. The head office set the "hard and fast" prices for all Buckeye products, but the sales offices had a "pretty free hand" on arranging delivery dates and service in general.[93] Contact was maintained between the corporate office and each sales office "two or three times a day" by telephone.[94] Annual sales meetings in Columbus also brought company officers and their sales representatives together. So did the occasional visits of Buckeye officials to the sales offices. Finally, both corporate officers and regional sales representatives took part in their industry's trade conventions, most importantly those of the Association of American Railroads and the Railway Supply Association.[95]

In terms of customers, Buckeye remained committed to a handful of railroads. In 1920–40, Buckeye sold its couplers to sixty-six customers, but eleven railroads accounted for two-thirds of all sales: the Baltimore & Ohio; the Chesapeake & Ohio; the Chicago, Milwaukee, & St. Paul; the Chicago, Rock Island, & Pacific; the Great Northern; the Hocking Valley; the New York Central; the Norfolk & Western; the Pennsylvania; the Union Pacific; and the Virginian. This emphasis on producing for a few major customers worked well in the 1920s, but it added to the problems Buckeye's officers faced in the following decade.[96] Few changes occurred in the 1940s and 1950s. A few lines continued to take the bulk of Buckeye's orders: the Baltimore & Ohio; the Chesapeake & Ohio; the Chicago, Milwaukee, St. Paul, & Pacific; the Chicago, Rock Island, & Pacific; the Great Northern; the New York Central; the Norfolk & Western; the Northern Pacific; the Pennsylvania; the Southern Pacific; and the Virginian.[97] Buckeye's inability to diversify its markets sorely hurt the company after the Second World War and, as we have seen, nearly led to the company's demise.

Sporadic and ineffective efforts were made to enter foreign markets. In 1923 S. P. Bush travelled to India and South Africa "to look after and foster the interests of the company."[98] Seven years later, Buckeye joined the other coupler companies in setting up the Foundries Export Company. The Foundries Export Company, working through yet a third corporation, the English Steel Corporation, coordinated the sales of couplers, bolsters, and side frames by the American companies to British-owned or -controlled railroads around the world.[99] The depression and the war halted attempts to expand sales overseas for two decades, but these efforts were renewed in the immediate postwar period. In early 1945 President Thomas noted that Buckeye was exporting "considerable tonnage" to Brazil and predicted that "export sales will be a factor in our business in the next two years."[100] Buckeye's new president, George Johnson, echoed these sentiments a year later. "Foreign markets" will be, he stated, "a source of business in the future."[101]

Such hopes proved chimerical. Foreign sales never became important for Buckeye. As one officer observed in 1957, "exports have been only a very small part of our sales."[102]

The years 1922 through 1959 brought few changes to sales or production methods at Buckeye. While the company pursued its quest for excellence in steel castings, it introduced few innovations in this period. Unlike its major competitors—National Malleable and American Steel Foundries, Buckeye made no attempts to move into the expanding market for steel castings in the automobile field. As one Buckeye executive accurately assessed the situation, "I think we just sort of settled down there and went along on what we had for awhile."[103]

Notes

1. William T. Hogan, *Economic History of the Iron and Steel Industry in the United States,* vol. 3 (Lexington, Mass.: D.C. Heath, 1971), pp.. 811–12, 878, 1001; Kenneth Warren, *The American Steel Industry, 1850–1970: A Geographical Interpretation* (London: Oxford University Press, 1973), pp. 214–19.

2. Gertrude Schroeder, *The Growth of Major Steel Companies, 1900–1950* (Baltimore: Johns Hopkins Press, 1953), p. 197.

3. Warren, *American Steel Industry,* p. 206.

4. William P. Conway, Jr., *Cast to Shape: A History of the Steel Castings Industry in the United States* (Rocky River, Ohio: Dillon, Liederbach, 1977), pp. 83–84, 89–90.

5. See Appendixes 1 and 2 of this book for the details of Buckeye's development.

6. "Minutes of the Meeting of the Board of Directors," October 2, 1923 (hereafter cited as "Directors Meeting").

7. Ibid., January 27, 1925, March 22, 1927.

8. Ibid., October 16, 1926, April 22, 1927.

9. Ibid., June 28, 1926, April 22, 1927.

10. Ibid., December 15, 1926.

11. Ibid., July 8, October 21, 1927, July 19, 1929.

12. Balance sheet figures for the 1920s.

13. "Minutes of the Stockholders Meeting," January 25, 1927 (hereafter cited as "Stockholders Meeting").

14. Ibid., January 31, 1928, January 29, 1929.

15. Anonymous, *National Malleable and Steel Castings Company* (Cleveland: no listed publisher, 1943), pp. 16–19.

16. Franklin Reck, *Sand in Their Shoes: The Story of American Steel Foundries* (Cleveland: no listed publisher, 1952), pp. 150–51.

17. On the early years of the Great Depression, see especially John Kenneth Galbraith, *The Great Crash* (Boston: Houghton Mifflin, 1961); Albert Romasco, *The Poverty of Abundance* (New York: Oxford University Press, 1965); Peter Temin, *Did Monetary Forces Cause the Great Depression?* (New York: W.W. Norton, 1976).

18. Hogan, *Economic History,* vol. 3, pp. 1119–20.

19. Interview by the author with John Elder, July 10, 1978.

20. Conway, *Cast to Shape,* 96.

21. "Stockholders Meeting," January 27, 1930, January 31, 1933.

22. Bernard Bellush, *The Failure of the NRA* (New York: W.W. Norton, 1975); Ellis Hawley, *The New Deal and the Problem of Monopoly* (Princeton, N.J.: Princeton University Press, 1966), part 1.

23. "Directors Meeting," July 14, 1933, January 17, 1934."

24. Ari Hoogenboom and Olive Hoogenboom, *A History of the ICC* (New York: W.W. Norton, 1976), pp. 119–27.

25. William Leuchtenburg, *Franklin D. Roosevelt and the New Deal* (New York: Harper and Row, 1963), p. 194.

26. Hogan, *Economic History,* vol. 3, p. 1120.

27. Conway, *Cast to Shape,* pp. 96, 101.

28. "Stockholders Meeting," January 30, 1934.

29. Ibid., January 25, 1938.

30. Warren, *The American Steel Industry,* 210.

31. Interview by the author with Lewis I. Day, June 5, 1978.

32. "Stockholders Meeting," January 31, 1939.

33. Balance sheet figures for the 1930s.

34. "Directors Meeting," October 17, 1930, January 25, 1938.

35. Buckeye Steel Castings, "Lists of Stockholders, January 26, 1937 and January 30, 1940."

36. C. A. Westberg to S. P. Bush, March 8, 1926, in Buckeye Collection.

37. "Directors Meeting," October 18, 1940.

38. Hogan, *Economic History,* vol. 3, p. 1339.

39. Ibid., p. 1120.

40. Howard Gilbert, *The Development, Operation, and Maintenance of A.A.R. Standard Couplers,* pamphlet, 1948, no place of publication, pp. 6–10, in Buckeye Collection.

41. "Directors Meeting," April 17, July 20, 1936.

42. Ibid., November 29, 1940, January 10, 1941.

43. Conway, *Cast to Shape,* pp. 88–89.

44. "Directors Meeting," January 14, 1938.

45. Elder interview, July 10, 1978.

46. This account is taken from Richard Polenberg, *War and Society: The United States, 1941–1945* (New York: J.B. Lippincott, 1972), chap. 1. See also: Jim Heath, "American War Mobilization and the Use of Small Manufacturers, 1939–1943," *Business History Review* 44 (Autumn 1972): 259–319; Eliot Janeway, *The Struggle for Survival: A Chronicle of Economic Mobilization in World War II* (New York: Weybright and Tally, 1951); Roland Stromberg, "American Business and the Approach of War, 1935–1941," *Journal of Economic History* 13 (Winter 1953): 58–78.

47. Hogan, *Economic History,* vol. 3, pp. 1121, 1193.

48. Conway, *Cast to Shape,* pp. 113–17.

49. Elder interview, July 10, 1978.

50. Interview by the author with Albert Stock, October 4, 1978.

51. Interview by the author with Marshall Cooledge, August 9, 1978.

52. Buckeye Steel Castings Company to Captain N. Cancilla, Tank and Combat Vehicle Division, Office of Chief of Ordnance, January 9, 1942; "Directors Meeting," January 9, 1942; "Stockholders Meeting," January 27, 1942.

53. Day interview, June 5, 1978. A major reason they wanted to build a new plant was that the federal government allowed businesses to amortize the costs of expansion over only five years, thus, as the historian Richard Polenberg has put it, "deflating taxable income while inflating earning capacity." See Polenberg, *War and Society,* p. 12.

54. Day interview, June 5, 1978; "Directors Meeting," April 14, 1942.

55. "Directors Meeting," May 1, 1942.

56. Interview by the author with Paul Crosier, July 10, 1978.

57. "Directors Meeting," July 16, 1942.

58. "Stockholders Meeting," February 15, 1944.

59. Ibid., March 27, 1945.

60. Warren, *American Steel Industry,* p. 242.

61. "Stockholders Meeting," February 16, 1943, February 15, 1944, March 27, 1945.

62. Ibid., February 15, 1945.

63. Conway, *Cast to Shape,* p. 114.

64. On reconversion, see Barton Bernstein, "The Debate on Industrial Reconversion: The Protection of Oligopoly and Military Control of the Economy," *American Journal of Economics and Sociology* 16 (April 1967): 159–72; Polenberg, *War and Society,* chap. 8.

65. "Stockholders Meeting," February 16, 1943.

66. Ibid., March 27, 1945.

67. "Directors Meeting," October 23, 1945.

68. Ibid., July 16, 1946; "President's Report to Stockholders, 1946."

69. Day interview, June 5, 1978.

70. Ibid.

71. "Directors Meeting," October 7, December 7, 1947.

72. Ibid., June 22, 1948.

73. Ibid., October 17, 1949.

74. "President's Report to Stockholders, 1949."

75. "Directors Meeting," December 5, 1950, July 11, October 5, December 4, 1951, January 8, July 1, October 20, 1952; "President's Report to Stockholders," 1950, 1951.

76. Buckeye Steel Castings Company, "President's Report to Stockholders," 1948, 1949, 1950, 1951, 1956.

77. Interview by the author with Leslie Roberts, June 27, 1978.

78. "Directors Meeting," November 29, 1946.

79. "Stockholders Meeting," March 23, 1954.

80. "Directors Meeting," July 6, October 18, 1955, March 27, 1956, March 26, 1957, March 25, 1958.

81. "Directors Meeting," January 13, July 20, October 15, December 17, 1954; "Stockholders Meeting," March 22, 1955.

82. "Stockholders Meeting," March 27, 1956, March 26, 1957, March 25, 1958.

83. Ibid., March 25, 1958.

84. Conway, *Cast to Shape,* pp. 125–139, 143, 157–158.

85. "Executive Committee Meeting," July 8, 1963.

86. Day interview, June 5, 1978.

87. Cooledge interview, August 9, 1978.

88. Ibid.

89. Interview by the author with Charles Pigott, June 14, 1978.

90. Ibid.

91. Interview by the author with George Johnson, Jr., April 21, 1978.

92. Ibid.

93. Pigott interview, June 14, 1978.

94. Johnson interview, April 21, 1978.

95. Cooledge interview, August 9, 1978.

96. Buckeye Steel Castings Company, "Sales, Net Tons, Couplers and Swivel Yokes, 1916–51."

97. Ibid.

98. "Directors Meeting," October 2, 1923.

99. Ibid., October 17, 1930.

100. "President's Report to Stockholders, 1945."

101. "Directors Meeting," July 16, 1946.

102. "Stockholders Meeting," March 26, 1957.

103. Elder interview, July 10, 1978.

chapter 5

MANAGEMENT, LABOR, AND CITY

Looking back upon his early experience at Buckeye in accounting and finance during the late 1930s, Lewis Day noted that many of the people in this department "grew up with the job."[1] What Day observed about those in accounting was true of the company as a whole. Even more than in the past, advancement came from within the company. Few new people were recruited from the outside in the years 1922 through 1959. Moreover, all of Buckeye's top management had engineering backgrounds. These twin circumstances help explain the conservative, and at times narrow, views they held of Buckeye's future. These views affected Buckeye's evolution as a business, and they influenced, as well, the company's relations with its labor force and the rest of society in Columbus.

Buckeye's Management

Professional education oriented toward engineering became increasingly common among Buckeye's management. As noted earlier, S. P. Bush, John Whitridge, and A. H. Thomas were all trained in mechanical engineering. Whitridge also became a member of the honorary engineering fraternity *Tau Beta Pi*. George Johnson came from an Ohio family long interested in iron works and joined Buckeye after graduating from Cornell University in mechanical engineering. Frank Bonnet, who became president in 1948, began at Buckeye immediately after finishing his studies in engineering at The Ohio State University. Since his family lived next door to the Wilbur Goodspeeds on Hamilton Avenue in Columbus, it was perhaps "only natural" for him to begin work at Buckeye.[2]

This engineering orientation continued after they began work at Buckeye. Thomas was a member of the American Society of

Mechanical Engineers and the Steel Founders Society, and Johnson also belonged to the latter organization. Bonnet was active in four such bodies: the American Society of Mechanical Engineers, the American Institute of Mining and Metallurgical Engineers, the American Foundryman's Society, and the Steel Founders Society.[3]

Buckeye's top management rose through the ranks, without exception. Whitridge, who took Bush's place as Buckeye's president in 1928, had been with the company for twenty-six years, and Thomas, who became president upon Whitridge's death in 1937, was also a veteran of many years. Johnson, who served as vice-president throughout most of the 1920s and 1930s and who became president in late 1945, started at Buckeye in 1906 and worked his way up through the company's various departments. Bonnet, who became a vice-president in 1937 and who assumed the presidency in 1948, began at Buckeye in 1909.[4]

Promotion from within typified the plant supervisory force as well as the top management at Buckeye. The careers of Paul Crosier and John Elder were characteristic of this process. Crosier graduated from The Ohio State University in civil engineering in 1935. "It was tough getting a job then," he recalled. Crosier was happy to hire on as an hourly worker in Buckeye's yard gang. He transferred to the plant's mechanical department around 1939 and was in charge of some of the wartime building. He soon became general foreman of the mechanical department. After the war, he went into the finishing department, and in 1961 he became the chief plant engineer.[5] Elder had worked at Buckeye in the maintenance department while an electrical engineering student at The Ohio State University. Upon his graduation in 1929, he went to work for the American Bridge Company in Pittsburgh, only to return to Buckeye when laid off by American Bridge in 1934. Hired as an engineer for the mechanical department, he became, first, assistant superintendent and then superintendent of the mechanical, power, and yard departments in the late 1940s and early 1950s.[6]

Like most American businesses, Buckeye possessed no real management training program for most of the interwar years. Johnson, as his son later recalled, "just like a lot of the apprentices, went through most of the departments." He worked his way up through the operating, engineering, and sales divisions. His rise was "just a natural evolution."[7] Bonnet, as one company officer recalled, had a business career which "involved growing up in the foundry."[8] Starting as a molder's helper, he soon became a special apprentice in the production engineering department and, after about a year in sales, the assistant mechanical engineer for the foundry. During the First World War, Bonnet was in charge of the forge department, and in 1919 he became the assistant plant superintendent responsible for all foundry, core, and open-hearth operations. In the 1920s and 1930s Bonnet's experiences were further broadened by service in various supervisory capacities.[9]

Buckeye did initiate something of a training program in 1937 and 1938 when the company recruited about twenty engineering graduates from Purdue and The Ohio State University.[10] Paid only "nominal salaries," they spent eighteen months going from department to department learning the ropes. The trainees spent about two or three months in each department working and observing operations. At the end of this program, each chose what part of the foundry he would enter. On-the-job training, then, complemented the theoretical education of Buckeye's management. "When they were molding, they carried cores," remembered Jack Dawson, a Buckeye foreman in the 1940s, about the trainees. "They worked on the open-hearth, they tapped heats, they worked in the finishing department, they worked all over."[11]

What was true of Buckeye's management also held true of its directors. Most stayed at their posts until they died or retired, and, as was typical of American businesses in this period, few were independent, outside directors. Walter Bowler, who became a director in 1918, was the husband of one of Frank Rockefeller's daughters. Alexander Brown, elected as director in 1923, was a Cleveland businessman who had owned stock in Buckeye since at least 1901. He replaced Thomas Goodwillie who resigned from the board because of advanced age. William Nash, a longtime Buckeye stockholder and the husband of another of Frank Rockefeller's daughters, became a director upon Bowler's death five years later. George Archer was elected to the board when John Deshler died in 1929. Archer was president of the Commercial National Bank, the institution Wilbur Goodspeed had earlier headed. (The Commercial National Bank was eventually acquired by the City National Bank.) Joseph Frantz, a trustee of the Battelle Memorial Institute and a director of Armco, became a director upon T. P. Linn's demise in 1930. John H. McCoy, the president of the City National Bank, became a Buckeye director in 1938.[12] John W. Galbreath, a prominent Columbus businessman, joined the board in 1950. A good friend of the McCoys, Galbreath was also a director of the City National Bank. William Tracy, another Columbus business-man, was elected two years later.[13]

Buckeye's officers were deeply involved in Columbus's civic af-fairs. For most of the 1920s Bush was mayor of Marble Cliff, a middle-class suburb of Columbus, in which he lived. It was in this position that he met John Bricker, then city attorney, who would later become a United States senator from Ohio and a Buckeye director. Bricker recalled that Bush had "a big stone house . . . a beautiful mansion," in which the city council "always met." Bush, concluded Bricker, "thoroughly enjoyed" being mayor.[14] Bonnet served as president of the Bexley city council for sixteen years (Bex-ley was another Columbus suburb).[15] As before, Buckeye's man-agement belonged to the "right" social clubs. Whitridge, Thomas, Johnson, and Bonnet all belonged to the Columbus Club, and John-son once served as its president. All except Johnson were members of the Rocky Fork Country Club and the Columbus Country Club. In addition, Thomas belonged to the University Club and the Lake Placid (New York) Club. They also became increasingly active in Co-lumbus businesses. Thomas served as a director of the Huntington National Bank, Midland Mutual Life, and the Sugar Creek Coal and Mining Company. Johnson was also a director of the Huntington National Bank, and Bonnet served as a director for the City National Bank and the Ohio Federal Savings and Loan Association.[16]

As the wide range of their local activities shows, Buckeye's of-ficers had become, to use a well-known phrase, "big fish in a small pond." They were among the most important business and social leaders in Columbus. They were accepted by others in the city's social and economic leadership, and this leadership was then a relatively closed group dominated by local business leaders. As one Buckeye director correctly observed, "Columbus wasn't as big then [in the 1930s and 1940s] or as diversified. Everybody knew every-body else in business around town."[17]

Labor

Deeply wedded to their local community, Buckeye's officers con-tinued to express a paternalistic concern about their workers' welfare. Genuine humanitarianism, combined with good business sense and a desire to avoid unionization, mandated improvements in working conditions at the steel plant. In 1924 the company raised the roof of the south molding lean-to and improved the building's ventilation, as the plant superintendent put it, to "lower costs and lessen labor turn-over."[18] Six years later, Buckeye's officers raised the roof of the north molding lean-to and installed a heating system in the east end of the foundry, as one explained, to "give us an abundance of light, ample heat, making it as desirable a place to work as any other in the shop."[19] Buckeye's management also co-operated with other companies on these matters. In 1929 F. G. Bennet, who had headed Buckeye's safety department since 1910, was chosen by members of the metals section of the National Safety Council to chair a committee to study the accident problem in foundries.[20]

Unfortunately, no records dealing specifically with wages and hours of work at Buckeye during the interwar years have survived.[21] However, it is likely that Buckeye followed national and regional trends and switched from twelve to eight-hour shifts in the early 1920s. Wages probably rose somewhat, at least for skilled workers. By 1920 Columbus molders made $7.04 for an eight-hour day, and pattern makers received $9.90 for nine-hour days.[22] Unskilled workers made much less. In 1929 all workers in the American steel industry earned an average of $3.20 per day; those in the Great Lakes, $3.36. These wages were actually considerably lower than the $4.40 that even unskilled workers received during the First World War.[23]

With the coming of the Great Depression, wages fell. In 1931 Buckeye lowered wages and salaries 10 percent, and a further 20 percent reduction came in the following year.[24] In making these reductions, Buckeye was following the pattern established by most iron and steel companies. Wages dropped 24 percent for common laborers in iron and steel mills across the nation in 1929–33.[25] However, those with jobs were probably glad to have them at whatever wage. Most Buckeye workers were laid off during the early and mid-1930s. In April 1934 the company was operating only one furnace.[26] Jobs were, as Lewis Day recalled, "very scarce." Even as recovery began in 1934–36, the work force, he remembered, was "reduced substantially," with people "either laid-off or put on reduced schedules."[27] In this situation, John Elder later recalled,

Buckeye tried to "hold onto their key employees and cut back the number of days and number of hours of work in order to spread the work around."[28] Conditions gradually improved. If, as is likely, Buckeye followed wage trends in Ohio's steel industry, much of the ground lost between 1929 and 1933 was made up later in the decade. This improvement came in part through government action (the National Industrial Recovery Act of 1933 set minimum wages for the steel-castings industry) and in part through the recovery of the economy.

Workers at Buckeye, as elsewhere, also sought to help themselves through unionization. The National Industrial Recovery Act seemed to encourage independent unionism.[29] However, as happened at United States Steel and Bethlehem Steel, the union set up at Buckeye was a company union, not a truly independent union belonging to a national or international federation. In 1933 company employees, working closely with management, formed a Shop Employees Association.[30] A committee of twenty-eight people, evenly divided between representatives of labor and management, ran the body, and it had no collective-bargaining power.[31] It was, as one company officer later described it, "more of a social-educational program." The association was, he recalled, "primarily dominated by management, and it was a device, in part, to stall off the formal efforts of the United Steelworkers."[32] The constitution of the organization set forth its limited powers:

> The purpose of this plan is to provide an easy, convenient, and regular means of exchanging such ideas as will be mutually helpful to both employees and management, and to talk things over freely and without restraint; to give the employees a voice in matters of mutual interest, including safety, sanitation, hours of work, wages, and other working conditions; to provide an orderly and expeditious procedure for the prevention and adjustment of differences; and to afford a means through which the Management may furnish information of interest to employees regarding the company's affairs.[33]

Not surprisingly, Buckeye's management, working through the Ohio Manufacturers' Association, opposed congressional passage of the Wagner Act in 1935.[34] As finally enacted, this law gave employees the effective power to organize unions of their own choice and to bargain collectively with management. It prohibited management discrimination against unionists and made difficult the establishment of company unions. Not until the 1940s, however, did the steelworkers unionize Buckeye.

The composition of Buckeye's labor force probably remained relatively unaltered during the interwar period. Again, because of the lack of records, it is impossible to determine precisely the make-up of the work force. However, if it is assumed (as many with Buckeye say was the case) that most workers lived near the steel plant in Columbus's South Side district, some conclusions can be reached. First, a growing number, probably 10 percent to 15 percent, of Buckeye workers were black. The migration of blacks to Columbus during the First World War raised the city's proportion of black residents from 7 percent in 1910 to 9.4 percent a decade later. By the late 1920s sociologists were listing the South Side as one of ten districts in Columbus with a sizable black population.[35] Still, most of Buckeye's workers were white, and about 14 percent of them were of foreign birth. For the first time in its history, Buckeye had a substantial number of Appalachian workers. Moving north after the First World War, many Appalachians came to Columbus, and by 1940 perhaps 20 to 22 percent of Buckeye's workers had been born in West Virginia and Kentucky.[36]

Living conditions for many of Buckeye's South Side workers were in need of improvement. An examination of housing conditions among blacks uncovered numerous cases of overcrowding, and many houses were found to be "of poor repair."[37] Buckeye's officers tried to ameliorate this situation. In 1925, at the urging of S. P. Bush, the company's directors voted to retain rather than sell company landholdings along the Groveport Pike. The reason for this decision was that "quite a number of our colored employees and those of other plants had located near the property" and that "it was desirable to provide suitable quarters for community gatherings, religious services and other public events."[38] A year later, Bush again pointed out to his firm's directors that "the plight among the colored people of Columbus is in many cases deplorable," and persuaded them to contribute $3,500 to a $35,000 fund the city was raising to set up a camp for blacks.[39] Finally, at the suggestion of A. H. Thomas, the directors guaranteed a real estate loan to black employees for the construction of the Mount Carmel Baptist Church and Community Center in 1928. They did so to boost "the morale and efficiency of our colored employees."[40]

The Second World War led to major changes in the relationship between Buckeye and its work force. More than in the past, the company's operations suffered from absenteeism and a manpower shortage caused by the wartime scarcity of labor. Concurrently, the company underwent an organizing drive by the United Steelworkers of America, a campaign which proved successful in 1942. Postwar strikes in 1945 and 1946 further complicated the labor picture.

The wartime labor shortage affected nearly all of American business. Like other manufacturing concerns, Buckeye suffered from the scarcity of labor. Despite the company's increase in business, the size of its work force remained stable: 1,345 hourly employees in 1941, 1,333 in 1943.[41] There never seemed enough men to do all the jobs. At Buckeye the wartime motto was, one general foreman later recalled, "if he was warm, hire him."[42] Buckeye's management perennially decried the lack of qualified labor. In late 1943 they complained that "absenteeism and [a] skilled manpower shortage" were "restricting our output" and contributing "to increased costs and a narrowing profit margin."[43] In that year they purchased eighty-three acres of land from the American Rolling Mill Company for use, in part, as a "recreation center [for] our own employees" as one way to attract workers to Buckeye and cut down the turnover rate.[44] Yet, the problems persisted. In 1944 President Thomas complained that "earnings are decreasing due to a curtailment of operations arising from a labor shortage and also due to the replacement of experienced workers by inexperienced workers resulting in a decline of efficiency."[45] A year later, Buckeye's president reiterated that "on account of the scarcity of labor, absenteeism, and decreased efficiency, operations were difficult and output was restricted."[46] There was some truth to these statements, as 516 Buckeye workers left the firm's employ to join the armed forces. One-half of them later returned to work in the steel plant.[47]

In their search for workers, Buckeye's officers employed larger numbers of blacks and Appalachians. Because of the lack of records, it is impossible to document precisely how the composition of Buckeye's work force changed, but foremen and officers at Buckeye recall intensified efforts to hire larger numbers of blacks and

Appalachians during the war years. As was typical of American industry during this period, blacks received mainly unskilled jobs. The yard department, remembered Paul Crosier, was "predominantly black." By way of contrast, the mechanical department, made up of skilled workers, "as far as the machinists, electricians, millwrights, and so forth were practically all white." The supervisors and foremen were also "all white."[48]

As mentioned earlier, it was during the 1930s that workers secured the right to form unions and bargain collectively with management, first as part of the National Industrial Recovery Act of 1933 and, more importantly, with the passage of the Wagner Act two years later. The Congress of Industrial Organizations (CIO) which John L. Lewis of the United Mine Workers and others formed in 1935 and 1936 was quick to take advantage of the new opportunity. While the older craft-oriented American Federation of Labor (AFL) hesitated, the CIO moved into many of the United States' mass-production industries. In the late 1930s the CIO, as a proponent of industrial unionism, organized America's auto, rubber, and steel industries.[49] In early 1937 the Steel Workers' Organizing Committee (SWOC), a CIO affiliate, secured recognition as a bargaining agent from United States Steel without a strike. While not winning all it desired, SWOC laid the groundwork for the unionization of the company's plants.[50] Violence accompanied organizing drives at the "little steel" companies—American Rolling Mill, Bethlehem, Inland Steel, National Steel, Republic Steel, and Youngstown Sheet and Tube. The most notorious event occurred on Memorial Day, 1937, when police killed ten strikers trying to picket Republic Steel's Indiana Harbor Plant. This incident, combined with other factors, slowed the organizing campaign, but by the close of 1941 SWOC had unionized most of little steel. However, even at the outbreak of war, many small and medium-sized plants, including Buckeye, remained non-union.[51]

The unionizing drive began at Buckeye in 1941. On March 3 of that year SWOC chartered Local Union Number 2342; and working through this body, SWOC organizers sought to win support for unionization from Buckeye's labor force.[52] Harry Mayfield, then head of the SWOC local which had just unionized Timken Roller Bearing in Columbus and later a leading Steelworkers official in Ohio, recalled that it was SWOC organizers more than local union leaders who spearheaded the drive at Buckeye. Ward Wolcott and Howard Porter, acting directors of SWOC (from 1942 on, the United Steelworkers of America) District 24 from 1936 to 1941 and 1941 to 1948, respectively, were particularly important. So was John Gwilt, a SWOC staff representative.[53] The task of these organizers was formidable, for unions had little hold on Buckeye laborers (except some skilled workers) when they started their unionizing campaign. A memo drafted by SWOC organizers listed the status of unions in various parts of Buckeye's plant on August 22, 1941, as shown in Table 5.[54]

Over the next year the United Steelworkers officials labored day in and day out to win support for Local 2342. They held weekly meetings at the Croatian Hall on Reeb Avenue on Columbus's South Side to explain the benefits of unionization to Buckeye workers. Similar meetings were also convened in the "Little Italy," a South Side nightclub, and in workers' homes. The United Steelworkers opened a special field office on South Parsons Avenue near the Buckeye plant to serve as an organizational center.[55] Harry Mayfield, who became involved in the unionizing campaign at Buckeye, remembered the situation there:

> We used every known organizing trick in the book. We had sound cars that we had out in front of the plant at shift-change time, and we talked to employees coming out and going in. We parked right across the street from the plant

Table 5
Workers and Unionization at Buckeye Steel

DEPARTMENT	EMPLOYEES	UNION STATUS
Foundry	450	practically nothing
Chipping room	200	fairly good
Coupler building	250	practically nothing
Mechanical	100	good
Cranes and electrical	200	weak
Pattern [shop]	50	inclined to AFL
Yard	400	weak, but attitude toward union good

SOURCE: "Buckeye Steel Castings Co.—SWOC Local Union 2342, August, 22, 1941," in the Columbus office of the United Steelworkers of America, p. 1.

gate; there was a bar-joint over there at the time. And, we put leaflets out at every shift. This went on for a number of months, and finally we got recognition.[56]

As Mayfield noted, the Steelworkers succeeded in unionizing Buckeye—but not without a fight. At the outset of their organizing campaign, Buckeye's officers displayed what one union officer called "a distinct coolness toward collective bargaining." Company officers turned down a request for a meeting with the union in November 1941 with the statement, "We do not believe that you represent a majority of our employees, and we therefore will not meet with you."[57] However, Buckeye's management never went as far in opposing unionization as many steel companies. As officers in a local company with strong ties to their community, Buckeye's management did not want to blacken their corporation's public image. Comparing his experiences in trying to organize the Columbus plant of the Timken Roller Bearing Company and Buckeye Steel, Mayfield found a sharp contrast:

It was not the same as Timken. Timken used every conceivable, in our words at least, unfair labor practice, gimick there was. This was not true of Buckeye Steel Castings. You have to remember that Buckeye Steel Castings Company is an old-line Columbus family. They had a lot of home ties in Columbus. They were not vicious. I'm not saying they wanted us to organize, but they did not use all of the, what we would term, gimicks to fight unionization. They were more realistic.[58]

The election on unionization took place in October 1942. It was a clear victory for the United Steelworkers; they won a majority of the ballots cast. Of the 1,260 ballots, the United Steelworkers received 712 votes; the International Molders Union, an AFL affiliate, won 149; and 399 employees voted for no union.[59] Following the election, the Steelworkers began negotiating their first contract with Buckeye's management. This process was protracted, for the union officials and company officers differed on a number of basic considerations. Only after the Steelworkers, reporting "no success" in their efforts at negotiation, appealed to the War Labor Board (a federal government agency), was an agreement hammered out and signed in July 1943.[60]

As expected, it was a compromise. The company recognized the union as the only bargaining agent for Buckeye workers, but did not institute an automatic checkoff system for union dues. Company and union agreed upon a forty-hour workweek with overtime for additional work, and both also approved a one-week paid vacation for eligible employees each year. However, the contract said nothing about a minimum wage; the Steelworkers wanted $0.78 per hour set as the minimum. Seniority was another thorny issue. The union wanted seniority to count for more than the ability to perform work and physical fitness in decisions on promotions or layoffs, but in the final contract seniority was to count only when the other "factors are relatively equal." Seniority was determined by department, rather than the plant as a whole. An elaborate grievance system was set up, but it, too, followed the wishes of management more than those of union officials. Finally, it was agreed that the contract would remain in force for one year.[61]

Despite the peaceful unionization at Buckeye, points of friction between labor and management remained, and in 1945–46 the company suffered from the first work stoppages and strikes in its history. In October 1945 the core makers walked out, closing the steel plant for about two weeks. The dispute involved a disagreement as to what constituted a full day's work. The core makers claimed that the completion of 600 units of work made up a day worked. The company wanted to require a full eight-hour shift, if it was necessary to stay that long in order to secure an output of cores needed to balance the foundry schedule. The strike was peaceful, and on October 23 the union agreed to binding arbitration. The issue was soon settled in favor of the company.[62]

More serious and long-lived was a strike which closed down Buckeye's operations for most of the first quarter of 1946. This work stoppage was part of a nationwide strike called by the United Steelworkers. The main issue was wages. During the war years the Steelworkers had agreed to what was known as the "Little Steel Formula" of July 16, 1942 as the guideline in setting wages. In essence, this formula said that wages could rise only 15 percent over what they had been on January 1, 1941. As a result, many unionists complained that wages failed to keep pace with inflation. With the coming of peace, the Steelworkers voted for a nationwide strike in late November 1945 to secure a wage increase averaging 18½ cents per hour.[63] The vote at Buckeye was 584 for the strike, 385 against it.[64]

The strike began on January 21, 1946, as 750,000 steelworkers walked off the job across the nation. In Columbus eight firms closed their plants when 8,000 workers left their posts and set up picket lines.[65] The Columbus walkouts were peaceful, with many strikers who were ex-servicemen wearing their uniforms on the picket lines. Within a few days, the strike closed several more Columbus plants, and despite intensely cold weather, students from The Ohio State University, carrying signs reading, "Solidarity Forever," "Workers and Students Unite and Fight," and "Right Pay Means Better Lives," marched in support of the strikers.[66]

The strike lasted about six weeks. In mid-February about one-quarter of the 200,000 steelworkers off the job in Ohio returned to work, when United States Steel, Republic Steel, and a few other firms settled on the union's terms. But in Columbus, the strike dragged on.[67] As the strike continued, violence flared up at Buckeye. On March 3, "massed pickets threw stones and brickbats" at a car leaving the company's steel plant with laborers who had gone back to work the day before.[68] The strike at Buckeye finally ended on March 9. Union officials and company officers signed a new contract good through April 30, 1947. In return for an average 18½ cents per hour raise, the Steelworkers agreed to a "no-strike" pledge. "We are very happy about the whole set-up," declared Buckeye's president. He had reason to be happy. Unlike most companies, Buckeye had to pay no retroactive wages as part of its settlement. Moreover, the new contract contained "additional security clauses" which Buckeye's management hoped "will be helpful to our supervisory forces in increasing production.[69] By the end of 1946, President George Johnson could inform his company's directors that relations with the Steelworkers had "improved somewhat" and that "absenteeism had been reduced.[70]

There can be little question that unionization, combined with the general return of prosperity during the Second World War, benefited Buckeye's workers in economic terms. Between 1941 and 1946 the average hourly wage paid at Buckeye rose from $0.91 to $1.25, an increase of 37 percent. The number of hours worked per week fell, from an average of 44.4 in 1945 to 37.5 in 1946. These figures were about the same as those for the steel-castings industry as a whole. In 1946 the industry's average wage per hour was $1.25, and the average number of hours worked each week stood at 38.8.[71]

In the 1950s Buckeye's labor relations and the composition of the company's labor force continued to evolve along the lines laid down in the war years. No radical departures from the past took place; rather, trends already begun were carried farther.

In the years after the Second World War, both blacks and white Appalachians continued to move north in search of better economic, social, and cultural opportunities.[72] Many ended up in Midwestern cities like Columbus, where they often displaced earlier migrants in hard, dirty jobs in such places as steel mills and foundries. Appalachians came to work at Buckeye Steel in two closely related ways. Often caught short of manpower during times of peak demand, Buckeye's officers actively recruited new workers from the South and Appalachia. As Bill Buffington, Buckeye's vice-president of manufacturing, explained, recruiters for Buckeye "brought busloads [of new workers] up" from south of the Ohio River at various times through the 1950s.[73] Once at Buckeye, these newcomers attracted still more migrants to the steel plant. Family ties were of great importance in bringing workers to Buckeye. "If a brother gets a job, he recommends it to his brother or his cousin," Phil Bordan, Buckeye's personnel manager, observed, "and there is a kin-family relationship out in the plant that is unbelievable." Buckeye's management welcomed this situation, according to Bordan, because "friends and relatives usually stay" at the steel plant, thus reducing its turnover rate.[74]

Relations between Buckeye's officers and union officials became more amicable, as the company's management accepted the reality of unionization. As we have seen, the United Steelworkers of America (local 2342) of the CIO came to represent Buckeye's labor force in the early 1940s. In 1948 the company's pattern makers established their own union, a local of the Pattern Makers League of North America, an AFL craft union.[75] Jim West, who had been with the federal government in labor relations, joined Buckeye to manage the company's relations with these unions; and it is to West's skillful handling of the issues that much of the industrial peace at Buckeye can be traced. Harry Mayfield, one of the leaders of the United Steelworkers, remembered West as "a realist . . . one of the leaders in this area on industrial democracy." West, Mayfield believed, "could have broke our union in nothing flat," but chose instead to deal "with us on a fair-and-square basis." However, as Mayfield also explained, "By the same token, Jim West was able to convince a lot of our committees to take less than what they could have gotten, if it hadn't been for Jim West."[76]

The issues at stake in labor negotiations changed over time. During the 1940s and 1950s "seniority was always the key issue," Mayfield recalled.[77] As noted earlier, seniority counted for less than other factors in determining promotions and layoffs at Buckeye Steel, as specified in the company's original contracts with the Steelworkers. By the late 1950s the Steelworkers had won the right to have seniority matter more than other considerations in the determination of these items. Fringe benefits grew in importance as bargaining issues. In 1947 the company set up an employee hospitalization plan, and hospital benefits were increased on a regular basis in later years. Paid vacations for employees, which had begun in 1943, were broadened in scope as time progressed. In 1950 Buckeye set up its first pension plan for hourly employees, and this plan, too, grew in depth and breadth throughout the 1950s. In 1959 a Supplemental Unemployment Benefit Plan came into being. Wages, of course, were a constant issue in labor relations at Buckeye Steel. Between 1941 and 1964, the average hourly wage at Buckeye rose by $1.85, about the same as the $1.90 increase at United States Steel, the base for the industry as a whole.[78]

In preparing to negotiate contracts with Buckeye, a Steelworkers staff representative would meet with a negotiating committee elected by the local union members. The staff representative would explain to the local negotiating committee what the Steelworkers' current wage and benefits policies were. (The Steelworkers had a wage policy committee which drafted standard policies for the union's entire membership, based upon what happened in basic steel.) The staff representative and the local negotiating committee, after agreeing upon what their demands would be among themselves, opened talks with company officials.[79] The actual negotiations usually went fairly smoothly. The talks in August 1963 were typical of the negotiating process at Buckeye. Seven meetings between Buckeye officers (led by Jim West) and union officials took place between August 6 and August 30. At first, a broad range of subjects were discussed, but as the conferences continued, the issues of wages and insurance benefits became paramount. By the sixth meeting, West was requesting both sides to "get down to brass tacks" to resolve the items still in dispute. This was soon done, and after some give and take, a new contract was signed in September.[80]

Company and Community

Columbus continued to develop as a major American city in the 1920s and 1930s. By 1940 Columbus had grown to 306,000 people, an increase of nearly 70,000 despite the hard times of the Great Depression. The downtown area continued to change with the construction of a civic center. In 1921 fire destroyed the city hall, but thirteen years later, Edgar T. Wolfe, the publisher of the *Ohio State Journal* and a member of Columbus's municipal planning commission, broke ground for the east wing of the new city hall, thus initiating the final stage of that building's completion. Even earlier, the American Insurance Union Building soared above the rest of the downtown area. The air age came to Columbus with the establishment of Norton Field in 1923 and Port Columbus six years later. City services began catching up with urban needs in these years. The completion of O'Shaughnessy Dam on the Scioto River in 1925 assured Columbus of an adequate supply of pure water for the first time, and a year later the city's police and fire departments were completely motorized. New "White Way" lighting graced downtown streets, which were further modernized by the installation of up-to-date traffic lights.[81] As in most cities, this growing modernity had a dark side. In 1934 the city council found it necessary to consider a special ordinance to stop "bootlegging" in night clubs which held only 3.2-beer permits.[82] Three years later, Columbus found itself in the midst of a syphilis epidemic. City health authorities estimated that there were 40,000 cases in Columbus, and the Community Fund set aside $4,000 to fight the disease (the city council appropriated an additional $2,000).[83]

Industrial development, while slowing, remained a bulwark of the Columbus economy. By 1930 about 40 percent of the city's total payroll came from manufacturing and construction, a situation prompting the Chamber of Commerce to claim that "while not to be rated as a Pittsburgh or Gary," Columbus possessed an industrial base "which many urban centers not serving as state capitals would be happy to boast of." The industrial segment of Columbus was diversified; Columbus never became an automobile center like Detroit or a steel city like Pittsburgh. Iron, steel, and machinery plants accounted for nearly 30 percent of Columbus's industrial payroll; food products, leather products, paper and printing, and vehicles and parts accounted for about 10 percent each; and textiles, stone products, lumber, and chemicals were responsible for about 5 percent apiece.[84] New companies continued to enter Columbus, most notably Timken Roller Bearing and Ford Motor, and older industries expanded, especially the shoe and mining machine industries.[85] Beginning a trend that would continue in later years, an increasing number of products made in Columbus found overseas markets. Direct exports of industrial machinery alone totaled more than $2,000,000 for the years 1922 through 1926.[86]

Despite the changes and additions to Columbus's economy, Buckeye remained one of the city's most important manufacturers, and Buckeye's presence continued to be felt through the company's support of philanthropic organizations. At S. P. Bush's suggestion in 1923, Buckeye's directors participated in the formation of Columbus's Community Fund as a way to further centralize philanthropy in the city, and Bush became vice-chairman of the fund's board of directors two years later.[87] Throughout the 1920s Buckeye's directors contributed $13,000 annually to the fund, a sum amounting to about 1.5 percent of Buckeye's net earnings, a proportion considerably higher than the national average.[88] Buckeye also gave large sums directly to agencies of immediate aid to Buckeye employees or to bodies emphasizing self-help and improvement to Columbus citizens. Buckeye donated $2,500 to Children's Hospital in 1922, $1,000 to the South Side Settlement House in the same year, $500 to the South Methodist Episcopal Church, and $7,500 to the YMCA in 1923.[89]

The Great Depression of the 1930s gravely injured the Columbus economy. In January 1931 the *Ohio State Journal* editorialized that "Our present emergency is greater than that brought about by any cyclone, fire, flood, or other sudden catastrophe."[90] A month later, 300 unemployed marched through downtown Columbus to the mayor's office, where they presented petitions asking for food for the jobless, a suspension of eviction laws, and free supplies and food for school children.[91] Statistics tell the grim story of the Depression's impact on Columbus. The value of manufactured goods produced in the city fell from $212,000,000 in 1929 to $90,000,000

just three years later, and the number of employed industrial
workers in Columbus dropped from 26,600 to 17,600 in the same
period.[92] Not even the diverse nature of its economy could save Columbus from devastation.

Just when it was most needed, corporate giving to philanthropy
declined nationally and locally. By 1935 the situation was so desperate in Columbus that the city's United Fund officers employed
sociologists at The Ohio State University to investigate the attitudes
of contributors and ways to increase their donations. The findings
of the study were unnerving. "In a word," the investigators reported, "the Community Fund is not generally accepted by its large
supporting public as an integral and effective part of the community organization of Columbus.[93]

Unlike most businesses in the United States, Buckeye increased
its corporate giving in the early 1930s. In 1931–33 the firm raised its
annual contributions to the Fund to $16,000 "in view of the pre-
vailing conditions."[94] However, as their company continued to suf-
fer from losses, Buckeye's officers cut back their donations to
$10,000 in 1934 and 1935.[95] Due to "the long continued period of
losses," they further reduced their contribution to $8,000 in 1936
and 1937.[96] In 1938 Buckeye's management considered ending its
support "in view of the present unfavorable operating condition of
the Company," but finally decided to make another $8,000 dona-
tion "in view of the fact that many of the families of our employees
availed themselves of the benefits of some of the agencies."[97] With
an improvement in business, they raised the contributions to $9,000
in 1939 and 1940.[98] Buckeye's officers also kept making donations
to organizations of special interest to their employees. In 1940 they
gave $500 to the White Cross Hospital (now the Riverside
Hospital), because "there was direct value derived from it by some
of our employees," and another $1,000 to the Red Cross.[99] A fear
of social unrest may also have motivated some of Buckeye's contributions. In 1937–40 the company gave $2,500 to the YMCA,
because "its influence was of a stabilizing character."[100]

Buckeye's officers also continued to play important roles in the
development of business organizations in Columbus and Ohio.
John Whitridge, Buckeye's president in 1928–37, was treasurer of
the Ohio Manufacturer's Association between 1932 and 1936; and,
working with W. J. Bennett, Buckeye's secretary-treasurer and also

an OMA member, he introduced a new financial system to the organization.[101] The Columbus Chamber of Commerce also attracted the attention of Buckeye's management. In 1920 the firm held seventy-five memberships, the largest number owned by any single corporation, and in 1938 the company began giving the chamber $1,000 annually "in order to support their program in a substantial manner."[102] A. H. Thomas, Buckeye's president in 1937–45, served as vice-president of the chamber for several years.[103]

The Second World War caused significant alterations in Columbus's economy. New businesses entered the city. The most obvious wartime influence was the construction of the $14,000,000 Curtis-Wright aircraft plant, which was employing 12,000 workers as early as 1940. In all, $53,000,000 were invested in Franklin County (of which Columbus was the major part), as new plants were built and old ones expanded. The importance of iron and steel companies like Buckeye to Columbus's economy, however, began declining. Only $6,000,000 of the new construction went into iron and steel companies. This relative decline continued after the war, as additional new businesses came to Columbus. In the late 1940s and 1950s, for instance, General Motors and Westinghouse put up large plants on the city's west side.[104] Despite this industrial growth, Columbus did not become a city dominated by industry. In fact, its economy grew more diversified among industry, government, education (as the home of The Ohio State University and several other institutions), and a wide variety of commercial and financial businesses as time progressed. With an increasingly diverse economic base, the city grew to 376,000 people in 1950 and 471,000 ten years later.[105]

The relative decline of their company as part of Columbus's economy did not immediately lessen the participation of Buckeye's officers in city affairs. Contributions to philanthropy continued unabated. The Franklin County War Chest handled Columbus's philanthropic needs during the war years. Buckeye contributed $65,000 to this body, 1.4 percent of the total contributions to it, in 1943–46, and Buckeye's president A. H. Thomas served as a member of the organization.[106] Buckeye also contributed to specific causes: $40,000 to the Red Cross in 1942–47; $4,300 to the YMCA and YWCA in 1941–46, and $1,000 to the Mount Carmel Hospital in 1946.[107] Buckeye gave primarily to organizations benefiting its employees. The YMCA received support, because it was again thought "that our Company derives benefit from the YMCA, both directly and indirectly," and the Mount Carmel Hospital won favor, because "for many years this hospital has taken care of our injured employees."[108] In all, Buckeye's contributions to philanthropy came to 5 percent of its net earnings during the war years, again much more than the national average.

During the late 1940s and the 1950s Buckeye continued its strong support of philanthropic organizations. Corporate giving varied significantly from year to year, generally being most substantial when net earnings were highest. On the whole, Buckeye's philanthropic contributions averaged about $41,000 per year, 2 percent to 5 percent of the company's net earnings—a proportion considerably higher than the national average and a percentage greater than that for other Columbus companies.[109] Much of this giving went, as in the past, to the Community Fund and its successor organization, the United Appeal. Buckeye contributed about 1 percent of the total raised by the United Appeal throughout the 1950s.[110] Specific organizations also continued to win Buckeye support. Hospitals, the YMCA, the YWCA, the Salvation Army, the Red Cross, the Central Ohio Heart Association, and the South Side Settlement House all received strong backing from the firm.[111]

Several motives lay behind Buckeye's contributions. Some organizations, like the Mount Carmel Hospital, continued to be supported because they were "used for our employees."[112] Then, too, Buckeye's officers identified closely with Columbus and wanted to improve their city. As Lewis Day later explained, all of Buckeye's top management were "natives of Columbus" who believed "they had an obligation to support the worthwhile endeavors or projects in the community."[113] Small and medium-size businesses have usually given a higher proportion of their earnings to philanthropy than have big businesses, precisely because, as in Buckeye's case, their owners or officers feel strong ties with their neighborhoods or localities. It is perhaps more difficult for a national firm with offices and plants across America to understand the value of supporting local philanthropic organizations.[114]

Buckeye's officers also remained involved in local business organizations. Frank Bonnet was a director of both the Ohio and the Columbus Area chambers of commerce. He belonged to the Columbus Industrial Association as well. As a vice-president at Buckeye in the 1950s, William Heimberger was a director of the National Association of Manufacturers and, closer to home, a director of the Development Committee for Greater Columbus.[115]

Buckeye Steel in Decline

The continued involvement of Buckeye's officers in community affairs masked the economic decline of their company. As we have seen, by the 1950s, especially the latter part of the decade, Buckeye faced major problems. Most basically, the corporation found itself tied too closely to a single highly cyclical and shrinking market— American railroads. This fate was not inevitable; other steel-castings companies avoided it. For instance, the American Steel Foundries Company (Amsted) responded to the same situation Buckeye faced by diversification. In the late 1940s railroads accounted for 90 percent of Amsted's sales, but the company soon moved into new areas with the acquisition of the Pipeline Service Company in 1955, the South Bend Lathe works four years later, and the Oconee Clay Products Company in 1963. By 1965 nonrailroad sales accounted for one-half of Amsted's output.[116] The nature of Buckeye's management, more than any other factor, explains Buckeye's failure to respond adequately to the corporation's economic difficulties.

Buckeye's continued reliance upon in-house promotion and dependence upon men with engineering and railroad backgrounds may have helped the company in the short run, but probably hurt it in the long run. On the one hand, by the time they had reached the top, Buckeye's executives knew their business well and had established valuable contacts with other businessmen. For instance, George Johnson's personal contacts with Charles Bradley and Charles Young helped keep the Chesapeake & Ohio and the Pennsylvania railroads buying from Buckeye. On the other hand, these policies stifled innovation and retarded the development of new products. Educated in one specialty, engineering, Buckeye's management had a hard time seeing beyond their field of expertise. "There wasn't much in the way of innovation," recalled one officer, and Buckeye's executives "had a tendency to resist change."[117] These attitudes made it difficult for Buckeye's management to understand changes occurring in American society and business in general and in the railroad industry in particular. It was a lack of vision about the future of the steel-castings industry on the part of Buckeye's management that explains the decline of their company. The position of Buckeye's officers in Columbus society exacerbated this problem. They had "arrived" and had been accepted socially. This situation had a positive side. As we have seen, Buckeye contributed very heavily to local philanthropic organizations precisely because its management identified so closely with Columbus. However, the situation also had a negative side. Buckeye's management became too comfortable, too complacent. As leaders in Columbus, they failed to perceive changes taking place beyond their city's boundaries, and this contributed to Buckeye's decline.

Frank Bonnet, Buckeye's president between 1948 and 1960, typified the strengths and weaknesses of the corporation's management. Like other Buckeye officers, Bonnet possessed important business connections. After working at Buckeye, one of Bonnet's brothers went on to become the major purchasing agent for the New York Central Railroad, a good Buckeye customer. Moreover, Bonnet was John G. McCoy's father-in-law. This was an important connection, because McCoy's father, John H., headed the City National Bank in Columbus, the bank that was Buckeye's major source of credit. As we have seen, Bonnet was also very active in local politics, business organizations, and philanthropic bodies. But his horizons were limited. Bonnet had worked his way up through the ranks at Buckeye; and, as Lewis Day observed, he "never really got away from manufacturing." He was "pretty much autocratic" and resisted the introduction of new production and accounting methods at Buckeye. He opposed the use of computers to report on molds made and cast.[118] Or, as John Elder recalled, Bonnet "blew his top every once in a while . . . he was pretty demanding" but also "fair and square."[119] Unable to see beyond his specialty, Bonnet could not lead Buckeye in badly needed new directions.

Notes

1. Interview by the author with Lewis Day, June 5, 1978.
2. Ibid.
3. Columbus *Dispatch,* July 30, 1936, May 29, 1952, March 12, 1953.

4. Interviews by the author with : John Bricker, May 23, 1978; Day, June 5, 1978; George Johnson, Jr., April 21, 1978; and Charles Pigott, June 14, 1978. One reason for this longevity is that Buckeye's officers continued to be well rewarded for their services. Throughout the 1920s the president (who also served as general manager) earned about $30,000 annually, the working vice-presidents around $20,000, and the secretary-treasurer about $12,000. Moreover, Buckeye's profit-sharing plan added significantly to these salaries. In the late 1920s the company's top five executives were dividing an annual bonus of some $70,000. In the 1930s salaries and bonuses were decreased, but they remained high for the steel castings industry. See "Minutes of the Meeting of the Board of Directors," January 30, 1922, March 30, 1923, January 29, 1924, January 26, April 20, June 28, 1926, January 25, 1927, January 31, 1928, January 29, 1929, January 28, 1930, January 27, 1931, January 26, 1932, January 31, 1933, January 30, 1934, January 29, 1935, January 28, 1936, January 26, 1937, January 25, 1938, January 31, 1939, January 30, 1940 (hereafter cited as "Directors Meeting").

5. Interview by the author with Paul Crosier, July 10, 1978.

6. Interview by the author with John Elder, July 10, 1978.

7. Johnson interview, April 21, 1978.

8. Day interview, June 5, 1978.

9. "Directors Meeting," May 5, 1960.

10. Day interview, June 5, 1978; "Directors Meeting," April 18, 1938.

11. Interview by the author with Jack Dawson, July 5, 1978.

12. "Directors Meeting," January 30, 1922, June 7, 1923, January 31, 1928, January 29, July 19, 1929, July 18, December 10, 1930, October 17, 1935, January 25, October 13, 1938.

13. Day interview, June 19, 1978; interview by the author with John Bricker, May 23, 1978.

14. Bricker interview, May 23, 1978.

15. Columbus *Dispatch,* August 14, 1962.

16. Ibid., July 30, 1936, May 29, 1952, March 12, 1953.

17. Bricker interview, May 23, 1978.

18. A. H. Thomas, "Memorandum: Proposed Foundry Building Improvements, 1930."

19. Ibid.

20. *Foundry* 57 (January 1, 1929): 42.

21. Buckeye disposed of many of its older records to make room for new material in the 1960s. The Ohio State Industrial Commission also threw out its older records on individual firms in the 1960s.

22. Ohio State Industrial Commission, *Bulletin, Union Scale of Wages and Hours of Labor in Ohio* (Columbus, October 1920), p. 19.

23. Carrol Daugherty et al., *The Economics of the Iron and Steel In-*

dustry, vol. 2, Bureau of Business Research, University of Pittsburgh Monographs (New York, 1937), p. 748. The Great Lakes region included much of Ohio.

24. "Directors Meeting," October 15, 1931, July 26, 1932.

25. Daugherty, *Economics,* vol. 2, p. 748.

26. "Directors Meeting," April 17, 1934.

27. Day interview, June 5, 1978.

28. Elder interview, July 10, 1978.

29. On labor in the 1930s, see Irving Bernstein, *The Turbulent Years* (Boston: Houghton Mifflin, 1971).

30. "Directors Meeting," January 17, October 17, 1933.

31. *The Buckeye Steel Castings Company, Employee Representation Plan,* pamphlet, unpaged, no place of publication, in Nationwide Insurance Company archives, Columbus, Ohio.

32. Day interview, June 5, 1978.

33. *Employee Representation Plan,* pamphlet in Nationwide archives.

34. Ohio Manufacturers' Association, "Minutes of the Meeting of the Executive Committee, April 11, 1935," at Ohio Manufacturers' Association headquarters in Columbus, Ohio. The Ohio Manufacturers' Association is hereafter cited as OMA.

35. Mary Louise Mark, *Negroes in Columbus* (Columbus: The Ohio State University Press, 1928), pp. 7, 23-24.

36. William Kaufman, *The Neighbors of the South Side* (Columbus: The Ohio State University Press, 1943), p. 18.

37. Mark, *Negroes,* p. 57.

38. "Directors Meeting," October 15, 1925.

39. Ibid., December 15, 1926.

40. Ibid., October 25, 1928.

41. "President's Report to Stockholders, 1945."

42. Interview by the author with Paul Crosier, July 10, 1978.

43. "Directors Meeting," October 19, 1943.

44. Ibid., July 16, 1943.

45. Ibid., November 28, 1944.

46. "President's Report to Stockholders, 1945."

47. Ibid.

48. Crosier interview, July 10, 1978; Day interview, June 5, 1978; Elder interview, July 10, 1978.

49. Irving Bernstein, *Turbulent Years,* chaps. 7-15; Melvyn Dubofsky and Warren Van Tine, *John L. Lewis* (New York: Quadrangle, 1977), part 3.

50. Dubofsky and Van Tine, *Lewis,* pp. 272-77.

51. Bernstein, *Turbulent Years,* pp. 485-90, 727-29.

52. "In the Matter of Buckeye Steel Castings Company, Columbus,

Ohio and the United Steelworkers of America, Local 2342, National War Labor Board, Case No. 5-D-50," in United Steel Workers of America, District 27, Subdistrict 5, Columbus, Ohio papers, at the Ohio Historical Society.

53. Interview by the author with Harry Mayfield, August 26, 1978.

54. "Buckeye Steel Castings Co.—SWOC Local Union 2342, August 22, 1941," p. 1, in the Columbus office of the United Steelworkers of America.

55. Ibid.; Mayfield interview, August 26, 1978. The United Steelworkers of America was formed out of SWOC in May 1942.

56. Mayfield interview, August 26, 1978.

57. "In the Matter of Buckeye and the United Steelworkers."

58. Mayfield interview, August 26, 1978.

59. Columbus, *Citizen,* October 17, 1942; Columbus *Dispatch,* October 17, 1942.

60. "In the Matter of Buckeye and the United Steelworkers."

61. Ibid.; "Agreement between the Buckeye Steel Castings Company and the United Steelworkers of America, Local Union No. 2342," in Buckeye archives, legal documents file.

62. "Directors Meeting," October 23, 1945. See also Columbus *Citizen,* October 12, 13, 16, 20, 23, 1945; Columbus *Dispatch,* October 11, 12, 16, 23, 1945; *Ohio State Journal,* October 12, 13, 17, 1945.

63. Bernstein, *Turbulent Years,* p. 730.

64. *Ohio State Journal,* November 29, 1945.

65. Columbus *Citizen,* January 21, 1946; Columbus *Dispatch,* January 21, 1946.

66. Columbus *Citizen,* February 17, 1946.

67. Columbus *Dispatch,* February 17, 1946.

68. *Ohio State Journal,* March 3, 1946.

69. "Directors Meeting," April 18, 1946; "President's Report to Stockholders," 1946. See also: Columbus *Citizen,* March 9, 1946; Columbus *Dispatch,* March 9, 11, 1946; *Ohio State Journal,* March 9, 11, 1946.

70. "Directors Meeting," November 29, 1946.

71. "President's Report to Stockholders," 1945, 1946.

72. On the Appalachian and black migration into Ohio, see Gene B. Petersen, Laure M. Sharp, and Thomas F. Drury, *Southern Newcomers to Northern Cities: Work and Social Adjustment in Cleveland* (New York: Praeger, 1977).

73. Interview by the author with Bill Buffington, June 27, 1978.

74. Interview by the author with Phil Bordan, June 27, 1978.

75. "President's Report to Stockholders," 1948.

76. Mayfield interview, August 26, 1978.

77. Ibid.

78. The contracts between Buckeye Steel and the Steelworkers and Pattern Makers are available in the legal documents section of the Buckeye archives at company headquarters. Many of the contracts are also available in the United Steelworkers of America, District 27, Subdistrict 5 Papers at the Ohio Historical Society.

79. Mayfield interview, August 26, 1978.

80. "Minutes of Union-Management Negotiation Meeting," August 6, 8, 9, 15, 19, 23, 30, 1963, in Buckeye's legal documents, corporate headquarters.

81. Betty Garrett and Edward Lentz, *Columbus: America's Crossroads* (Tulsa, Oklahoma: Centennial Heritage Press, 1980), pp. 119–121; *Ohio State Journal,* September 22, 1927, November 28, 1934.

82. *Ohio State Journal,* May 8, 1934.

83. Ibid., March 10, 1937.

84. Roderick Peattie, *Columbus, Ohio: An Analysis of a City's Development,* (Columbus, 1930), pamphlet, p. 32.

85. Garrett and Lentz, *Columbus,* pp. 119–20.

86. Peattie, *Columbus,* pp. 37–38.

87. Columbus Community Fund File, 1925, William O. Thompson Papers, box 3-e-9, The Ohio State University archives; "Directors Meeting," June 7, 1923.

88. "Minutes of the Annual Meeting of Stockholders," March 30, 1923, January 29, 1924, January 27, 1925, January 26, 1926, January 31, 1928, January 29, 1929, January 28, 1930 (hereafter cited as "Stockholders Meeting"). Money given to the Community Fund went to such organizations as the YMCA, the YWCA, the Boy Scouts, the Campfire Girls, hospitals, and settlement houses. See also Morrell Heald, *The Social Responsibilities of Business: Company and Community, 1900–1960* (Cleveland: Case Western University Press, 1970), chap. 5.

89. "Directors Meeting," October 6, 1922, June 7, 1923, April 22, 1927.

90. *Ohio State Journal,* January 5, 1931.

91. Ibid., February 26, 1931.

92. Henry Hunker, *Industrial Evolution of Columbus, Ohio* (Columbus: The Ohio State University Press, 1958), pp. 56–67.

93. Mary Mark, "The Contributor and the Community Fund," typescript essay, 1935, in The Ohio State University Library.

94. "Directors Meeting," October 17, 1930, October 15, 1931, October 24, 1932; "Stockholders Meeting," January 27, 1931, January 26, 1932, January 31, 1933, January 30, 1934.

95. "Directors Meeting," October 17, 1933, October 16, 1934.

96. Ibid., October 17, 1935, October 9, 1936, September 14, 1937; "Stockholders Meeting," January 26, 1937, January 25, 1938.

97. "Directors Meeting," October 13, 1928.

98. Ibid., October 18, 1939, October 8, 1940; "Stockholders Meeting," January 30, 1940, January 28, 1941.

99. "Directors Meeting," April 15, June 14, 1940.

100. Ibid., March 23, 1937, June 16, 1938, June 13, 1939, June 14, 1940.

101. OMA, "Board of Trustees Meeting," November 30, 1932, December 19, 1934, January 7, 1936, in OMA archives, Columbus, Ohio.

102. *Columbus Forward: Report of the Activities of the Columbus Chamber of Commerce, 1919-20,* pamphlet, Columbus, 1920, p. 86; "Directors Meeting," January 20, 1947.

103. Columbus *Dispatch,* May 29, 1952.

104. Garrett and Lentz, *Columbus,* pp. 135, 147; Hunker, *Industrial Evolution of Columbus,* pp. 58-59.

105. Garrett and Lentz, *Columbus,* p. 174.

106. "Directors Meeting," October 22, 1942, October 19, 1942, October 17, 1944, October 23, 1945, October 17, 1946.

107. Ibid., June 12, 1941, January 9, April 14, 1942, February 15, December 29, 1944, March 27, July 19, 1945, January 18, November 29, 1946, January 20, 1947.

108. Ibid., December 20, 1944, July 19, 1945, January 18, 1946.

109. "Stockholders Meeting," March 23, 1948, March 22, 1949, March 28, 1950, March 27, 1951, March 25, 1952, March 24, 1953, March 23, 1954, March 22, 1955, March 27, 1956, March 26, 1957, March 25, 1958, March 24, 1959, March 22, 1960.

110. In 1957 Buckeye gave $30,000 of the United Appeal's $3,280,000 total, and in the following year the company contributed $30,000 to the $3,388,000 total. See "Directors Meeting," October 8, 1957, October 17, 1958.

111. "Directors Meeting," July 2, December 9, 1947, December 8, 1948, October 17, 1949, January 10, 1951, October 16, 1953, January 12, 1955, January 11, December 11, 1956, March 25, 1958, January 8, 1962.

112. Ibid., January 10, 1951.

113. Day interview, June 5, 1978.

114. Heald, *Social Responsibilities of Business,* pp. 262-63.

115. Columbus *Dispatch,* August 14, 1962.

116. For the details on Amsted, see the quarterly editions of *Moody's Handbook of Common Stocks* (New York: Moody's Investors Service, Inc.).

117. Day interview, June 12, 1978.

118. Ibid., June 5, 1978.

119. Elder interview, July 10, 1978.

chapter 6

REBIRTH THROUGH DIVERSIFICATION, 1960–1980

The 1960s were pivotal years at Buckeye, for in that decade the corporation's management began a massive diversification effort. Moving first into areas related to railroad castings, they soon entered businesses completely foreign to their past experiences— plastics, juvenile products, precision metal parts, communications, and others. In his report to Buckeye's stockholders in 1976, Rowland Brown, the company's president throughout the 1970s, summarized well what the corporation had accomplished. "Balance," he stated, "is the word that best describes what has occurred in your company and is the keystone of our further growth." Buckeye, he continued, would "achieve a high rate of growth through a combination of internal market and product development and market share with external growth by acquisition of companies, products, and technologies."[1]

Buckeye's diversification took place as part of a general movement in American business. Since the 1920s, and especially in the years following the Second World War, American business firms have become increasingly diversified in the goods they produce and the activities in which they engage.[2] In the 1960s the diversification drive and the accompanying growth of conglomerates were the big news of the business world. Statistics suggest the extent of diversification. In 1966 about 60 percent of the 1,517 business mergers reported by the Federal Trade Commission were across industry lines, and a year later 46 of *Fortune*'s top 500 firms were conglomerates. For a variety of reasons, the trend toward diversification slowed in the early 1970s, only to speed up again later in the decade.[3]

Four major reasons led to this spurt in diversification and conglomerate activity. First, some corporations diversified as defensive maneuvers. Companies of this type were looking for more profitable investment opportunities for their funds. Secondly, some businessmen diversified and formed conglomerates on the assumption that all businesses, no matter how diverse, could best be managed by a small group of executives in the head office. These executives argued that they could coordinate the accounting, planning, and financial services of the many divisions to the benefit of the whole company. They called this concept "synergism," by which they meant that expertise acquired in one area of business could be carried over to another to the benefit of both. Or, as businessmen often expressed this idea in shorthand: $2 + 2 = 5$. Government actions also spurred diversification. While it sometimes brought antitrust proceedings against other forms of big business in the 1950s and 1960s, the federal government took no actions against conglomerates. Finally, the great profits sometimes reaped by promoters putting together conglomerates attracted businessmen into this field and hastened the spread of conglomerates.[4]

The Beginning of Diversification

Managerial changes spurred diversification at Buckeye. In 1959 John G. McCoy, the head of the City National Bank, joined Buckeye's board of directors, and six years later he became the chairman of the board. A graduate of Ohio's Marietta College and possessing an MBA from Stanford University, he was prepared to lead Buckeye in new directions. A second major managerial change occurred in 1963 with the recruitment of William Henderson from outside the company as a vice-president at Buckeye. One year later Henderson became Buckeye's president, the first outsider to do so in seventy-eight years. Possessing an MBA from Northwestern University and a Ph.D. in economics from the University of Wisconsin, Henderson was a man of intense drive. The youngest captain in the Rangers during the Second World War, he had a varied business career in the 1940s and 1950s. From 1956 on Henderson had worked as a management consultant with McKenzie and Company, and by the time he came to Buckeye was well versed in the intricacies of diversification.[5]

Both McCoy and Henderson understood Buckeye's problems and were willing to try to find new solutions. Neither was satisfied with the status quo. McCoy saw two closely related questions facing Buckeye, he later recalled: "How were you going to treat the present management properly, and yet infuse new blood in the organization, and what were you going to do with a corporation that basically served a dying industry?'' One of McCoy's initial actions as a director was to work out a supplement to the company's pension plan which allowed its elderly top management to retire gracefully on an adequate stipend. And they did. Frank Bonnet, who was McCoy's father-in-law, stepped down as president after twelve years in office.[6] Henderson later explained that he came to Buckeye because the company offered "an opportunity to be innovative and creative." As he put it, "I felt the challenge would be substantially greater where there was a need to substantially or radically change the thrust or course of a business."[7]

Led by a reinvigorated management, Buckeye entered an era of diversification and innovation during the 1960s. At the core of the thoughts and actions of Buckeye's officers lay a desire to reduce their company's dependence upon the highly cyclical and declining railroad industry. In mid-1960 Buckeye's directors urged that "prompt steps be taken to investigate activities in fields other than through the production and sale of steel products."[8] This was necessary, McCoy explained at the time, "in order to stabilize and make more continuous its [Buckeye's] operations."[9] Henderson later recalled the situation in much the same way. Upon coming to Buckeye, he found the company "tied almost wholly to the railroads." The possibilities of vertical and horizontal integration were, he thought, severely limited, because "the steel castings business is an island unto itself." Therefore, he concluded, "it was obvious that we had to get into an unknown area."[10]

When Henderson took over at Buckeye, he retained Marathon Associates of Cincinnati to do the preliminary screening for an acquisition program. Working with those at Marathon, he systematically examined ninety industries for acquisition prospects.[11] As Henderson explained to Buckeye's stockholders, only certain types of companies were sought:

> Your Company desires diversification in order to provide a broader base for future growth and to minimize heavy dependency on a single industry. . . . Three relatively dissimilar business situations appear to be most logical as prospective diversification opportunities. They include:

1. Businesses which tend to generate income independent of the business cycle.
2. Manufacturing companies producing proprietary products and serving industrial needs.
3. Companies either utilizing castings or serving the railroad market, where a combination with Buckeye would create economies not available to each alone.[12]

Over the next two years, Buckeye's executives mulled over many possibilities. Two companies received particular attention. Buckeye nearly bought Orton Crane and Shovel in late 1965, but pulled back at the last minute, because its purchase would place Buckeye in direct competition with several of its best customers for industrial castings, Bucyrus-Erie and Ohio Locomotive Crane.[13] Still more protracted were Buckeye's efforts to buy the Hydraxtor Company, a maker of commercial laundry equipment in Chicago and Moline. This company seemed to offer many advantages. Most importantly, it was in "a rapidly growing market subject to different cyclical factors than Buckeye" and was perceived as giving Buckeye the chance to enter an expanding but fragmented industry. Henderson hoped that if the acquisition of Hydraxtor proved successful, similar businesses might be purchased, giving Buckeye a major position in the industry.[14] However, these negotiations also fell through, largely because of the reluctance of Buckeye's directors to enter such unknown waters.[15]

Little came, then, of Buckeye's first attempts to acquire other companies. Diversification was, Day recalled, "mostly given lip service." That is, he believed, "everyone agreed it was the thing to do, but no one did too much about it." Several factors militated against Buckeye's early acquisition program. First, Buckeye's officers and those of the businesses considered for purchase could not agree upon price. Buckeye's management was unwilling to offer prices high enough to close the deals. Second, Buckeye's directors harbored a lingering hesitancy about moving into new areas. There was a reluctance, Day felt, "to bite the bullet and go."[16] Finally, Henderson found that the systematic approach to acquisition simply did not work, as he later explained:

What we found was that what we had been looking for had been picked over so badly that we were getting the dredgings. . . . An attempt to plan along methodical lines was extraordinarily difficult. . . . So, what we did was to look and say, "OK, let's find something that becomes available and have the guts to take the plunge."[17]

Before 1967 diversification within Buckeye's steel plant proved more successful than diversification through acquisitions. Buckeye's officers sought to expand their output of cast armor and industrial castings. Buckeye had been a supplier of cast steel armor for America's defense needs during the Second World War and the Korean War. In 1960 Buckeye, as a subcontractor for Chrysler, began to revitalize its cast armor program. Over the next few years Buckeye stepped up its production of tank armor, and in 1965, the firm won a major order to make cast armor gun shields for the Sheridan tanks produced by the Allison Division of General Motors.[18] Industrial castings represented another departure for Buckeye. The company had long produced some industrial castings, but they had always been secondary to the railroad business. (Industrial castings were used in such things as cranes, shovels, and earth-movers.) In mid-1962 the Bucyrus-Erie Company offered Buckeye a chance to supply it with 500 to 600 tons of castings per month, and Buckeye eagerly embraced this opportunity.[19] Later in the year Buckeye hired W. Dan Reuter, a graduate in engineering formerly with Allis Chalmers, to increase the industrial business of the firm. Progress was slow, however; for Reuter had a hard time convincing potential customers that Buckeye, which they viewed as strictly a producer for railroads, was serious about entering and staying in the industrial castings market. Yet, as obstacles were overcome, industrial castings came to account for a growing share of Buckeye's steel-castings sales in the late 1960s.[20]

It is rare that a company's diversification efforts proceed as smoothly as hoped. Nowhere was this clearer at Buckeye than in the company's abortive attempt to produce a new type of casting, cast iron soil pipe. In the early 1960s, most of the nation's soil pipe was produced in the South and Southwest, and Buckeye's officers thought they could capture much of the Midwestern market because of lower raw material and transportation costs. In early February 1962 the board of directors voted to begin work on the project. Some $2,000,000 were appropriated to convert a foundry building to cast iron soil pipe production, and the target production start-up

date was set for April 1, 1963.[21] After some delay, the soil pipe facilities began operations in September of that year. As Jack Dawson, who was in charge of the soil pipe foundry, remembered it, the
plant was "beautiful," boasting two cupolas, overhead monorails
to speed up pouring, and a high-speed fittings line.[22] But it did not
work. In November 1963 Henderson noted that Buckeye was having "considerable difficulty" with the pipe-making machinery.[23]
This difficulty was never remedied. The problem lay with the equipment used to cast the soil pipe. It employed the then new technique
of centrifugal casting. While this method looked fine on paper, it
did not work well in practice. As Dawson later explained, the casting machine was "very, very complicated" and "too highly engi-
neered."[24] By April of 1964 the soil pipe division had accumulated
a net operating loss of $335,000, and in June, Buckeye's directors
voted to terminate the program "on the assumption the soil pipe
machine will not work."[25] The company wrote off the entire experiment as an immediate loss against earnings.[26]

To handle the continuing railroad work and the growing industrial castings and armor-castings businesses, Buckeye's officers
initiated a sorely needed program to improve the steel plant. As
Henderson pointed out in 1964, modernization was "necessary and
urgent," because "at the present time the plant is operating under
almost impossible conditions which must be corrected if the company expects to remain in the steel castings business."[27] To improve
the situation, the company spent $8,500,000 between 1963 and
1966.[28] Two changes were of particular importance. In 1964–65
Buckeye's officers installed a Universal (Hermann) Moldmaster at
a cost of $2,800,000. Capable of automatically turning out 240
molds in an eight-hour shift, this machine reduced production costs
by cutting the need for labor.[29] By early 1966 it had become, according to Henderson, "the key to profitable operation" in the
steel plant.[30] Equally significant was the company's switch from
open-hearth to electric melting furnaces. Installed in 1965, a thirty-
ton electric furnace replaced all the open-hearth facilities. It had
definite advantages: it melted faster, required fewer repairs, and
lasted longer than the open-hearth furnaces. Above all, it offered
"big savings" in the labor expense.[31] In its first year of operations,
the electric furnace lowered the cost of producing a ton of steel
from $62 to $55 per ton, and in 1966 Buckeye's management was
considering the installation of a second electric furnace.[32]

Like a caterpillar in its cocoon, Buckeye was undergoing a meta-morphosis in the mid-1960s. Spurred by an energetic management, the company was entering new types of steel-castings businesses. The steel plant was undergoing a long-needed, massive renovation program. Yet, much remained to be done. As late as 1965 railroads accounted for 90 percent of Buckeye's sales, and the cyclical nature of their buying still determined Buckeye's fortunes.[33] Much had been said, but little accomplished, in diversifying beyond steel castings, and the company had as yet made no acquisitions.

The First Acquisitions

Buckeye's officers renewed their acquisition efforts in 1967 and 1968. With their steel plant modernization program going well and their attempts to enter the industrial castings market beginning to show signs of success, they turned, once again, to new areas. In remarks to Buckeye's stockholders in March 1967, Henderson made clear that no possibility would be overlooked in the quest for acquisitions:

> Buckeye is vigorously pursuing acquisitions. . . . We expect to follow both an integrated and conglomerate approach to acquisition. By integrated, we mean acquiring companies which should generate economic savings because they serve common markets, use the same methods of distribution, have relatively similar manufacturing technologies, or common supply sources. The conglomerate approach means we do not want to overlook profitable opportunities in new markets where entirely different capabilities are required.[34]

In fact, Buckeye had already made its first acquisition by the time Henderson was delivering these remarks. Just a few weeks earlier, Buckeye had bought Earl Fisher Plastics of Reynoldsburg, Ohio. With sales of $1,600,000 in 1966, Earl Fisher made a full line of plastic baby accessories (training cups, feeding sets, nursery toys, and diaper pails) and also marketed plastic floral products through Woolworth, Kresge, and Grant.[35] This acquisition quickly led to others. In November 1967 Buckeye bought Millington Plastics of Upper Sandusky, Ohio, a company with sales of over $5,000,000 in the industrial molding market. Its main market lay in plastic parts for automobiles.[36] Three months later, Buckeye acquired

Hamilton Plastics of Cincinnati, Ohio. Like Millington Plastics, Hamilton Plastics was a custom molder. The company produced precision plastic parts for nonautomotive customers.[37] Finally, Buckeye acquired Warren Molded Plastics of Mineral Ridge, Ohio in March 1968. Like Millington and Hamilton, Warren manufactured molded plastic parts. It produced almost wholly for automobile companies.[38]

Buckeye's move into plastics, as Lewis Day remembered it, was "more happenstance than it was deliberate."[39] It was the conglomerate approach to acquisitions that Henderson described to Buckeye's stockholders in March 1967. Earl Fisher Plastics was brought to Buckeye by Jim Jones, a Columbus lawyer then dabbling in arranging corporate mergers. A personal friend of Henderson, Jones knew Buckeye was on the prowl for acquisitions. The possibility of buying Earl Fisher was particularly appealing, because it was accompanied by the offer of Millington Plastics. As Henderson later described the situation, "The fact that it was Fisher plus Millington was really the key. Jim Jones said, 'If you buy Fisher, I can deliver Millington.' "[40] With the acquisition of Earl Fisher and Millington, the purchase of additional plastics companies seemed a natural way for Buckeye to expand. Yet, even the later purchases were largely unplanned. Looking back over Buckeye's plastics acquisitions, Henderson concluded that Buckeye went into plastics "only because that's the first thing that came along that was available." It took place "absolutely by chance"; there was "no predetermined move at all to go into plastics."[41]

While Buckeye's entrance into plastics was fortuitous, it made logical sense. The plastics business was more "consumer-oriented" than the steel-castings industry, and it offered an alternative to the railroad business cycle. "Plastics permitted us," Henderson recalled, "to go into a consumer business and a totally different cycle." Plastics offered still other advantages. The plastics industry was, at the time, fragmented among many small producers. It was the type of industry Buckeye could become well established in from scratch. "There were hundreds of small guys out there, and economies of scale were going to decide their ultimate profitability," Henderson later explained. Plastics was, he believed, "a field in which we could build a position."[42]

Buckeye thus became a diversified business in the late 1960s. By 1969 the plastics companies already accounted for 37 percent of Buckeye's sales.[43] In recognition of the altered nature of their company, Buckeye's stockholders changed its name to "Buckeye International, Inc." in 1967. They also amended the corporation's charter to allow the company "to engage in any endeavor or pursuit that is profitable."[44] At the outset, however, troubles hampered the plastics operations. After making a small profit in 1968, the plastics companies, taken as a whole, reported a loss in 1969.[45]

Buckeye faced three types of problems in trying to make the plastics companies profitable. The first was managerial. In most cases, the former owners of the plastics companies had run their operations as one-man shows, and when they retired, as most did upon selling out to Buckeye, they left gaps difficult to fill. As Henderson noted in early 1969, this situation caused problems: "Where we have had to provide new management, we've had to live with a learner's curve."[46] Second, in their eagerness to diversify, Buckeye's officers bought companies of dubious value. Nowhere was this clearer than with the purchase of Warren Molded Plastics. The initial price was low, only $250,000; but the company was, as Day recalled, "a dog on the verge of bankruptcy." Large sums were required to renovate its plant.[47] The same was true of all the other plastics companies to some degree. All required fresh capital for improvements and, in some cases, relocation. Finally, exacerbating the other problems, was the nature of the plastics industry. A relatively new industry composed of mainly mom-and-pop operations, the plastics business was a scene of fierce competition. In time Buckeye would, as Henderson predicted, entrench itself well. But, initially, Buckeye had a hard time differentiating its products from those of its many competitors and suffered from the industry's low profit margins. As late as 1971, Buckeye's officers were describing plastics as "a very unstable and still immature industry" marked by "severe price competition."[48]

The difficulties Buckeye's management had with plastics slowed their diversification drive. "We are going to catch our breath in 1970," noted Buckeye's president, "We do not plan to expand."[49] In fact, Buckeye made no new acquisitions in 1969–71. Yet, this pause soon ended, and in 1972 Buckeye entered a second period of diversification.

Additional Acquisitions

A new management led Buckeye in making additional acquisitions. Henderson had succeeded in leading Buckeye into new paths
of development, a very considerable achievement given the inertia
into which the company had fallen in the 1950s. Change, however,
had been accomplished only at some cost. Henderson tended to run
Buckeye by himself without building up an organization needed to
manage the corporation's more and more diversified operations.
"The big problem," McCoy later explained, "was that he was a
one-man operator, and he was not able to communicate with his
people."[50] Moreover, being a very hard worker himself, Henderson
was perceived by those under him as expecting too much from
them. In his attempts to revitalize Buckeye, he came across as a
very demanding and, at times, abrasive person. "To change the
method of operation, I'm sure I was a difficult person in those
days," Henderson later explained, "I recall meetings in which I
became extraordinarily difficult."[51] All of this "just reached the
point," Day remembered, "where he became ineffective" as a
leader and was asked to resign.[52]

Buckeye's directors first considered one of their own, Lewis Day,
as president. Born and raised in Ohio, Day graduated as a business
major from The Ohio State University in 1935. He began at
Buckeye as a clerk in materials controls, but he quickly caught the
eye of the company's secretary-treasurer who "drafted" Day to
work with him in his office. Here Day dealt with "general corporate information" which, he believed, was "very helpful in giving me an understanding of the business." Day played a major role
in negotiating the reconversion contracts with the federal government after the Second World War. Following the war, his rise
within Buckeye continued without interruption. Under president
George Johnson he became assistant comptroller, and in 1955 he
took over as comptroller. In 1961 he became secretary-treasurer,
and four years later he was elected a director. Finally, in 1968, he
became vice-president in charge of finance.[53] Described by Henderson as "an extremely conscientious individual absolutely dedicated
to the welfare of Buckeye," Day took over as acting chief executive
officer, vice-president, and secretary-treasurer when Henderson
resigned.[54]

Although he had grown up with Buckeye, Day was receptive to

new ideas and favored a continuation of diversification. At the same time, his long service with the company made him familiar with all of its operations and key personnel. As head of Buckeye, Day held the company together in preparation for further growth. "He saved our lives," McCoy later stated.[55] Day, however, declined the presidency when it was offered him. He did so, he later explained, because he thought a person of wider business experience should be in charge of Buckeye.[56] Then, too, as McCoy recalled, Day was approaching retirement age and may not have wanted the responsibility of being president.[57]

With this turn of events, Buckeye engaged a management search firm to look for a chief executive officer. Buckeye's directors instructed the search firm, as McCoy remembered: "We want somebody that will communicate better, that will build an organization, that will weld it together." In short, they were hoping to find "a contrast" to Henderson.[58] The directors were also anxious to locate someone specifically skilled in running decentralized, diversified businesses. Day later explained the situation:

> The Board felt that since the company was diversified to a certain extent, it needed a management, or at least a chief executive officer, that was a little more broadgauged than the ones we had had up to that point in time. . . . We were looking for someone with a proven track record and in a primarily diversified company. Specific experience in steel castings was not a prerequisite.[59]

Rowland C.W. Brown, whom the search firm found for Buckeye, fit these requirements well. Brown received his undergraduate education at Harvard, finishing in 1947 after serving in the Marines as a fighter pilot during the Second World War. He then attended the Harvard University Law School, receiving his law degree in 1950. During the Korean War, Brown acted as counsel for the Industrial Materials Division of the Economic Stabilization Agency (he later called this "an accelerated course in the real world of heavy industry") before going back into the Marines. After Korea he became the general counsel for the Machinery and Allied Products Institute (MAPI), a trade association engaged in economic research for heavy industry. At MAPI Brown was particularly active in advising American companies how to set up overseas operations. Brown left the association in 1959 to join Dorr-Oliver (a member firm of MAPI) in a variety of capacities. In 1967 he became this diversified firm's president, but in 1968 Curtis Wright acquired Dorr-Oliver in an unfriendly takeover, and Brown found it difficult to work in the new situation. He was ready to move when Buckeye approached him, and he became Buckeye's president and chief executive officer in mid-1970.[60]

Like Henderson before him, Brown came to Buckeye because he believed the company offered a chance to be innovative and creative, but he viewed the opportunity in different terms than had Henderson. He was primarily interested in setting up a systematic type of management and in guiding the company along rational courses of future development. In short, Brown viewed himself as something more of an organizer and, perhaps, something less of an empire builder than Henderson. As Brown later recalled his thoughts upon joining Buckeye:

> My feeling was that it was a company badly in need of professional management experienced in diversified operations, decentralized operations. . . . They needed internal management development. . . . They needed to develop some sort of strategies for what the hell they were going to do or not do. . . . And, if anybody had any ego as a chief executive, this was an ideal place to start from almost scratch.[61]

Brown spent much of his time fashioning a management system and arranging financing appropriate for Buckeye's new form (see the next chapter for these topics), but at the same time he renewed his corporation's diversification drive. In this campaign Buckeye's officers followed more of a planned approach than they had in their purchase of the plastics companies, at least in their broad strategies. As in the past, they were particularly interested in acquiring companies whose sales and income cycles would counter or balance those of the steel foundry. They defined this as meaning that Buckeye should enter consumer goods rather than capital goods industries, that they should enter less capital-intensive businesses (the steel business remained highly capital-intensive), and that they should try to avoid energy-intensive industries. Energy became a major concern around 1975, particularly because the steel foundry was a very heavy user of electricity. However, despite the formulation of these rational strategies, the actual timing of acquisitions continued to take place, as McCoy later explained, "more by accident" than by planning.[62]

One reason Brown could lead Buckeye into further diversification was his success in improving the performance of the plastics companies. Taken as a whole, they rebounded from their loss in 1969 to report substantial profits in the 1970s. In fact, in some years it was only the profits from plastics that kept Buckeye afloat, as other divisions reported losses.[63]

Brown and others improved the plastics operations in several ways. Brown required the managers of each company to look more closely than they had in the past into the strengths and weaknesses of their businesses. At the same time, he brought in outside consultants to investigate market possibilities more carefully. He also sought to improve the management of the plastics operations. When he joined Buckeye, Brown found the plastics companies working in an uncoordinated fashion, "each with their own discrete set of markets . . . each buying materials on their own, each doing their own engineering." In the early 1970s he improved communications between the companies, and then in 1975 he combined them into one cohesive unit, the plastics group, with Richard Warnick as its general manager.[64] Capital was also needed to improve and relocate the plastic plants, and this Buckeye either provided itself or secured from outside sources. All the plant improvements stressed the increased production of injection-molded plastic parts for automobiles at the very time automobile companies were trying to reduce the weight of their cars to meet federal government gasoline consumption standards. It is not surprising, in light of this coincidence, that plastics became profitable.

With its plastics operations on a sound footing, Buckeye could expand into new areas, and between 1972 and 1976 the company acquired four businesses in fields as varied as electronics and juvenile products.

The Bethandale Corporation, a producer of precision metal parts for automobiles located in Mentor, Ohio, was the first of Buckeye's new acquisitions. Lewis Day handled the purchase. Bethandale was brought to Buckeye by a Cleveland broker who knew, as

Day put it, that Buckeye was "acquisition-minded." Already in the automotive supply business with its plastics companies, Buckeye proved eager to buy Bethandale, and Day quickly closed the negotiations with the company's two partners, Dick Brosius and John Newton. The sale was completed in 1972.[65]

As had been the case with the plastics companies, problems plagued Bethandale's early operations as part of the Buckeye organization. Most basic were managerial difficulties. With Buckeye's backing, Bethandale took on new jobs that stretched its organization thin. Brosius, who stayed on as Bethandale's president (reporting directly to Day in Columbus), found it hard to break away from his former "one-man operation," until forced to. "We had an awful lot of work," he remembered, but "very little organization."[66] Buckeye helped solve this problem by bringing in new officers to assist Brosius: a manufacturing manager, a personnel manager, and a chief engineer. Labor problems also cut into earnings, most notably a six-week strike in 1974. Then, too, Bethandale's very success in securing new jobs created temporary difficulties. In 1973 Buckeye had to secure $1,750,000 in loans to finance a major expansion program at Bethandale so that it could fulfill its new contract obligations.[67] After losses in 1974 and 1975, Bethandale returned a profit in 1976. Profits continued to be made over the next two years, and by 1978 Buckeye's officers were calling Bethandale "a gem" of an acquisition.[68]

Buckeye's second purchase in the 1970s was Peterson Baby Products. Located in Los Angeles, Peterson was a manufacturer of high-quality juvenile products, most notably a car seat for infants. The purchase of Peterson, Brown later explained, was Buckeye's "most planned acquisition." On paper it was, he believed, "as well conceived a plan as you could put together."[69] And, in fact, Peterson seemed to offer many opportunities for Buckeye. The intent was to combine Peterson with Buckeye Plastics (formerly Earl Fisher Plastics), which was also in juvenile products. The two firms together would then command a major share of their market, roughly 22 percent. They would also complement each other's operations: Peterson was a west coast firm strong in tubular metal products, while Buckeye Plastics in Ohio was in plastics goods.[70]

From the outset, Peterson had problems as part of Buckeye. Some of these were left over from earlier times. In the late 1960s and early 1970s, Peterson had nearly tripled its sales, moving from its regional market into the national market for the first time. Peterson's management had a difficult time handling this expansion. According to Day, "the business was too big for these people" and "they couldn't get their arms around it."[71] Nor did Peterson's high-quality products compete well in the mass market. As Warnick later explained, "You don't take a Cadillac and try to push it in the Chevrolet marketplace."[72] Still other problems arose. It proved difficult for Buckeye's top management to stay in close touch with Peterson's California operations which were, Warnick later noted, "a long way from home base."[73] Even more basically, the decline in the United States' birthrate hurt Peterson's sales. "We were wrong," Brown admitted, "on the projections in terms of births."[74]

Peterson never made a profit for Buckeye. Nothing Buckeye's management tried—the importation of new managers, the provision of new financing, or other steps—proved capable of turning Peterson around. As early as late 1974, Brown was considering the "disposal or closing down of Peterson in order to put an end to the cash drain."[75] In late 1977 he was still trying to bring "the operation at least to the break-even position while pursuing its ultimate divestiture."[76] In 1976–78 Buckeye's officers cut back and relocated Peterson's operations, and in late 1978 they finally sold them at a large loss.[77] "It's always easier," Brown later ruefully observed, "to get into something than it is to get out."[78]

Two minor purchases completed Buckeye's second acquisition drive. The Micro Communications Corporation of Waltham, Massachusetts, an electronics firm in the microprocessor and minicomputer fields, was bought in 1975. Brown viewed this purchase as a type of diversification that would make Buckeye "less dependent in the future on capital-intensive and energy-intensive operations."[79] At the time they gained control of Micro, Buckeye's officers viewed it as a research and development project unlikely to return a profit for several years. Such proved to be the case, as Micro operated at a loss for the remainder of the 1970s. Finally, Buckeye acquired a small California company, the Hollowform Corporation, in 1976. This business produced cross-linked polyester resins used in manufacturing boat hulls, agricultural tanks, and tops for camper trucks. No further purchases took place.[80]

Even while Buckeye entered its second phase of diversification, steel castings remained a key part of the Buckeye picture. In 1970 steel castings accounted for roughly three-quarters of Buckeye's sales, and in 1977 they still made up two-fifths of the sales. As had been true throughout Buckeye's history, the performance of the steel-castings division remained erratic. "The cyclical nature of the business," recalled John Hughes, who took over as the head of Buckeye Steel Castings in 1971, "made me sick."[81] Profitable years—1971, 1974, 1975, and 1977—alternated with unprofitable or marginal ones, 1972–73 and 1976.[82]

Buckeye was not alone in the problems it faced in steel castings. Difficulties were hurting most companies in the industry. Increased costs of production—labor expenses, the cost of installing expensive (but nonproductive) pollution-control devices, and the ever-rising prices of raw materials—bit sharply into profits. At the same time, the reliance of some companies upon railroads for their markets hindered their economic advance. Steel-castings companies continued to close their doors, fifty-two in the years 1966–73. Those companies which continued to grow and remain profitable did so through diversification. As we have seen in chapter four, American Steel Foundries pursued this path as early as the 1950s. Others survived only as divisions of diversified companies. This was the fate of National Malleable, another long-time Buckeye competitor. National Malleable remained closely tied to railroads and, failing to launch any diversification program of its own, was acquired by the Midland-Ross Corporation in 1965.[83]

In an attempt to solve its problems, Hughes led Buckeye Steel Castings through a diversification program, a task for which he was well prepared. As Brown explained, Hughes's skills were "broader and different and beyond those in the foundry industry."[84] Hughes was used to large, decentralized businesses. After serving as a B-24 pilot in the Pacific during the Second World War, Hughes went to work for the American Machine and Foundry Company in Brooklyn as a methods engineer. By the mid-1950s he had become the general manager of the company's Brooklyn plant, and in 1962 he took command of its overseas operations. Three years later, he resigned to become head of Champion Spark Plug's new European venture. Here he established manufacturing operations "from the ground up." Once this was accomplished, however, "boredom set in." An energetic, restless man, Hughes returned to the United States where he became the general manager of Gould National Battery's marine and automotive battery division. He was at this post when contacted by a consultant who put him in touch with Brown, and after "a very long, in-depth talk" with Brown, Hughes elected to come to Buckeye.[85]

Hughes was quick to expand the diversification of steel castings begun by Henderson and others in the 1960s. Renewed emphasis was placed upon industrial castings, and a reinvigorated sales effort attracted and held important customers—the Terex Division of General Motors, Northwest Engineering, Bucyrus-Erie, Mack Truck, Clark Equipment, and others. Industrial sales composed one-fifth of Buckeye Steel Castings' sales in 1972. The proportion grew as the decade progressed. By 1978 about two-fifths of Buckeye Steel's sales were industrial castings.[86] Buckeye also expanded its role as a cast armor producer. Still more important was the company's movement into the mass transit field. Buckeye entered mass transit almost by accident. "We stumbled into it," recalled Hughes. General Steel Industries of St. Louis had long been producing trucks for mass transit cars. This business proved unprofitable for General Steel, and the company incurred losses in it. Hughes met General Steel's chairman of the board by chance at a trade meeting in 1973, and they worked out an agreement beneficial to both their firms. Buckeye became the sole American licensee to produce the truck designed by General Steel. This business prospered. As Brown noted in the fall of 1974, "the margins" were "very good." In 1977 Buckeye Steel did $6,500,000 worth of what Hughes labeled "very profitable" business in mass transit components.[87]

To handle these varied needs, Buckeye accelerated the modernization of its steel plant. Between 1969 and 1972 Buckeye's board of directors approved some $5,400,000 in appropriations for capital improvements for the steel plant, and in 1973 Brown could accurately report that a "major expansion" was underway.[88] Much of this amount, $1,500,000, went into pollution-control devices mandated by the state and federal governments. More, however, was spent, as in the past, to make Buckeye Steel's operations more efficient. In 1971, for instance, Buckeye set up a scrap fragmentizer designed to shred 6,000 automobiles a month, thus producing a new low-cost source of high-grade scrap for the electric furnace.[89]

Reducing the labor expense remained a prime concern of Buckeye's officers. As Henderson explained in 1968:

> Our principal consideration with new equipment is to take the labor out of the job. If labor is required we must take the skill out of labor. We can no longer live with the situation where it may take a man a year to learn a new skill. Equipment must be provided that will enable a new man to operate relatively efficiently within four to six weeks and at a standard pace within two or three months.[90]

During the mid-1970s, Buckeye's management drafted a comprehensive, long-range plan for the improvement and expansion of the steel plant. Costing $16,000,000, the plan envisioned changes in virtually all of Buckeye Steel's operations. The heart of the plan, however, lay in the installation of a second electric furnace. The new furnace, Buckeye's officers hoped, would both increase their plant's output of steel castings and ensure the reliability of this production, should the first furnace ever have to be shut down. At a cost of $2,600,000, a new twenty-ton electric furnace was placed on the line in December 1978.[91]

By the late 1970s, the potential that Buckeye's management had seen in diversification in the 1960s was being realized. Tremendous growth resulted from the diversification effort. There was a nearly tenfold increase in Buckeye's sales between 1960 and 1977, and assets rose by a factor of six in the same years. By 1978 Buckeye ranked 955 on *Fortune*'s list of America's top 1,000 industrials.[92] Profits did not keep pace with the rise in sales. As we have seen, specific problems troubled many of the acquisitions. In addition, Buckeye suffered from managerial and organization difficulties, the topics of the next chapter.

Buckeye's diversification program most closely resembled the efforts of those corporations that entered new fields as a defensive strategy. Faced with unstable and declining sales to railroads, Buckeye went into new areas as a matter of survival. While it never became a true conglomerate, Buckeye was like such companies as Textron and Borden in their growth patterns. Worried about low profits in milk products, Borden went into chemicals, cosmetics, fertilizers, and fast foods. Textron found itself trapped in the declining textile industry in the 1940s, and over the following two decades sought escape by expanding into a myriad of fields ranging from aerospace products to fountain pens. Buckeye's evolution was similar, though on a much smaller scale. In less than twenty years, Buckeye changed dramatically from a one-product, single-division company into a multidivisional corporation offering many products to an ever-wider variety of customers.

This transition was difficult, perhaps especially so for Buckeye, because it was a medium-sized rather than large company, with relatively few reserves to draw upon in hard times. Luck and the personal whims of its officers played as much of a role in the success of Buckeye's diversification program as did sound, rational planning. Buckeye was particularly lucky (the move was unplanned) to enter the molded plastics field just as automobile companies were beginning to use more plastics in their car bodies. In fact, Buckeye's most highly planned acquisition, Peterson Baby Products, turned out to be the most disastrous. Chance and the personality of executives continue to play large roles in American business, particularly in the world of small- and medium-sized businesses.

Notes

1. Buckeye International, *Annual Report* (hereafter cited as *Annual Report*), *1976*.

2. See, especially, Alfred D. Chandler, Jr., *The Visible Hand* (Cambridge, Mass.: Harvard University Press, 1977).

3. The Editors of *Fortune,* ed., *The Conglomerate Commotion* (New York: *Fortune,* 1970), pp. 8–15. A conglomerate was defined as a business operating in at least eight different unrelated fields.

4. John Didrichsen, "The Development of Diversified and Conglomerate Firms in the United States, 1920–1970," *Business History Review* 46 (Summer 1972): 202–219; Charles Gilbert, ed., *The Making of a Conglomerate* (Hempstead, New York: Hofstra University Press, 1972).

5. Interview by the author with William Henderson, August 19, 1978; interview by the author with John McCoy, September 12, 1978.

6. McCoy interview, September 12, 1978.

7. Henderson interview, August 19, 1978.

8. "Minutes of the Executive Committee Meeting" July 8, 1960 (hereafter cited as "Executive Committee Meeting").

9. "Minutes of the Meeting of the Board of Directors" July 11, 1960 (hereafter cited as "Directors Meeting").

10. Henderson interview, August 19, 1978.

11. "Directors Meeting," July 12, 1965; Henderson interview, August 19, 1978.

12. "Minutes of the Annual Meeting of Stockholders," March 23, 1965 (hereafter cited as "Stockholders Meeting").

13. "Directors Meeting," July 12, 1965; "Executive Committee Meeting," June 14, September 13, December 13, 1965.

14. "Directors Meeting," July 12, September 13, 1965, March 22, 1966; "Executive Committee Meeting," May 10, June 14, 1965, September 12, 1966.

15. Interview by the author with Lewis Day, June 12, 1978; Henderson interview, August 19, 1978.

16. Day interview, June 12, 1978; Henderson interview, August 19, 1978.

17. Henderson interview, August 19, 1978.

18. "Directors Meeting," October 11, 1965; "Executive Committee Meeting," September 11, 1961, February 12, 1962.

19. "Executive Committee Meeting," June 11, 1962.

20. Day interview, June 12, 1978; Henderson interview, August 19, 1978; interview by the author with W. Dan Reuter, July 5, 1978; "Stockholders Meeting," March 26, 1963, March 22, 1966.

21. "Directors Meeting," January 8, March 27, 1962; "Executive Committee Meeting," February 12, May 14, September 10, 1962.

22. Dawson interview, July 5, 1978.

23. "Executive Committee Meeting," November 8, 1963.

24. Dawson interview, July 5, 1978.

25. "Executive Committee Meeting," May 5, June 8, 1964.

26. Ibid., October 12, November 9, 1964, September 9, 1968.

27. Ibid., January 13, 1964.

28. Ibid., January 13, 1964, March 23, 1964, September 12, 1966.

29. Ibid., May 11, June 8, November 9, 1964, September 13, 1965.

30. "Directors Meeting," January 10, 1966.

31. Dawson interview, July 5, 1978.

32. "Directors Meeting," June 13, 1966; "Executive Committee Meeting," November 8, 1965.

33. "Stockholders Meeting," March 22, 1966.

34. Ibid., March 28, 1967.

35. Ibid.

36. "Directors Meeting," October 9, November 13, 1967.

37. "Stockholders Meeting," March 26, 1968.

38. "Directors Meeting," March 26, 1968.

39. Day interview, June 12, 1978.

40. Henderson interview, August 19, 1978.

41. Ibid.
42. Ibid.
43. "Stockholders Meeting," March 24, 1970.
44. Ibid., March 28, 1967.
45. Ibid., March 25, 1969 and March 24, 1970.
46. Ibid., March 25, 1969.
47. Day interview, June 12, 1978.
48. "Stockholders Meeting," March 23, 1971.
49. Ibid., March 24, 1970.
50. McCoy interview, September 12, 1978.
51. Henderson interview, August 19, 1978.
52. Day interview, June 19, 1978.
53. Ibid., June 5, 1978.
54. Henderson interview, August 19, 1978.
55. McCoy interview, September 12, 1978.
56. Day interview, June 19, 1978.
57. McCoy interview, September 12, 1978.
58. Ibid.
59. Day interview, June 19, 1978.
60. Interview by the author with Rowland C.W. Brown, September 20, 1978; Day interview, June 19, 1978.
61. Brown interview, September 20, 1978.
62. McCoy interview, September 12, 1978.
63. *Annual Reports, 1971–77.*
64. Brown interview, September 20, 1978; interview by the author with Richard Warnick, September 14, 1978.
65. Interview by the author with Dick Brosius, August 23, 1978; Day interview, June 12, 1978; McCoy interview, September 12, 1978.
66. Brosius interview, August 23, 1978.
67. "Directors Meeting," March 27, 1973, October 23, 1974; "Executive Committee Meeting," June 25, December 11, 1973.
68. *Annual Reports, 1974, 1975;* "Directors Meeting," May 11, 1976; interview by the author with John Hughes, June 27, 1978.
69. Brown interview, September 20, 1978.
70. Ibid.; Day interview, June 12, 1978; "Directors Meeting," July 7, August 18, 1972, October 1, 1973.
71. Day interview, June 12, 1978.
72. Warnick interview, September 14, 1978.
73. Ibid.
74. Brown interview, September 20, 1978.
75. "Executive Committee Meeting," June 26, 1974; "Directors Meeting," October 23, 1974.
76. "Directors Meeting," February 10, 1976, November 1, 1977.

77. Ibid., February 8, 1978.
78. Brown interview, September 20, 1978.
79. "Directors Meeting," June, 1975.
80. *Annual Reports, 1976, 1977.*
81. Hughes interview, June 27, 1978.
82. *Annual Reports, 1971-77.*
83. William P. Conway, Jr., *Cast to Shape: A History of the Steel Castings Industry in the United States* (Rocky River, Ohio: Dillon, Liederbach, Inc., 1977), pp. 141-61.
84. Brown interview, September 20, 1978.
85. Hughes interview, June 27, 1978.
86. *Annual Report, 1972:* "Directors Meeting," October 21, 1975, October 26, 1976; Hughes interview, June 27, 1978.
87. "Directors Meeting," October 23, 1974; "Executive Committee Meeting," June 25, 1973; Hughes interview, June 27, 1978.
88. "Directors Meeting," July 14, 1969, March 24, 1970, January 11, 1972; "Executive Committee Meeting," February 8, 1971, December 11, 1973.
89. *Annual Report, 1971.*
90. "Stockholders Meeting," March 26, 1968.
91. Brown interview, September 20, 1978; Hughes interview, June 27, 1978.
92. *Fortune*, June 19, 1978, p. 188.

chapter 7

MANAGING THE
DIVERSIFIED COMPANY

Buckeye's transition from a well-established producer of steel castings to a multidivisional, diversified corporation was not easy. Diversification necessitated major changes in the management of the company. The centralized type of management adequate for the control of the steel company proved incapable of handling Buckeye's increasingly diverse operations and in the 1970s gave way to a new decentralized management structure. This change affected more than simply Buckeye's top officers, for the very nature and meaning of the company were altered. Running Buckeye as a decentralized corporation required "a different style" and "different senses" of its management, Rowland Brown recalled.[1] Even the corporation's sales methods and financing felt the impact of diversification.

Managerial Change

Significant managerial changes began even before diversification was well underway. When he came to Buckeye, William Henderson initiated a major overhaul of the company's management. Most importantly, Henderson began an Operations Improvement Program in mid-1963. A four-man team headed by an outsider examined the work of Buckeye's various departments "to locate problem areas" and "to work out the best solution to the problems."[2] By the end of the year, the team had reviewed the accounting department and made recommendations which its members thought would save Buckeye $100,000 annually.[3] At about the same time, Henderson established an Operations Control Center to coordinate incoming customer orders for steel castings with production runs, a task formerly done (or all too often not done) by four separate departments.[4] Henderson also set up a new cost-accounting system for the steel foundry which tightened management's control over production costs.[5] Finally, Henderson instituted major changes in Buckeye's managerial personnel. He moved men from position to position in an attempt to match their abilities with Buckeye's needs, and in a major break with previous practices, he brought in new people from outside the company to fill some of Buckeye's middle-management positions.[6]

All of Henderson's actions represented central management's efforts to restore their control over Buckeye's operations, and all led to a centralization of power in Buckeye's head office. None of Henderson's activities was accepted easily. "The new management," recognized Henderson in 1964, "has also been a disturbing influence in that it is a new way of life for many people."[7] The reasons for this feeling are understandable, for Henderson's changes inevitably stepped on peoples' toes. For instance, most of the savings in the accounting department were made by firing sixteen of its members.[8] In his response to the problems Buckeye faced, Henderson resembled the managers of earlier corporations caught in similar situations. For example, when General Motors was teetering on the edge of bankruptcy in the early 1920s because the head office had lost control over the company's operations, its officers moved to centralize power in their hands, thus restoring managerial control over the firm.[19] With his boundless energy, Henderson continued to run Buckeye with a highly centralized management structure throughout the 1960s.

However, with the purchase of the plastics companies and then the continued acquisitions of the 1970s, running the increasingly diversified company became too much of a job for any one person at the top. As Buckeye's operations became geographically dispersed and more and more separated by market and process, Henderson's centralized system of management proved inadequate. Richard Warnick, who became the head of Buckeye's automotive division, summed up the situation well:

> You don't run a diversified organization with different geographic locations without a good, strong management base. They were used to working in a self-contained South Parsons Avenue [steel foundry] complex. If you had a problem, you could walk out on the [foundry] floor, basically analyze the problem in five to ten minutes, walk back in the

office and hopefully solve it. When you have five plants now scattered around Ohio, the problems may not even get to you for two or three months. You can't be everywhere all of the time.[10]

Under Rowland Brown's leadership, Buckeye's officers devised a decentralized system of management to meet their company's changing needs. The corporate office took charge of grand strategy for the company, while the divisions carried out the day-to-day operations. This system evolved over time. The former steel foundry became the steel division. The plastics companies (exclusive of Earl Fisher) became the plastics group in 1975 and, with the addition of Bethandale, the automotive group two years later. Finally, Earl Fisher Plastics and Peterson Baby Products were linked to form a juvenile products group. Other acquisitions—Micro Communications, for instance—were still in the developmental phase and not part of a division.[11]

Buckeye's head office, composed of President Brown and his legal and financial staff, set the policies for the company and planned its overall growth. Corporate headquarters decided company stances on such issues as environmental protection, labor relations, legal problems, and so forth. Brown and the other corporate officers also supervised the operations of divisions. Brown had direct access to the controller of each division and ensured that the controllers "know that they have a primary responsibility to the chief executive officer and corporate comptroller rather than just to the local [divisional] people."[12] In this way the head office was assured of a flow of accurate information from the divisions. The corporate office also exercised control over the divisions through its power over budgetary appropriations. Any unplanned capital expenditure of over $500 had to be approved by the head office.[13] Rowland Brown explained well his role as Buckeye's chief executive officer in 1978:

> My job is really not to run the company, or even to know in depth the markets, the technologies. . . . My job, as I see it, is to establish a corporate philosophy. . . . I am the chief planner of the company. . . . Putting together the right kind of people and having a system for developing people has got to be one of my major concerns.[14]

Buckeye's officers conferred regularly with the company's directors, and in the 1960s and 1970s the directors regained much of the power they gave up during the company's middle years. In 1965 the board reestablished the three-man executive committee (which had lapsed around 1926) to advise Buckeye's president between their quarterly meetings. In 1971 the board set up a finance committee to aid management in long-range planning, and three years later the board formed an audit committee.[15] As was the case in other companies, Buckeye's directors took a more active role in running the corporation.[16] Paul Craig, a professor of economics and public administration at The Ohio State University and a Buckeye director, accurately described the board's function in 1979:

> I think the board of Buckeye is a board that is reasonably active. . . . I hope that we do not get into the day-to-day management or the routine management. But, I think that we are not a passive board. The board does play an active role in the strategic decisions of the company.[17]

As was also increasingly the case in American business, more and more of Buckeye's directors were outside directors, people not employed by the corporation. However, while less important than in the past, ties of friendship and business acquaintance continued to attract men as directors to Buckeye. Craig described the ties of friendship that led to his election to Buckeye's board, a typical situation at the company:

> In odd ways not directly associated with the corporation I knew many of its directors. . . . I have known Lew Day for many years . . . through various contacts at the OMA. I had known Mr. McCoy for many years through consulting at the bank [City National Bank]. I had known Rowland Brown through the Torch Club and other civic-community activities. And, I knew John Galbreath [a Buckeye director], and I knew John Bricker [another Buckeye director]. So, in a sense, I did not know the company very much, but I knew the people that were in one way or another associated with it.[18]

The importance of similar ties can be seen by examining how others became directors. John Bricker, a former governor of Ohio and United States senator from Ohio, joined the board in 1960. Bricker had known S. P. Bush and others at Buckeye during the company's middle years and was a close friend of John Galbreath. He and Galbreath had played baseball in high school, and in 1978 Bricker described Galbreath as "the longest-time friend I've got in Columbus." It was Galbreath who suggested Bricker as a director. John Fulford, the president of Jeffrey Manufacturing in Columbus, joined Buckeye's board of directors in late 1962. "There has always been," Lewis Day has noted, "a business relationship between this company and Jeffrey." Fulford was also a director of the City National Bank.[19] Eugene Miller, president of Cooper Industries, became a director in 1965 primarily through the influence of Henderson. Frank Durzo, Jeffrey's new president, replaced Fulford on Buckeye's board late the next year. James Earl Rudder, president of Texas Agricultural and Mechanical University, became the first academic to sit on the board. Henderson's commanding officer in the Second World War, he also joined the board in 1966. Frederick Jones, who owned the Buckeye Mutual Insurance Company and whose family owned Jackson Iron and Steel, was brought onto the board two years later through McCoy's influence. William Caples, the president of Kenyon College and a former vice-president of Inland Steel, joined the board in 1971. He had come to know McCoy when the City National Bank contributed to Kenyon's development fund. William Ferguson, the president of Ashland Chemical Division of Ashland Oil, was also elected to the board in 1971. James Phillips, an associate of John Galbreath, became a Buckeye director a year later, as did Robert Crane, the president of Crane Plastics in 1973. Finally, Paul Craig joined the board in 1975, and John Havens, an Ohio financier, became a Buckeye director in 1976.[20]

The division heads ran the daily operations of the firm, and in this work they enjoyed a fair degree of autonomy, as long as they produced profitable results. Warnick, the head of the automotive group, described his position: "Basically, I am in charge of the shooting match." He kept track of things through written reports, the telephone (he estimated he spent 20 percent of his time on the telephone), and by visiting the various plants in his group, a task which took, he judged, about one and one-half days each week. Quarterly management meetings, two planning sessions per year, and special projects meetings also kept him in touch with the operations of Bethandale and the plastics companies.[21] Below the division heads, the general managers of the individual companies also had considerable clout. Dick Brosius, for one, felt he had "excellent autonomy" as the head of Bethandale.[22]

This system of decentralized management generally worked well at Buckeye in the 1970s. Only when a division consistently lost money, as was the case at Peterson Baby Products, did the corporate office step in to drastically alter operations. Nowhere was this generally harmonious relationship between the head office and the divisions more evident than in Buckeye's approach to long-range planning. Long-range planning began at Buckeye with Henderson's presidency. In 1966 he assigned planning "a number 1 priority."[23] It was necessary to do so, Henderson later explained, because "it is easy to get lost, caught up in day-to-day details."[24] Out of necessity, perhaps, planning under Henderson was, according to Lewis Day, "pretty much dictated to the operating divisions."[25] Brown changed this situation. As Buckeye diversified, the division officers were brought into the planning process. In the late 1970s division officers worked with their staffs to prepare short- and long-range plans. Using these plans, the corporate officers worked out long-range growth strategies for the company as a whole. These plans were, in turn, revised year by year in light of Buckeye's actual performance.[26]

Buckeye's managerial system, then, underwent a two-stage development in the 1960s and 1970s. Henderson concentrated power in the head office as a prerequisite to leading the company in new directions. With the crisis past and with Buckeye's operations growing increasingly diversified, Brown established a more decentralized system of management. Buckeye's managerial evolution again closely resembled that of General Motors and many other large American corporations. Once General Motors survived its crisis, its management developed a decentralized management structure based upon its different automobile lines.[27] Not all companies have been as fortunate as General Motors and Buckeye in striking a happy balance between the responsibilities of their head offices and those of the operating divisions. When the head office of General Dynamics lost control of the company's Convair Division, the corporation came close to bankruptcy, losing $425,000,000 in just two years during the early 1960s.[28]

Sales

Diversification led to major changes in Buckeye's sales picture. As Buckeye moved into plastics and other items, its management scrapped the regional sales structure in favor of one organized by product line. The New York sales office was moved to Westfield, New Jersey in 1963 and then closed later in the decade. The Chicago office shut its doors in 1971. From this point on, all steel-castings sales were made from the offices of the Columbus steel plant, while still other sales organizations developed to service the plastics companies.

The steel-castings business became increasingly competitive as time progressed. By 1963 Buckeye, as its president noted, was engaged in serious price competition with its rivals.[29] Five years later "severe" competition led to 15 percent price cuts on railroad products, and Buckeye was forced to lay off one-third of its work force.[30] Such competition continued in the 1970s. "Competition is very, very severe," observed John Hughes, the president of Buckeye Steel Castings, in mid-1978. There was, he noted, "no competition on quality or delivery or that sort of thing." Rather, "it is all price competition."[31]

It was the growing competition in railroad castings, combined with the continued cyclical nature of the railroad business, that led Buckeye to move into industrial castings. This proved difficult to do. As previously noted, many customers were skeptical about Buckeye's long-range commitment to this field and were reluctant to place orders with Buckeye. As president, Henderson tried to overcome this hesitancy by personally visiting each customer twice a year. He also promised complete satisfaction on all orders within ninety days. "I was a real bear," he later recalled, in making the steel plant's management live up to this promise.[32] Henderson was assisted by W. Dan Reuter in his attempts to increase industrial castings sales. Hired specifically to raise industrial castings sales, Reuter visited some 175 potential customers during 1962 and 1963. After these visits he narrowed the list of possible customers to fifty, of whom twenty-five or so came to buy from Buckeye. In securing orders, price competition, service, and the right contacts all played roles. Word of mouth was also "important." Most of Buckeye's customers were well acquainted with each other and exchanged information on their suppliers. "All of these fellows know one another," Reuter explained, "They play cards together and go to ball games together."[33]

Buckeye's officers also sought to increase their income from foreign sales, usually by licensing foreign companies to produce Buckeye products. In 1963 Buckeye's management explored licensing possibilities with companies in Japan, Belgium, Argentina, Turkey, South Africa, India, and Canada.[34] Further negotiations took place in the mid- and late 1960s. In 1965 Buckeye officials briefly considered investing $2,500,000 in a South African foundry, but soon rejected that possibility.[35] More typically, Buckeye reached an agreement in the same year with the Kawasaki Rolling Stock Company of Japan to manufacture railroad car trucks under a Buckeye patent, and a year later Henderson traveled to Colombia, Australia, and Japan in search of additional business.[36] Further work occurred in the 1970s, and, while precise figures are not available, Buckeye's income from foreign sales and licensing agreements rose in the later part of the decade.

As previously mentioned, Buckeye Steel Castings' sales were centralized in the offices of the Parsons Avenue Plant during the 1970s. This was done for two basic reasons: First, to cut costs. With improvements in transportation and communications, Buckeye's officers came to view the regional sales offices as expensive white elephants. Then, too, they thought that moving the salesmen to Columbus would keep them in closer touch with what was going on in the steel plant, especially in the product-development field. In 1978 Buckeye Steel Castings' sales department consisted of five men, each of whom specialized in one type of product—railroad castings, mass transit work, industrial castings, and so forth. As had been hoped, expenses were low. Buckeye's expense/sales ratio was one of the lowest in the industry.[37]

Buckeye International handled the sales of its other divisions differently. The sales work of the divisions was decentralized. Peterson Baby Products sold through manufacturers' representatives, which was also how the plastics companies handled their sales in the late 1960s and early 1970s. There was considerable duplication of effort by this method, and in the mid-1970s Buckeye moved to tighten things up. In late 1975, when one of the major manufacturers' representatives handling Warren Molded Plastics' accounts died, Buckeye took over the sales enterprise, renaming it Buckeye

Sales, Inc. This move was designed, according to Day, to "do a more effective job of marketing at less cost." In the late 1970s Buckeye Sales with its office in Detroit, took over most of the sales responsibility for Buckeye's automotive group. Buckeye International's sales effort came, then, to resemble closely the rest of the corporation. It was decentralized, with each major division possessing a high degree of autonomy over how its products were sold.[38]

Financing Diversification

Buckeye's expansion during the 1960s brought changes to its finances, because, for the first time in many years, the company's retained earnings failed to meet its capital requirements. This situation first became apparent in 1963-64, when Henderson initiated the major improvement program for the steel plant. In early 1963 Buckeye began negotiating a loan agreement with the City National Bank, which was headed by John G. McCoy. Later that year, Buckeye's officers closed the deal, securing a $3,000,000 revolving credit arrangement with the City National Bank and the Chemical Bank of New York. By June 1965 all the borrowed funds had been repaid.[39] Buckeye's officers also altered their company's equity capital structure. In 1959 they redeemed all of the preferred stock to "effect substantial current savings."[40] In 1960 Buckeye's directors voted to increase the authorized number of shares of common stock from 240,000 to 500,000, and between 1964 and 1968 they approved annual 10 percent common stock dividends each year "to provide [the] impression of stockholder interest and growth." It was hoped that the stock dividends would also "appeal to potential subscribers of a new issue."[41]

Buckeye stepped up its quest for outside funds during the late 1960s. Retained earnings failed to cover the costs of capital improvements at the steel plant. Moreover, the corporation had also started acquiring other companies. Most of these purchases were made for cash rather than through an exchange of securities, for Buckeye's stockholders and officers did not want to dilute the ownership of their business.[42] Buckeye's management again turned to the City National Bank and negotiated a revolving credit agreement for $8,000,000 in 1969. By October of that year Buckeye had used all but $1,000,000 of the loan.[43] At about the same time, the corporation's equity capital structure underwent major alterations.

In 1968 the company's common stock was split 3:1, and a new issue of 300,000 shares of preferred stock was authorized (but not actually issued). It was anticipated that the stock split would increase the market for Buckeye shares.[44]

Buckeye's search for capital led the company to use new methods of raising money in the 1970s. The relocation and modernization of several of the newly acquired plastics plants were financed through State of Ohio Industrial Revenue bonds, and in 1971 State of Ohio Air Quality Revenue Bonds were used to finance the steel plant's air pollution equipment.[45] In 1971 Buckeye's officers briefly considered borrowing $5,500,000 for fifteen years from the Prudential Insurance Company, and three years later they considered "long-term, secured financing" from several of their major customers. Nothing, however, came of these efforts.[46] In 1975 Buckeye's management began exploring the possibility of public and private stock and bond placements, an investigation that bore fruit with the flotation of $5,000,000 in Buckeye notes by the Ohio Company in 1977.[47] At the same time, Buckeye continued to draw upon the City National Bank for funds. In 1972 Buckeye's management secured a new $6,000,000 revolving loan with that institution and, once again, the Chemical Bank of New York, a credit line which was increased in the following year. These arrangements were replaced by a three-year $5,000,000 revolving credit loan from the City National Bank in late 1975.[48]

Buckeye's expansion and diversification had an impact upon virtually all of the company's operations. The officers evolved a decentralized management system to meet their firm's changing needs and even the corporation's sales and financial structures underwent transformations. Less changed were Buckeye's relations with its labor force and the Columbus community in general.

Notes

1. Interview by the author with Rowland Brown, September 20, 1978.

2. "Minutes of the Meeting of the Executive Committee," June 10, 1963 (hereafter cited as "Executive Committee Meeting").

3. Ibid., November 8, 1963.

4. Ibid., May 13, 1960; interview by the author with William Henderson, August 19, 1978.

5. "Executive Committee Meeting," June 8, December 14, 1964.

6. Henderson interview, August 19, 1978.

7. "Executive Committee Meeting," May 11, 1964.

8. Buckeye Steel Castings Co., "Operations Improvement Project: Accounting Department, July–September 1963," in the possession of Henderson.

9. Alfred D. Sloan, Jr., *My Years with General Motors* (New York: Macfadden-Bartel, 1965).

10. Interview by the author with Richard Warnick, September 14, 1978.

11. Buckeye International, *Annual Reports* (hereafter cited as *Annual Reports*), *1975–1977*.

12. Brown interview, September 20, 1978.

13. Interview by the author with Lewis Day, June 19, 1978.

14. Brown interview, September 20, 1978.

15. "Minutes of the Meeting of the Board of Directors," June 22, 1971 (hereafter cited as "Directors Meeting"). "Executive Committee Meeting," June 14, 1965, May 21, 1974.

16. *Forbes,* May 15, 1976, devotes much of the issue to the changing nature and roles of directors in American business.

17. Interview by the author with Paul Craig, April 2, 1979.

18. Ibid.

19. Day interview, June 19, 1978; interview by the author with John Bricker, May 23, 1978.

20. Ibid.; *Annual Reports, 1971–77;* "Directors Meeting," January 11, 1965, January 10, July 11, 1966, July 8, 1968, March 23, 1971, March 28, 1972, March 23, 1976.

21. Warnick interview, September 14, 1978.

22. Interview by the author with Dick Brosius, August 23, 1978.

23. "Executive Committee Meeting," June 13, 1966.

24. Henderson interview, August 19, 1978.

25. Day interview, June 19, 1978; "Executive Committee Meeting," June 13, 1966.

26. Interview by the author with Robert Marshall, June 20, 1978.

27. Alfred D. Chandler, Jr., *Strategy and Structure* (Garden City, N.Y.: Doubleday, 1966), part 3.

28. Richard Smith, *Corporations in Crisis* (Garden City, N.Y.: Doubleday, 1963), chaps. 3–4.

29. "Directors Meeting," September 9, 1963.

30. Henderson interview, August 19, 1978; "Minutes of the Annual Meeting of Stockholders," March 25, 1969 (hereafter cited as "Stockholders Meeting").

31. Interview by the author with John Hughes, June 27, 1978.

32. Henderson interview, August 18, 1978.

33. Interview by the author with W. Dan Reuter, July 5, 1978.

34. "Executive Committee Meeting," May 13, June 10, September 9, 1963.

35. Ibid., December 13, 1965, February 14, 1966.

36. "Directors Meeting," July 11, 1966; "Stockholders Meeting," March 22, 1966.

37. Reuter interview, July 5, 1978.

38. Day interview, June 19, 1978; Warnick interview, September 14, 1978.

39. "Directors Meeting," January 14, 1963; "Executive Committee Meeting," May 13, July 8, September 9, December 12, 1963, March 24, December 14, 1964, June 14, 1965.

40. "Directors Meeting," July 13, 1959.

41. Ibid., January 11, 1960, July 13, 1964, March 23, 1965, January 10, October 10, 1966, November 13, 1967, November 11, 1968.

42. Henderson interview, August 19, 1978; "Stockholders Meeting," March 26, 1968.

43. "Directors Meeting," October 13, 1969; "Executive Committee Meeting," May 12, September 8, 1969.

44. "Directors Meeting," October 9, 1967, March 26, 1968; "Executive Committee Meeting," February 14, 1966; "Stockholders Meeting," March 28, 1967.

45. "Directors Meeting," June 22, 1971; "Executive Committee Meeting," February 11, 1972.

46. "Directors Meeting," October 28, 1974; "Executive Committee Meeting," September 14, December 14, 1971.

47. "Directors Meeting," July 9, 1975, October 26, November 16, 1976, February 8, 1977.

48. Ibid., January 11, August 18, 1972, July 24, 1973, April 23, December 10, 1975, February 10, 1976.

chapter 8

LABOR AND COMMUNITY

Labor relations at Buckeye and the connections between Buckeye and the rest of the Columbus community were a complex blend of change and continuity after 1959. Unionization altered the corporation's labor picture, but did not cause a great increase in labor strife at the company. Buckeye's acquisition program forced some changes in Buckeye's labor policies, for labor relations, mirroring alterations in the nature of the company itself, were handled on an increasingly decentralized basis. These same trends were apparent in Buckeye's relationships with the rest of Columbus. The company continued to contribute to the same types of community projects as in the past, but the methods and mechanisms of giving changed somewhat.

Working at Buckeye

Reflecting alterations in the composition of Columbus's population, Buckeye Steel's labor force came to include more and more blacks and Appalachians. By 1978 Buckeye's work force was 35 percent black and 65 percent white. According to Phil Bordan, Buckeye Steel's personnel manager, the white segment was "overwhelmingly" Appalachian in background.[1] The foreign ethnic groups which had been important earlier became less significant as time progressed. Bill Buffington, Buckeye Steel's vice-president in charge of manufacturing, recalled this change. "I found that when I first came here in the early 1950s," he remembered, "we did have a lot of the foreign element in the plant, and they started being replaced very rapidly."[2]

Like other corporations in the United States' basic productive industries, Buckeye encountered what its management viewed as increasingly serious problems with the performance of its work force.

Central to these difficulties, according to both company officials and some labor union officers, was a changing attitude toward work. Despite continuing technological innovation, much of the labor at Buckeye Steel remained, as Bordan put it, "a backbreaking, hard job."[3] Given this situation and the rising expectations of Americans about their places in society, it became more and more difficult to motivate workers and, especially, to get them to identify with their jobs. Harry Mayfield, who headed the United Steelworkers' subdistrict office in Columbus during most of the 1950s and 1960s, commented upon the "different outlook" of present-day workers toward their jobs in 1978. Post-Second World War workers, Mayfield believed, had needs and desires different from those of workers during the 1930s and early 1940s:

> Their needs and so forth are different than existed then. . . . Back then the main idea was just to have a union in order to have some guarantees of not being fired, and recognition, and so on. The needs were minimal. . . . Also, that era of people had a different attitude toward work and work habits. I mean that they were used to long hours and hard work, and steady work. And, they wanted work so badly they worked under almost inhuman conditions. That's not true today. The pace is different. And, in many respects, it is more difficult today to convince the average worker that's just coming into plants as to the necessity of production.[4]

The turnover rate and absenteeism, both of which had long been concerns for Buckeye's management, remained problems in the 1960s and 1970s. In 1964 Buckeye's president asserted that "our inability to maintain a stable hourly workforce" was cutting into Buckeye's profits, and two years later William Henderson observed that "maintaining the workforce" was "a continuing problem."[5] According to Bordan, absenteeism and the turnover of workers, especially among those new to the job and unused to industrial discipline, were still problems at Buckeye Steel in the late 1970s:

> We still have a turnover problem. . . . It's with the younger worker. . . . They would rather have more time off [for] their own pleasures or pursuits. . . . There is a moment of truth

that occurs, and the employee says, "I don't care how much they pay me, I don't want to do this kind of work." The magnitude of the plant scares people . . . the size, the physical size and the heat.[6]

Closely related to the turnover problem was that of quality control. Buckeye's officers, like those of other corporations, believed that as workers lost interest in their jobs, the quality of their work declined. As we have seen, one of the motives behind Henderson's capital-improvement programs for the steel plant was a desire to lessen the skills needed to perform any given task. Skilled labor, Henderson believed, was both expensive and, all too often, unavailable. Substituting machines for men, he hoped, would both decrease the costs of production and increase the quality of Buckeye's products. Yet, despite capital expenditures, the problem of quality control, as viewed by Buckeye's management, remained serious. "As long as they can get by with it," some workers, Buffington observed, will "produce anything they can, just as long as they can get their paychecks."[7] Bordan agreed and added that quality improvement was going to be "a long program," because "you've got to develop pride in the workers."[8]

Again like the managers of other companies, Buckeye's officers perceived still other problems as affecting their labor force. Vice of various sorts troubled the steel plant. As Buffington put it, vice is "a constant battle here." Drugs and alcohol, Bordan and Buffington believed, were particularly irksome. Drug usage was, they thought, especially troublesome. "We have narcotics like everyone else has narcotics," Bordan observed in 1978.[9] Race relations proved to be less of a difficulty. While some racial friction existed at Buckeye, this was not a major cause of concern. In the 1960s and 1970s blacks became "on-line supervisors" at the steel plant, and some began to advance into middle-management ranks.[10] In mid-1978 Buffington summarized the changes which he had seen occur at Buckeye since the early 1950s:

I've seen it [race relations] change tremendously. In the shower room we used to have actually three sections within the main shower. We had a foreign section which was made up mostly of Hungarians and Czechs. And, then we had the black section and the white section. And, they were all fenced off individually. Now it's one, main, open shower room.[11]

Buckeye Steel's management tried to cope with these problems in several ways. They set up incentive systems designed to speed production, while at the same time improving the quality of their plant's production. They also initiated training and counseling programs for steel plant employees.

During the 1930s, 1940s, and 1950s, Buckeye Steel's time-study department drew up work standards for the wide variety of foundry tasks. "Our time-study job," remembered Frank Lewis who was engaged in the task, "was to measure the work as it existed and develop a work standard." As drafted, the standards included an incentive system. Workers were paid a money rate per hundred units produced, and the standards set generally allowed workers to make about 25 percent more in pay than the guaranteed base rate, but to receive this they had to increase their output by about 50 percent. According to Lewis, this scheme worked fairly well. "Our work pace was pretty good in those days," he observed.[12]

Buckeye's management refined this system in the 1960s and 1970s. Under President Henderson's leadership, the time-study department evolved into a full-scale industrial engineering department with separate sections for methods engineering, estimating, and pricing. Lewis and others began attending industry-wide seminars and visiting rival foundries to become acquainted with the most modern developments in industrial engineering. This led to changes in the organization of work throughout the steel plant. Rather than simply accepting the status quo as they had in the past (in the 1940s and 1950s only foremen and superintendents could make changes in work patterns), the industrial engineers began planning how tasks would be done at different work stations throughout the steel plant—as Lewis put it, "who does what at what speeds." Buckeye Steel also switched to a standard hours system, under which tasks and working times were designed so that the average worker could earn a 25 percent premium.[13]

Buckeye Steel's officers also set up training courses for its employees. As was typical of industrial enterprises, the company operated an orientation program for all new workers. It dealt with employee benefits, union membership, and job safety. The company also ran specific training programs for skilled occupations—welders, mobile equipment operators, and the like. Less successful was Buckeye's college tuition refund program, for the number of workers taking advantage of it was low. Perhaps most promising for the future is a Career Development Program initiated by Buckeye Steel's personnel department in the late 1970s. A guidance program, it seeks through personal interviews with individual employees to "find out just where they want to go and what they want to do." Finally, Buckeye Steel's management became increasingly active in Columbus area programs to fight drug abuse.[14]

As noted in an earlier chapter, most contract negotiations were settled amicably at Buckeye in the years after the Second World War, but several strikes did take place. In 1963-64, negotiations broke down with the pattern makers. Two issues were involved. First, the pattern makers wanted a $0.46 per hour wage increase, while Buckeye was prepared to grant only a $0.04 raise. Perhaps even more importantly, the pattern makers disliked some of the changes recommended by an Operations Improvement Study for the work of the pattern shop. As Henderson noted in May 1964, "the men generally are extremely wary and in some cases are resisting the changes." A strike ensued during the fall of 1964, but it was soon settled by concessions on the part of both the company and the union.[15] During March 1966, a strike by the steelworkers for higher wages (Buckeye initially offered an increase of $0.38 per hour spread over three years, the steelworkers wanted $0.69) shut down the steel plant for three weeks.[16] A strike by the steelworkers closed nearly all operations at Buckeye Steel during the opening months of 1978. The major issue was again wages. Under the new contract which ended the strike, the wages of beginning employees increased from $5.23 per hour to $7.78 between 1979 and 1981.

With Buckeye's diversification, the company's labor relations changed a bit in the 1970s. Buckeye International's head office set up a vice-president in charge of human resources to oversee and coordinate all of the company's personnel policies. The brunt of the daily relations with labor, however, was borne by executives at the divisional level. For instance, the automotive group had an office to handle contract negotiations with the Allied Industrial Workers, the United Auto Workers, and the Teamsters. At times the work of the corporate and the division levels overlapped. During the 1978 steelworkers strike, to cite one example, the negotiations, as Lewis Day explained the situation, were "handled entirely by the division," but "there was lots of conversation between Mr. Hughes and Mr. Brown."[17]

Company and Community

In the broadest sense, the changes going on at Buckeye mirrored alterations occurring in Columbus's economy. Like Buckeye, Columbus experienced growth in the postwar period. The population of Columbus rose from 376,000 in 1950 to 546,000 thirty years later.[18] Columbus and central Ohio grew at a rate faster than the national average or the average of the north central states as a whole. Columbus's employment figures outpaced those of the state, as well. Between 1960 and 1970, employment in Columbus increased by 21 percent, while that in the state climbed by only 16 percent. Columbus, with its continuing growth, more nearly resembled southern cities than its Midwestern neighbors Cleveland and Akron.[19]

Columbus's growth, again like Buckeye's, was achieved through diversification. Manufacturing declined in its relative importance in the city's economy; in 1950 manufacturing employed 25 percent of Columbus's workers; by 1970, only 23 percent. Columbus grew as a service center, a locus of finance and insurance, and as a governmental center. By 1974 only one of the city's ten largest employers was a manufacturing concern. Most were in other fields of activity.[20] Reflecting this change, Columbus's downtown was revitalized by a series of corporate building projects in the 1970s— the Banc Ohio headquarters, the Nationwide Insurance Building, and the Ohio Center, a convention and hotel complex.[21] Symbolizing its diversification beyond steel-castings, Buckeye moved its corporate headquarters from the steel plant in South Columbus to the City National Building, a dazzling skyscraper in the heart of Columbus's financial district.

As their city evolved, Buckeye's officers continued to play significant roles in its development, despite a relative decline in their company's economic importance to Columbus. Yet here too, Buckeye's diversification caused some alterations in the behavior of its officers.

Speaking in 1978, Rowland Brown well summarized the complexities of the public's reaction to corporate involvement in community affairs:

> Corporate involvement in community affairs has become an increasingly complex subject—surrounded by controversy. . . . Some complain that we are too involved, spend too much of our time on community affairs and invest too much of our shareholders' earnings. Others resent our involvement and complain that we try to exert too much leadership—in this case described as pressure. And finally, there are those critics who feel our efforts are too meager, our commitment directed too much to maintaining the status quo, too remote from the inner city.[22]

Despite its pitfalls, Buckeye continued its long tradition of engagement in public affairs.

Buckeye remained a mainstay of corporate funds for philanthropic organizations in Columbus. However, as the company's profits fell in the early 1960s, so did its giving. The company's officers deferred action on requests for contributions from the Boy Scouts and Children's Hospital in 1962 "in view of the loss sustained for the year 1961," and in 1963 they put off a request from the Columbus Hospital Federation for the same reason.[23] Buckeye gave $30,000 to the United Appeal campaign in 1961, but the directors reduced this to $24,000 in the following year "in view of the current business conditions and the requirements for the plant improvement and soil pipe programs."[24] A further decrease to $20,000 due to the "tight cash situation" came in 1963, and that level of giving was maintained, with slight increases, through 1966.[25]

As in so many other matters, diversification brought changes to corporate philanthropy at Buckeye. The head office in Columbus continued to make decisions on major contributions, but division heads and plant managers assumed some responsibility. For instance, while Buckeye International contributed to the United Way in Columbus, Bethandale gave to Mentor, Ohio's United Way drive.[26] To handle contributions, Buckeye International's officers set up a nonprofit corporation, the Buckeye International Foundation, in 1968. Endowed with $250,000, the foundation was empowered to make contributions for "education, religious, charitable, scientific, or literary purposes." Established partly for tax reasons, the foundation was dissolved in the mid-1970s.[27] After that, Buckeye's officers and directors decided on contributions on an annual basis. In late 1977 they drew up, for the first time, formal "Charitable Contribution Guidelines." According to these guidelines, Buckeye's giving would amount to, as "a rough rule of thumb," 2 to 3 percent of pretax earnings. "First priority should be given," the guidelines stated, "to aiding on-going charitable operations as distinct from capital fund drives."[28]

While the mechanism of giving changed somewhat, the nature of Buckeye's contributions remained relatively constant. The United Way (the successor to United Appeal) campaigns continued to win strong support from Buckeye. The head office contributed an annual average of $22,000 to the Columbus drives in the 1970s.[29] Buckeye companies also gave to the campaigns in their localities.[30] Particular projects also garnered Buckeye's backing. The YMCA, the Salvation Army, and hospitals continued to receive funding from Buckeye. In May 1976 the company gave $30,000 to the South Side Settlement House, because "a number of employees of the Steel Division and their families reside in the neighborhood of the Settlement House and are beneficiaries of many of its services." Four months later, Buckeye contributed $5,000 to the Hannah Neil House for the same reason. The company also began setting aside funds for cultural projects, $25,000 for the Columbus Association for the Performing Arts in 1971 and $25,000 for the Columbus Gallery of Fine Arts a year later.[31]

Buckeye continued its corporate giving for several reasons. Chief among them, as in the days of S. P. Bush, was Buckeye's officers' conviction that they had a duty to improve society. This belief, as in times past, was tinged with a bit of paternalism. Buckeye generally gave to conservative, old-line causes which its officers felt were "best" for Columbus. "We contribute to those institutions," Lewis Day explained in 1978, "that have been in place for some time and which we know do a constructive job for the community."[32] Other reasons dictated Buckeye's giving. By helping create what they considered a better community, Buckeye's officers hoped to attract high-caliber business executives to Columbus (and Buckeye) and to improve social and economic conditions in Columbus in general. Asked why his company gave so heavily to local organizations, Rowland Brown replied:

> If you want a good management, a good work force, an environment in a community that's easy to bring people into, you'd better hope that that community is a healthy one. . . . In the long run, our ability to economically survive and do well depends upon the economic and social health of the city we are in, the state we are in, and the country we are in.[33]

Given this attitude, it is not surprising to find that Buckeye executives were, as always, very active in community affairs. William Henderson, although extremely busy with changes at Buckeye, found time to head Columbus's United Appeal drive for 1968. He did so, he later explained, because "if you couldn't depend on home-grown companies to provide leadership, how could you go to the foreign-owned [out-of-state] firms?"[34] Henderson was also a member of the Executive Board of the Central Ohio Council of the Boy Scouts of America and a trustee of Children's Hospital. Lewis Day was chairman of the Industrial Division of the United Way for two campaigns and served as treasurer of the Central Ohio Heart Association. Rowland Brown was a member of the board of trustees of the Columbus Association for the Performing Arts, the Jefferson Center, Alvis House, and the Columbus Urban League. In 1976 he served as both the industrial chairman and the associate general chairman of the United Way campaign. Perhaps most importantly, Brown chaired a citizen's committee to ease school desegregation in Columbus. He had the wholehearted backing of Buckeye's other executives in this endeavor. "It is important," Day explained, that desegregation proceeds smoothly, because "it affects the business climate of the City of Columbus." Moreover, he observed, Buckeye Steel's operations could be directly influenced. "The steel foundry, being an integrated, that is racially integrated business on its own," Day noted, "we don't want any potential conflict to carry over into that operation."[35]

The engagement of company officers in community projects extended to the division and plant executives. John Hughes was president of the Central Ohio Council of Boy Scouts, was a trustee of

Mercy Hospital, and served in several other organizations as well. As head of Warren Molded Plastics, Richard Warnick was active in hospital fund drives, United Way campaigns, local school board elections, and youth development projects. Various plant managers served on Little League organizations, United Way drives, school boards, and city councils.[36]

Buckeye's management also continued their involvement in business and professional associations. Day was president of both the Columbus Chapter of the National Association of Accountants and the Central Ohio Chapter of the Financial Executives Institute (he was a national vice-president of this latter body as well). Day also served as treasurer of the Ohio Manufacturers' Association in the early 1960s and won election as the organization's chairman of the board in 1977 and 1978. Henderson was president of the Railway Progress Institute for a time in the 1960s and acted as an informal adviser to the executive director of the Steel Founders Society. Brown was a member of many professional societies and their advisory boards. He was also a director of the Columbus Area Chamber of Commerce. Buckeye's plant managers reflected this concern for involvement in business groups, belonging to and sometimes heading local chambers of commerce, rotary organizations, and manufacturing associations.[37]

The leadership that Buckeye's officers and the officers of other corporations gave Columbus was one of the keys to the city's continued growth and development. In particular, it was this leadership that prevented the deterioration of the downtown area. Like Buckeye's officers, other Columbus businessmen identified closely with their city and worked together to prevent its decline. In the 1950s and 1960s they formed a Metropolitan Committee which successfully pushed for various city improvement bond issues. In the 1970s they erected major company headquarter buildings in the downtown area in a conscious move (and again a successful one) to avoid a flight of business to the suburbs. Asked why he decided to keep his large department store in downtown Columbus rather than open many suburban branches, Charles Lazarus replied, "in the '50s, we started this process because we firmly believed Columbus had that kind of opportunity to continue development of Downtown, and we have been doing it ever since."[38] Dean Jeffers, the head of Nationwide Insurance, noted that one reason his corporation built its new headquarters downtown was that, "I feel the role of major corporations in social affairs" is very "important."[39]

In his recent study of urbanization in the Lackawanna and Lehigh regions of Pennsylvania, the historian Burton Folsom, Jr. argues persuasively that it was the high quality of business entrepreneurship in Scranton and Bethlehem that pushed those cities ahead of their urban rivals.[40] Despite locational disadvantages, Scranton and Bethlehem triumphed because of the strong leadership of their businessmen. This situation also appears to have prevailed in Columbus. Most Columbus businessmen, like those at Buckeye, identified strongly with their local community and acted as boosters for it. Of course, the great danger in such a situation is the development of a narrow parochialism—the problem that afflicted Buckeye's management and perhaps other Columbus businessmen during the 1930s and 1940s. Happily, the movement of major out-of-state corporations like Borden and American Electric Power to Columbus in the 1970s has made the occurrence of such parochialism less likely in the future. Columbus should benefit from the blend of a strong, local business community leavened by the presence of national corporations with a broad range of experiences.

Notes

1. Interview by the author with Phil Bordan, June 27, 1978. In the 1970s Columbus had a population that was about 18 to 22 percent black. About two-thirds of the city's white population was first- or second-generation Appalachian.

2. Interview by the author with Bill Buffington, June 27, 1978.

3. Bordan interview, June 27, 1978.

4. Interview by the author with Harry Mayfield, August 26, 1978. In 1973 Mayfield was elected director of district 27 (Canton, Ohio) of the Steelworkers.

5. "Minutes of the Meeting of the Board of Directors" (hereafter cited as "Directors Meeting"), July 11, 1966; "Minutes of the Meeting of the Executive Committee" (hereafter cited as "Executive Committee"), September 11, 1964.

6. Bordan interview, June 27, 1978.

7. Buffington interview, June 27, 1978.

8. Bordan interview, June 27, 1978.

9. Ibid.; Buffington interview, June 27, 1978.

10. Ibid.

11. Buffington interview, June 27, 1978. Since the mid-1970s Buckeye has also employed fifty to sixty women in the foundry, and expects to employ more in the future.

12. Interview by the author with Frank Lewis, June 27, 1978.

13. Ibid.

14. Bordan interview, June 27, 1978; Buffington interview, June 27, 1978.

15. "Directors Meeting," October 14, 1963, "Executive Committee Meeting," November 8, 1963, May 11, September 11, December 14, 1964.

16. "Executive Committee Meeting," February 14, 1966.

17. Interview by the author with Lewis Day, June 19, 1978.

18. Betty Garrett and Edward Lentz, *Columbus: America's Crossroads* (Tulsa, Oklahoma: Centennial Heritage Press, 1980), p. 174.

19. The best source for Columbus's recent development is City of Columbus, *Overall Economic Development Plan Profile* (Columbus: Columbus Chamber of Commerce, 1976). The population of the Columbus SMSA increased from 637,000 in 1950 to 1,018,000 in 1970 (p. 26).

20. Ibid., pp. 54, 74. Columbus's ten largest employers in 1974 were: The Ohio State University (18,847 employees), state government (18,379), federal government exclusive of the military (13,299), public schools (8,342), Western Electric (8,217), Lazarus (6,987), city government (6,847), Nationwide Insurance (6,000), Ohio Bell (5,100), and Borden (5,000).

21. Garrett and Lentz, *Columbus,* p. 165.

22. Rowland Brown, "Remarks on Corporate Involvement in Community Affairs," address to the Northwest Area Council (Columbus), November 16, 1978.

23. "Directors Meeting," January 8, 1962, January 14, 1963.

24. "Executive Committee Meeting," September 10, 1962.

25. Ibid., September 9, 1963, September 11, 1964, September 13, 1965, May 9, 1966.

26. Interview by the author with Rowland Brown, September 20, 1978.

27. "Directors Meeting," July 8, 1968.

28. Ibid., November 11, 1977.

29. Ibid., July 14, 1970, September 14, 1971, October 24, 1972, October 23, 1974, July 9, 1975, September 27, 1977.

30. Ibid., October 21, 1975.

31. Ibid., March 28, 1976, October 21, 1975, May 11, 1976, September 7, 1976; "Executive Committee Meeting," May 11, 1971.

32. Day interview, June 19, 1978.

33. Brown interview, September 20, 1978.

34. Henderson interview, August 19, 1978.

35. Day interview, June 19, 1978.

36. Brown interview, September 20, 1978; Day interview, June 19, 1978.

37. Columbus *Dispatch,* August 14, 1962; Day interview, November 9, 1978; Henderson interview, August 19, 1978. For his civic and professional work, Brown received many honors: the Columbus Award, the Phi Delta Kappa Education Award for Leadership, the MIT Corporate Leadership Award, the Urban League Equal Opportunity Award. Brown was named Public Citizen of the Year by the Ohio Chapter of the National Association for Social Workers.

38. Columbus *Dispatch,* August 2, 1981.

39. Ibid.

40. Burton W. Folsom, Jr., *Urban Capitalists: Entrepreneurs and City Growth in Pennsylvania's Lackawanna and Lehigh Regions, 1800–1920* (Baltimore: Johns Hopkins University Press, 1981).

chapter 9

MERGER

As Buckeye entered the late 1970s, its officers were optimistic about the future and remained committed to the idea of growth through diversification. "Management will be constantly on the look-out for opportunities for investment," Lewis Day observed in 1978, "primarily in smaller companies that have good growth prospects."[1] Addressing his company's stockholders in the same year, Rowland Brown also observed that Buckeye needed to "broaden the scope" of its activities by "getting into many new ventures."[2] Such a future, however, was not to be, for Buckeye's officers soon discovered that their company was being eyed as a prospect for acquisition by other corporations.

Merger Prospects

This situation was not new at Buckeye, for as the company modernized its steel plant and entered additional fields, it became an increasingly attractive prize for other corporations. In 1964 an "unknown California company" tried to buy Buckeye stock in an acquisition move, and a year later the Evans Product Company of Detroit expressed interest in Buckeye.[3] The Budd Company, a producer of automotive and railroad equipment, made acquisition enquiries in 1966, and both the Compu Dyne Corporation and the Ametek Company did the same in 1969.[4] As William Henderson, Buckeye's president during most of the 1960s, recalled, Buckeye's officers were not interested in these approaches, and rebuffed them. "A lot of people came in and talked to us seriously," remembered Henderson. "We just said, 'what do you have to offer? No, we aren't interested in being one of fifty-six divisions which you have.' "[5]

In the 1970s the pressure upon Buckeye increased. In mid-1977

Buckeye's secretary and general counsel, Paul Ferrell, reported to the company's directors that "various measures" were being taken to protect Buckeye from "a bargain takeover bid," and three months later Buckeye's officers set up a special group to fend off "any unnegotiated tender offer."[6] Buckeye's management was opposed to being acquired by another company, in part because they had been through similar unfriendly takeover situations before (Brown with Dorr Oliver, Ferrell with United Fruit) and were, as Lewis Day noted, "gun shy." To avoid an undesired merger, they worked through politics. In the late 1970s the Ohio Manufacturers' Association, of which Day was chairman of the board, secured passage of an anti-takeover law by the state legislature. This law made it difficult for an out-of-state company to acquire an Ohio-chartered corporation in an unfriendly manner.[7]

By the late 1970s Buckeye was an appealing prize coveted by other corporations. Several factors made Buckeye attractive. Buckeye had by this time successfully completed its own diversification program. "We happen to have several very attractive assets, the foundry and our plastics, auto-related division, that are both needed in the world of the next decade," noted Paul Craig, a leading Buckeye director in April 1979.[8] By the summer of that year, Buckeye had a $260,000,000 steel-castings backlog, two years of orders, and the plastics division was doing well.[9] Buckeye had also eliminated past sources of losses, such as Peterson Baby Products.

Moreover, in the opinion of Buckeye's officers and many outside financial analysts, Buckeye's stock was underpriced; it did not, they thought, reflect accurately either Buckeye's present position or future potential. As early as 1977, *Forbes Magazine* listed Buckeye as one of the nation's "best buyouts"; for, as the journal pointed out, Buckeye's stock was selling at only $9 per share, while the replacement value of the company was about $40 per share.[10] A year later, *Business Week* observed that Buckeye had one of the nation's few modern foundries capable of meeting the growing demand for steel castings.[11] By May 1979, Buckeye's stock had risen to $20 per share, but stock market analysts were still recommending the purchase of the company's stock. A stock market newsletter put out by Prescott, Ball, & Turber concluded:

> We recommend purchase of Buckeye International as a speculative participation in the burgeoning business of rail-

road castings. Its past record has been spotty, but there is no
doubt that the steel castings market is booming, and there are
positive signs that Buckeye has taken steps to eliminate or
minimize the problems that have plagued it in the past.[12]

Dayton-Walther's Acquisition Attempt

In 1979 the Dayton-Walther Corporation of Dayton, Ohio
mounted a major effort to acquire Buckeye. Although ultimately
unsuccessful in its attempt to purchase Buckeye, Dayton-Walther's
effort heightened the interest other companies had in Buckeye. In
the end, Dayton-Walther's acquisition move served as a catalyst for
a successful merger overture from a different corporation.

Dayton-Walther was a manufacturer of parts for the heavy-
transportation, recreational-vehicle, and travel-trailer markets. Its
most important products were cast steel wheels and wheel assem-
blies for trucks and semi-trailers. A privately held company owned
by the Walther family, Dayton-Walther earned about $8,500,000
on sales of $189,000,000 in 1978.[13] By February 1979, Dayton-
Walther had purchased 5.9 percent of Buckeye's common stock,
and three months later the company owned slightly more than 10
percent of it. Most of the stock was purchased on the open market
at about $15 per share, but a large block was obtained in a private
sale from an institutional investor, the Chase Manhattan Bank.[14]
Dayton-Walther's officers maintained that these purchases were
for investment purposes only, but there was little doubt, at least in
the minds of Buckeye's management, that Dayton-Walther was trying to gain control of Buckeye.[15]

From the outset, Buckeye's officers viewed Dayton-Walther's
actions as an unfriendly takeover bid. Having just finished
rebuilding their company, Buckeye's management had no intention
of yielding control to someone else. Rowland Brown stated the
prevailing attitude of those at Buckeye in an interview at the time of
Dayton-Walther's purchases of Buckeye stock. "We aren't seeking
a merger partner and don't see why we should be interested in a
merger," noted Brown. "Our board feels quite comfortable with
the direction we're going in without outside assistance."[16]

Buckeye's officers saw no advantage in merging with Dayton-
Walther. As Brown noted, Dayton-Walther was "in a business not
in keeping with our long-term growth strategies." Moreover, the
company's overdependence upon cast-steel truck wheels at a time

when aluminum wheels were coming into use made it "quite vulnerable in terms of product technology."[17] Paul Craig made the same point. Because of Dayton-Walther's heavy dependence upon one product, Craig believed that the company "had serious problems emerging," and he wanted to be sure that Buckeye was not "ripped off" in a merger.[18]

Buckeye's management thought that their counterparts at Dayton-Walther were trying to use them. Buckeye's officers believed that Dayton-Walther's management desired to buy Buckeye as a way of acquiring a vehicle for becoming a publicly held corporation. Brown thought that "they felt they could use our shareholder base as a means of getting instantly a large public following."[19] Day viewed the situation in the same way. "Dayton-Walther was a closely held, family company," he noted, "and they were desperately looking for ways to go public."[20] In addition, the tactics of Dayton-Walther's management antagonized those at Buckeye. Craig later condemned Dayton-Walther's management for buying Buckeye's stock "surreptitiously" and "as cheaply as they could."[21] Day was especially incensed by Dayton-Walther's purchase of the large block of shares from Chase Manhattan, for he had thought that Buckeye had "an informal agreement" to buy back those shares, should they ever be put on the market. "For a few quick and dirty dollars," he later observed, institutional buyers "will sell you down the river."[22] Brown was more realistic, perhaps. He thought the gentleman's agreement was "wishful thinking" and "unrealistic." As he later recalled, "we were disappointed" with the sale, but not particularly surprised.[23]

For all of these reasons Buckeye's management decided to fight Dayton-Walther's takeover bid. Opposing Dayton-Walther proved difficult, for by the late 1970s, Buckeye's common stockholdings were widely dispersed in many hands. Buckeye's management no longer owned enough Buckeye stock to control their company. Moreover, a fair amount of Buckeye's stock was owned by institutional investors who might sell it to a third party. It was these circumstances that had enabled Dayton-Walther to buy Buckeye stock in the first place.[24] Buckeye attacked Dayton-Walther through a series of lawsuits charging that Dayton-Walther's tender offer to buy Buckeye stock was illegal, that Dayton-Walther's statements to the Securities and Exchange Commission were false and misleading, and that Dayton-Walther was violating both state and federal laws in trying to acquire Buckeye. Buckeye also purchased shares in the Citation Corporation, a business Dayton-Walther was also trying to buy. Then, as a minority stockholder in Citation, Buckeye's officers argued that Dayton-Walther had not made full disclosures to the Securities and Exchange Commission about that acquisition effort. This last maneuver with Citation was, Lewis Day recalled, "a dirty trick lawsuit, but, nevertheless, it was very effective." Dayton-Walther's officers replied that Buckeye's accusations were without merit, and countered with lawsuits of their own.[25]

Buckeye's management proved successful in their efforts. They first obtained a temporary restraining order preventing Dayton-Walther from obtaining any more Buckeye stock; then they reached an agreement with Dayton-Walther not to purchase additional Buckeye stock before January 15, 1980. Finally, Buckeye's opposition to Dayton-Walther's acquisition of Citation killed that venture; no merger between Citation and Dayton-Walther occurred. All of these actions, Day later remembered, "made Dayton-Walther very, very mad."[26] With any reconciliation impossible, Dayton-Walther abandoned its efforts to acquire Buckeye.

In late December 1979, Buckeye and Dayton-Walther dropped all the lawsuits pending against each other. Buckeye paid Dayton-Walther $500,000 as part of the agreement to end the litigation. In return, Dayton-Walther agreed to sell its shares of Buckeye stock to another corporation, Worthington International, a wholly owned subsidiary of Worthington Industries. Buckeye's merger experiences, far from ending, were really just beginning.[27]

Worthington Industries and Buckeye

Worthington Industries had been founded by John H. McConnell twenty-four years before, in 1955.* Located in Worthington, Ohio, a suburb just north of Columbus, the corporation began as a steel processor. Worthington purchased master coils of open tolerance steel from Armco, Bethlehem Steel, United States Steel,

*Part of this analysis was first presented as a paper, "An Inside Look at the Merger Process through Oral History," at the Business History Conference, May 5–7, 1981 in Philadelphia; this paper has been published under the same title in Jeremy Atack, editor, *Business and Economic History* (Urbana: University of Illinois Press, 1981), pp. 57–69. Used with the permission of the publisher.

and other companies. It then performed a series of operations—slitting, edge-rolling, cold reduction, roller-leveling, annealing, and pickling—to process the steel to very close tolerances for its final users. By 1979 Worthington was processing steel at six plants in Ohio, Kentucky, Illinois, South Carolina, and Maryland for over 1,000 companies in a wide variety of fields. Like Buckeye, Worthington Industries diversified during the 1970s. In 1971 the company entered a new field by purchasing the pressure cylinder business of Lennox Industries of Columbus, Ohio. Worthington manufactured disposable steel and aluminum cylinders to contain liquefied petroleum gas; these cylinders were then sold both to equipment manufacturers and end-product consumers. Through the acquisition of the U-Brand Corporation in 1978, Worthington began manufacturing and selling steel, iron, and plastic pipe fittings in the residential and commercial construction industry. In the late 1970s Worthington also opened operations in still other fields—reflective metallic coatings, hydraulic circuitry, and controls for lawn mowers.[28]

By 1979 Worthington had become a very healthy, diversified corporation. On sales of $278,000,000 the corporation reported earnings after taxes of $16,000,000, about $1.45 per share. The company's rapid growth and earnings attracted the attention of investors. In 1979 *Barron*'s, the *Financial World,* and *Fortune* all spotlighted the company as one of the United States' fastest-growing and most profitable corporations.[29] A statement by *Dun's Review* summarized investor analysis of Worthington Industries:

> Columbus, Ohio's Worthington Industries Inc. has racked up a financial record that would be the envy of any company. In the past decade, its earnings have grown at an annual compounded rate of 41%, return on capital has averaged 19%, and return on equity 28%.[30]

John McConnell was the man behind Worthington's growth record. A native of Weirton, West Virginia, McConnell worked in a National Steel mill there after graduating from high school. After serving in the navy and earning a degree in business administration from Michigan State University (while working nights in Lansing's Oldsmobile plant), he returned to the Weirton steel mill in the order department. He then joined a Pennsylvania-based steel warehouse as a commission salesman. It was while working in this capacity that McConnell decided to open his own business in Columbus, and with a $600 loan on his car and $1,200 in savings he founded Worthington Steel in 1955.[31] One of America's relatively few genuine Horatio Alger stories, McConnell explained what he thought were the reasons for his success in 1978:

> We have simply concentrated on what we think are the basics of good business. First, we have not tried to be the biggest but rather the best. We have specialized in areas where we can do a superior job. Second, we have practised the philosophy of treating our employees, customers, and suppliers the way they like to be treated. Third, we have established ourselves as the technological leaders in the industry.[32]

McConnell and others at Worthington first became interested in the possibility of acquiring Buckeye in the early fall of 1979, though as McConnell later observed, "of course, we've known about Buckeye for a long time."[33] Interest on Worthington's part was perhaps natural, for there were many links, in terms of personal connections, between Buckeye and Worthington. Paul Craig and Robert Crane served as directors of both companies; John McCoy, as head of the City National Bank, was a chief lender to both companies and was Buckeye's chairman of the board; John McConnell, in turn, had served as a City National director; and William Saxbe was both a Worthington director and the head of the law firm that represented Buckeye in its lawsuit against Dayton-Walther. Despite these connections, it was not until Dayton-Walther's attempted takeover of Buckeye that Worthington became interested in acquiring the Columbus corporation.

At a meeting between Worthington officers and stock market analysts in New York in September or October 1979, Buckeye's negotiations with Dayton-Walther were discussed. Shortly after this meeting, William McLaughlin, then Worthington's executive vice-president and treasurer, purchased 15,000 shares of Buckeye stock on his own account.[34] Over the next few months, Worthington's officers became increasingly interested in the prospect of acquiring Buckeye. Eventually, as McConnell later recalled, "we talked with John G. McCoy" about the possibility of purchasing

Buckeye. As McConnell emphasized, "We approached them [Buckeye's officers] . . . it was our initiative."[35] On November 29, 1979, Buckeye and Worthington announced that they were holding preliminary talks about the possible combination of the two companies, and on December 11 Worthington made a tender offer for up to 590,000 shares of Buckeye stock at $25 per share. As previously noted, Dayton-Walther agreed to sell its holdings of Buckeye stock to Worthington as part of these arrangements.[36]

Worthington's officers favored purchasing Buckeye for several reasons. Most importantly, McConnell was "very impressed" with Buckeye's "modern, well-equipped foundry." As he later explained, he thought there was "a great big market potential, other than railroads, that Buckeye could be participating in." He also thought that "the plastics division looked good" and had "a great profit potential." Then, too, personal, perhaps sentimental, reasons may have influenced those at Worthington. "The first reaction here was more out of civic pride and civic duty," McConnell recalled, "We hated to see Buckeye, that had been a fixture of this community for a hundred years, be taken over by a company in Dayton."[37]

The response of Buckeye's officers was mixed. Most wanted Buckeye to continue operations as an independent company; they did not want to merge with anyone. However, they realized that, given the nature of the company's stock holdings (in 1979 the officers and directors of Buckeye owned only 5.5 percent of their corporation's stock), a merger with or takeover by some other company was likely. Day characterized the Buckeye stock still in the hands of institutional investors as "hanging out there like a vulture waiting for something to happen," and, mixing his metaphors, Day noted that Buckeye's situation was "just like a dog in heat—once the scent gets out, you'll never be a virgin again." Day concluded that "if you are going to get married, you at least ought to be able to choose your marriage partner."[38] Brown was more reluctant to accept any company's acquisition overtures. "I didn't feel as desperate as some members of the board," he observed, "I tended to feel that we had more time on our side." But, as Brown noted, most of those with Buckeye welcomed Worthington with "a feeling of relief."[39] Referring to Worthington, Craig expressed the majority point of view:

I think our principal motive in seeking a merger once the idea came out was that we were not strong enough to fight off an acquisition. Therefore, the best strategy is to hunt a friendly one that we can have some control over. Negotiation would be arm's length and *quid pro quo,* rather than someone confronting us with the reality that they had bought us and that they were now going to use us. And, if we had not thought we were vulnerable, I don't think we would have sought a merger.[40]

More positive considerations also led those at Buckeye to come to favor a merger with Worthington. While he viewed Worthington as a "white knight" rescuing Buckeye from Dayton-Walther, Day recognized that Worthington had "a tremendous track record" and "a very good reputation in the investment community."[41] Craig, too, realized that Worthington had "an exceedingly good prior growth record" and concluded that Buckeye and Worthington would make "a good combination."[42] Brown had more doubts. While noting that Worthington had "a good track record," he questioned the company's future. Worthington possessed "no technologic innovations, no proprietary position, no franchised situation," he explained. Moreover, Brown was concerned about Worthington's management's ability to run the much larger diversified company resulting from the proposed merger.[43] As with those at Worthington, ties of sentiment predisposed Buckeye's officers to favor Worthington, because Worthington was a Columbus corporation. As Day observed, Buckeye's management wanted to avoid becoming "a satellite of a big conglomerate," and Worthington had "the advantage of being a Columbus-based company."[44] Craig later explained that "there was a kind of affinity of localism" involved in the merger and noted that Buckeye's officers felt "civic patriotism, a kind of chauvinism" in selling to another Columbus corporation.[45]

With the officers of Buckeye and Worthington in substantial agreement on the need and desirability of merger, negotiations proceeded smoothly. Worthington's tender offer for 590,000 shares of Buckeye stock was quickly filled, giving Worthington 36 percent of Buckeye's shares by late December 1979.[46] As the merger discussions continued, Worthington, with the approval of Buckeye's management, purchased more Buckeye stock and owned 44 percent of the total by late February 1980.[47] Finally, after more negotiations, the managements of Buckeye and Worthington agreed upon merging the companies through an exchange of stock, 1.5 shares of Worthington stock for each of the remaining Buckeye shares still outstanding. Buckeye's stockholders approved this arrangement at a special meeting in May 1980; and shortly thereafter, Buckeye went out of existence as a separate company, becoming a wholly owned subsidiary of Worthington Industries. After ninety-nine years of independent life, Buckeye became a division in a different company.[48]

As part of Worthington Industries, Buckeye continued its operations, but, as is typical after mergers, changes occurred. Buckeye's divisions were reorganized as two profit centers, steel and automotive; and peripheral operations—Hollowform, Micro-Communications, and others—were sold. Worthington's officers also streamlined the management at Buckeye. In McConnell's opinion, Buckeye was "top-heavy" in corporate management, and about one-half of Buckeye's corporate officers lost their jobs after the takeover.[49] As Brown, who left Buckeye to head another Columbus company, noted, "a merger is a very traumatic type of thing," for "your enterprise is being sold or transferred without you really being part of it."[50]

In 1981 Worthington's officers tried to integrate Buckeye's operations into those of the parent company. "Right now we want to get the shop in order on Buckeye," McConnell observed in March of that year, "We have still got a lot to do."[51] McConnell was generally pleased with the long-range implications of the merger. As he told his company's stockholders, the acquisition of Buckeye left Worthington "solidly positioned in the metal and plastics fields," with promising prospects for the future.[52]

In its disappearance as an independent company, Buckeye went through an experience that became increasingly common in the American business world during the late 1970s.[53] After what many business writers called the "great merger frenzy" peaked in the late 1960s, merger activity declined in the United States in the early 1970s. However, merger movements revived later in the decade.

Companies worth $12,600,000,000 merged in 1977, and two years later corporations valued at about $40,000,000,000 merged. These mergers were somewhat different than the conglomerate type of mergers common in the 1960s. Fewer of them cut across industry lines; more were between related companies. Here, too, the linking of Buckeye and Worthington was typical, bringing together two companies in the steel industry.

Notes

1. Interview by the author with Lewis Day, June 19, 1978.
2. "Rowland Brown's Remarks to Stockholders at the 1978 Annual Meeting," author's notes on the remarks at the meeting.
3. "Minutes of the Meeting of the Board of Directors" (hereafter cited as "Directors Meeting"), October 12, 1964; "Minutes of the Meeting of the Executive Committee" (hereafter cited as "Executive Committee Meeting"), February 14, 1966.
4. "Directors Meeting," October 10, 1966; "Executive Committee Meeting," November 10, December 8, 1969.
5. Interview by the author with William Henderson, August 19, 1978.
6. "Executive Committee Meeting," June 6, September 27, 1977.
7. Day interview, June 12, 1978.
8. Interviews by the author with Paul Craig, April 2, 1979.
9. Columbus *Dispatch,* June 10, 1979.
10. *Forbes Magazine,* April 18, 1977, p. 12.
11. *Business Week,* May 15, 1978, p. 123.
12. Prescott, Ball, & Turben, "Recommendations, May 2, 1979," one-page broadsheet in author's possession.
13. United States, Securities and Exchange Commission, "Schedule 13 D: Dayton-Walther and Buckeye International, February 8, 1979"; *Wall Street Journal,* June 12, 1979.
14. Columbus *Citizen's Journal,* June 7, 1979; Columbus *Dispatch,* June 6, 1979; United States, Securities and Exchange Commission, "Revised Schedule 13 D: Dayton-Walther and Buckeye International, April 30, 1979."
15. Interview by the author with Rowland Brown, March 10, 1980; Day interview, February 28, 1980.
16. *Wall Street Journal,* June 12, 1979.
17. Brown interview, March 10, 1980.
18. Craig interview, March 5, 1980.
19. Brown interview, March 10, 1980.
20. Day interview, February 28, 1980.
21. Craig interview, March 5, 1980.

22. Day interview, February 28, 1980.

23. Brown interview, March 10, 1980.

24. Buckeye International, "Shareholders of Record Holding 1,000 Shares or More of No Par Common Stock, November 19, 1979."

25. Day interview, February 28, 1980. See also a lengthy series of law briefs filed in the United States District Court for the Southern District of Ohio, Western Division (see especially October 24, 1979).

26. Ibid.

27. John McCoy to Dayton-Walther Corporation, December 19, 1979; *Wall Steet Journal,* December 24, 1979.

28. Worthington Industries, *Annual Report, 1979,* p. 1. See also: Blunt, Ellis, & Loewi, "Progress Report, Worthington Industries, May, 1979"; The Ohio Company, "Research, Worthington Industries, October 30, 1978"; Prescott, Ball, & Turben, "Recommendation, Worthington Industries, October 1, 1979."

29. *Barron's,* March 5, 1979; *Financial World,* August 15, 1979; *Fortune,* June 18, 1979.

30. *Dun's Review,* August 1979.

31. Biographic sketches of McConnell can be found in *Columbus Business Forum,* February 1978, p. 11, and Columbus *Dispatch,* May 10, 1979.

32. *Columbus Business Forum,* February 1978, p. 11.

33. Interview by the author with John McConnell, March 16, 1981.

34. Ibid.; Buckeye, "Shareholders, November 19, 1979."

35. McConnell interview, March 16, 1981.

36. United States, Securities and Exchange Commission, "Form S-14 Registration Statement: Worthington Industries, February 28, 1980," p. 7.

37. McConnell interview, March 16, 1981.

38. Day interview, February 28, 1980.

39. Brown interview, March 10, 1980.

40. Craig interview, March 5, 1980.

41. Day interview, February 28, 1980.

42. Craig interview, March 5, 1980.

43. Brown interview, March 10, 1980.

44. Day interview, February 28, 1980.

45. Craig interview, March 5, 1980.

46. Worthington Industries, "Offer to Purchase Not Less than 345,000 Nor More than 590,000 Common Shares of Buckeye International"; *Wall Street Journal,* December 24, 1979.

47. Columbus *Citizen-Journal,* February 20, 1980; *Wall Street Journal,* February 21, 1980.

48. Worthington Industries, *Annual Report, 1980,* p. 3.

49. McConnell interview, March 16, 1981.

50. Brown interview, March 10, 1980.
51. McConnell interview, March 16, 1981.
52. Worthington Industries, *Annual Report, 1980,* p. 7.
53. See, for instance: *Business Week,* September 17, 1979, p. 146; *TIme,* December 26, 1977, p. 49; *Wall Street Journal,* December 5, 1979, p. 1.

EPILOGUE

By 1980 Buckeye had nearly a one-hundred year history, and this history illustrated how successful small businesses often evolve in the United States. Buckeye's history also showed well the connections between corporate and community development. From the beginning, Buckeye, while a small or medium-sized business by national standards, was a large business by Columbus standards, and the company played significant roles in the city's evolution.

Beginning as a small malleable iron company in the early 1880s, Buckeye had to struggle simply to survive. Lacking any distinct products, it hovered on the brink of failure for nearly a decade. The malleable iron business proved to be highly competitive, and this fierce competition came close to killing Buckeye. Had Buckeye gone under, the company would have shared the most common fate of new, beginning businesses in the United States. According to *Dun and Bradstreet,* the annual death rate of American businesses has ranged between 115 and 240 per 1,000 concerns for the years 1900 through 1941. Many of these business failures were new companies. Even in the 1950s, about 60 percent of all failing businesses were under five years of age.[1]

Buckeye, however, became a flourishing corporation in the 1890s, despite the onset of a major depression which devastated the United States for much of the decade. As we have seen, no single factor explained Buckeye's success. Rather, it was caused by the confluence of several elements—the location of the company, the character of Buckeye's officers (particularly their willingness to innovate and their persistence in the face of adversity), government actions, and chance. Perhaps most significant were the personal and business connections of Buckeye's management. These ties brought in sorely needed capital and opened markets for Buckeye products during times of crisis. The importance of these personal relationships may well be the key to success in small business in general.[2] These friendships and connections were related to the position of Buckeye's officers in Columbus. They quickly established themselves as community leaders, and this circumstance helped them secure the needed financing and other advantages for their company. With their corporation economically viable, Buckeye's officers moved from malleable iron goods into the production of cast steel components for railroad equipment. By 1920 the company had clearly emerged as a leader in the nation's steel-castings industry. By this time Buckeye had also become a medium-sized corporation in the American economy. In 1917 a company possessing assets of $20,000,000 or more was a big business. Buckeye's assets in that year came to $7,300,000.[3]

The years 1922–59 saw slower expansion and change at Buckeye. Several reasons account for this slowing of Buckeye's advance. Most obviously, the economic climate of the United States in the 1930s did not favor growth. At a time when many businesses were failing, Buckeye did well to survive intact. Yet, the slowing of Buckeye's development began well before the Great Depression and lasted after it. The coupler agreement between Buckeye and other manufacturers continued in force, with a few lapses, between 1916 and the early 1940s. It retarded innovation at Buckeye and helps explain why the company failed to move into new areas. Perhaps even more important was the way in which Buckeye's top management viewed their corporation. They, quite simply, were happy with things the way they were. Their company was a leader in both its industry and the local Columbus business community. Buckeye and its officers had "arrived." Moreover, except for the mid-1930s, Buckeye was generally very profitable. Given this situation, it is understandable, if unfortunate, that Buckeye's officers were satisfied with the status quo. Nor is it surprising to find them spending increasing amounts of time and energy as leaders in both professional societies and Columbus civic organizations. Ironically, their growing interest in community activities outside of their business may be one reason they became less concerned about promoting rapid expansion at Buckeye.

The Second World War and its aftermath brought some changes to Buckeye, with major alterations occurring in the 1960s and

1970s. Caught in what they perceived as a highly cyclical and declining business, Buckeye's management turned to diversification as a solution to their problems. They both altered operations at the steel plant and acquired a host of companies in a variety of nonsteel businesses. In the process, Buckeye was reinvigorated, with growth and expansion once again characterizing the company's development. Finally, this renewal led to the acquisition of Buckeye by Worthington Industries in 1980.

Continuity more than change may be seen in Buckeye's relationship to the rest of Columbus. In both quantifiable and qualitative terms, the company and its officers played major roles in the socioeconomic development of Columbus and central Ohio. From the early 1900s to the present, Buckeye's officers have been extremely active in civic, business, and charitable organizations. Corporate giving to philanthropic organizations has also been consistently generous, far exceeding the national norm. Precisely because Buckeye has been a small to medium-sized company firmly rooted in one community for most of its history, it has been deeply involved in community affairs.

Notes

1. James Soltow, "Origins of Small Business Metal Fabricators and Machinery Makers, in New England, 1890–1957," *Transactions of the American Philosophical Society* 55 (December 1965): 6.

2. Ibid., especially pp. 16–30, 41–47. See also Mansel G. Blackford, *Pioneering a Modern Small Business: Wakefield Seafoods and the Alaskan Frontier* (Greenwich, Conn.: J.A.I. Press, 1979). On the most recent developments in small business, see *Wall Street Journal,* November 4, 1976, January 4, November 14, 21, 25, 29, December 2, 7, 1977.

3. Thomas R. Navin, "The 500 Largest American Industrials in 1917," *Business History Review* 44 (Autumn 1970): 360–86.

Appendix 1 _____

Table 6 _____
Output of Steel Castings, 1902–1979 (net tons)
(in thousands)

YEAR	BUCKEYE STEEL CASTINGS	U.S. INDUSTRY TOTAL
1902	2	
1903	17	
1904	15	326
1905	27	
1906	36	
1907	34	
1908	17	
1909	46	615
1910	50	
1911	19	
1912	68	
1913	62	
1914	33	659
1915	37	
1916	74	
1917	95	
1918	73	
1919	31	825
1920	63	
1921	13	
1922	51	
1923	72	1,254
1924	48	
1925	56	
1926	51	
1927	46	1,101
1928	51	
1929	72	1,531
1930	46	
1931	15	514
1932	4	
1933	6	312

SOURCE: Buckeye Steel Castings Company, "Minutes of the Annual Stockholders Meetings," in Buckeye Collection, the Ohio Historical Society.

Table 6 _____
Output of Steel Castings, 1902–1979 (net tons)
(in thousands)

YEAR	BUCKEYE STEEL CASTINGS	U.S. INDUSTRY TOTAL
1934	19	
1935	10	
1936	46	
1937	53	1,316
1938	9	
1939	30	
1940	46	798
1941	66	1,316
1942	61	
1943	66	1,929
1944	60	
1945	53	
1946	39	1,043
1947	51	
1948	66	
1949	32	
1950	37	1,462
1951	65	
1952	56	
1953	43	
1954	12	
1955	35	1,531
1956	61	
1957	57	
1958	18	
1959	28	1,413
1960	37	
1961	21	
1962	33	
1963	40	1,504
1964	57	
1965	59	1,961
1966	67	
1967	58	1,857
1968	58	
1969	62	
1970	63	1,724
1971	60	

Table 6 _____
Output of Steel Castings, 1902–1979 (net tons)
(in thousands)

YEAR	BUCKEYE STEEL CASTINGS	U.S. INDUSTRY TOTAL
1972	52	
1973	54	1,894
1974	55	
1975	56	1,937
1976	36	
1977	45	
1978	49	
1979	74	

Appendix 2 _____

Table 7 _____
Buckeye's Financial Data, 1895-1978
(in thousands)

YEAR	ASSETS	SALES (NET)	NET EARNINGS (AFTER TAXES)
1895	$ n.a	$ 237	$ 47
1896	515	374	100
1897	n.a	433	95
1898	n.a	865	236
1899	n.a	994	299
1900	n.a	920	182
1901	n.a	764	113
1902	1,609	698	75
1903	1,350	1,886	84
1904	1,433	1,377	27
1905	1,712	1,830	229
1906	n.a	2,206	272
1907	2,694	2,113	392
1908	2,727	976	86
1909	3,293	2,612	270
1910	2,976	2,914	614
1911	2,874	1,027	11
1912	3,845	3,652	650
1913	3,893	3,662	521
1914	3,953	1,902	245
1915	4,273	2,150	223
1916	5,295	5,298	908
1917	7,312	9,640	1,002
1918	8,140	9,847	762
1919	6,977	4,845	1,164
1920	9,086	9,623	1,207
1921	6,252	1,473	(370)
1922	7,106	5,296	647
1923	9,173	10,274	2,414
1924	8,457	5,357	943
1925	8,577	5,829	947
1926	8,330	5,234	720

SOURCE: Buckeye Steel Castings Company, "Minutes of the Annual Meetings of Stockholders," in Buckeye Collection, the Ohio Historical Society.

Table 7 _____
Buckeye's Financial Data, 1895-1978
(in thousands)

YEAR	ASSETS	SALES (NET)	NET EARNINGS (AFTER TAXES)
1927	8,352	4,483	741
1928	8,330	4,426	620
1929	9,114	7,030	1,257
1930	8,822	4,915	854
1931	7,581	1,431	(288)
1932	6,445	424	(575)
1933	5,908	570	(146)
1934	5,950	2,059	402
1935	5,598	1,121	167
1936	6,516	4,915	882
1937	7,086	6,363	1,046
1938	6,099	1,120	(236)
1939	5,649	3,776	708
1940	6,372	5,409	782
1941	7,704	8,605	930
1942	9,854	10,200	630
1943	9,905	12,514	621
1944	7,882	10,072	609
1945	7,613	8,516	435
1946	8,292	8,016	672
1947	8,842	11,100	875
1948	10,659	16,000	1,840
1949	9,242	9,000	826
1950	11,692	10,737	1,653
1951	13,918	20,723	1,522
1952	14,296	19,410	1,411
1953	13,832	16,226	1,324
1954	10,997	4,188	(345)
1955	12,987	11,870	1,074
1956	15,414	20,717	1,762
1957	14,935	21,252	1,675
1958	12,030	6,800	(596)
1959	10,242	12,046	454
1960	10,411	14,094	476
1961	9,391	8,717	(387)
1962	9,802	13,701	390
1963	12,062	16,544	811
1964	11,876	23,250	1,002
1965	14,072	24,886	1,217

Table 7 _____
Buckeye's Financial Data, 1895–1978
(in thousands)

YEAR	ASSETS	SALES (NET)	NET EARNINGS (AFTER TAXES)
1966	16,320	28,662	1,698
1967	21,359	28,751	1,889
1968	30,511	43,436	2,364
1969	34,714	43,990	1,012
1970	33,537	44,143	113
1971	31,431	47,942	1,615
1972	38,644	52,546	744
1973	51,597	76,613	(180)
1974	52,059	93,014	1,726
1975	51,555	111,666	3,935
1967	54,625	107,764	2,995
1977	62,221	124,772	1,885
1978	76,211	120,644	(790)

BIBLIOGRAPHIC ESSAY

Secondary works, books, and articles referred to in the notes have been useful in setting the background for this study. A list of secondary sources on business history would require many pages and still not be complete. Three studies, however, have been particularly helpful in explaining the evolution of American business and its relationship to changes in society and culture. Alfred D. Chandler, Jr., *The Visible Hand* (Cambridge, Mass.: Harvard University Press, 1977) is an excellent examination of the development of the modern business corporation and its management in nineteenth- and twentieth-century America. Thomas C. Cochran, *Business in American Life* (New York: McGraw-Hill, 1972) and Morrell Heald, *The Social Responsibilities of Business: Company and Community, 1900–1960* (Cleveland: Case Western Reserve University Press, 1970) relate changes in business to the larger social and economic alterations occurring in the United States.

Particular studies have been of aid in learning about the iron and steel industries. William Hogan, *Economic History of the Iron and Steel Industry in the United States* (Lexington, Mass.: D.C. Heath, 1971), 5 volumes, presents an excellent overview of the history of the industries. Also useful were Kenneth Warren, *The American Steel Industry, 1850–1970: A Geographical Interpretation* (London: Oxford University Press, 1973) and Gertrude G. Schroeder, *The Growth of Major Steel Companies* (Baltimore: The Johns Hopkins Press, 1953).

The history of the steel-castings industry is covered in William P. Conway, Jr., *Cast to Shape: A History of the Steel Castings Industry in the United States* (Rocky River, Ohio: Dillon, Liederbach, 1977). Buckeye's competitors are covered in two brief, popular works: Franklin Reck, *Sand in Their Shoes: The Story of American Steel Foundries* (Cleveland: no publisher listed, 1952) and an anonymous study, *National Malleable and Steel Castings Company, 1868–1943* (Cleveland: no publisher listed, 1943).

Much more research needs to be done on the history of Columbus, but some useful works are available. Betty Garrett and Edward Lentz, *Columbus: America's Crossroads* (Tulsa: Centennial Heritage Press, 1980), provides a general overview of the city's evolution. On the early history of the city, see: Osman Hooper, *History of the City of Columbus* (Columbus: Memorial Publishing Company, 1920); Alfred Lee, *History of the City of Columbus,* 2 vols. (New York: Munsell Publishing Company, 1930). A number of theses and dissertations also exist. Among the most useful are Andrea D. Lentz, "The Question of Community: The 1910 Street Car Strike in Columbus, Ohio" (Masters thesis, The Ohio State University, 1970) and Michael Speer, "Urbanization and Reform: Columbus, Ohio 1870–1900" (Ph.D. Dissertation, The Ohio State University, 1972). For an analysis of the economic development of Columbus, refer to Henry Hunker, *The Industrial Evolution of Columbus, Ohio* (Columbus: The Ohio State University Press, 1958). This work is particularly useful for developments in the late nineteenth and early twentieth centuries.

The heart of the research for this study was done in primary source materials. Newspapers, especially the Columbus *Dispatch* and the *Ohio State Journal,* and trade journals, particularly *The Foundry,* proved useful in checking specific items. General city directories and business directories were of aid in unraveling Buckeye's early history, as were various reports by the Columbus Board of Trade and the Columbus Chamber of Commerce. Government reports proved to be less helpful, but they did provide valuable data for the 1920s and 1930s. Manuscript collections were of most use. The S. P. Bush letters are in the hands of Mrs. Steward Clements of New Haven, Connecticut. Copies of these letters are available for use at the Ohio Historical Society in Columbus. The records of the Ohio Manufacturers' Association through 1940 were consulted. These are kept at the the organization's headquarters in Columbus. The Labor History Collection at the Ohio Historical Society contains papers of aid in understanding labor relations at Buckeye; see, especially, the Harry Mayfield and United Steelworkers papers.

Oral history interviews by the author were conducted with: John Bricker, Dick Brosius, Phil Bordan, Rowland Brown, Bill Buffington, Marshall Cooledge, Paul Craig, Lewis Day, Charles Henderson, William Henderson, John Hughes, George Johnson, Jr., Frank Lewis, Bob Marshall, John McConnell, John G. McCoy, Charles Piggott, W. Dan Reuter, Leslie Roberts, Albert Stock, and Richard Warnick. All of these interviews were tape recorded. Most were donated to the Ohio Historical Society at the completion of this study, and most of them are available for immediate use without restriction.

Most important, of course, have been the records of Buckeye International. These have been fully inventoried and organized by Andrea D. Lentz, a professional archivist and historical researcher. At the conclusion of this study they were donated to the Ohio Historical Society, where they are immediately available for use without restrictions. Buckeye, however, retains its legal documents and the minutes of its boards of directors, executive committees, and stockholders meetings since 1957 at corporate headquarters. Copies of the inventory of Buckeye's records, as prepared by Andrea D. Lentz, can be obtained from the Ohio Historical Society.

INDEX

About the Author
MANSEL G. BLACKFORD is Associate Professor of History at
Ohio State University in Columbus. His earlier works include *The
Politics of Business in California, 1890–1920,* and *Pioneering a
Modern Small Business.*